STREETWISE
ITALIAN
DICTIONARY/THESAURUS

STREETWISE ITALIAN

DICTIONARY/THESAURUS

The User-Friendly Guide to Italian Slang and Idioms

Nicholas Albanese
Giovanni Spani
Philip Balma
Ermanno Conti

McGraw·Hill

New York   Chicago   San Francisco   Lisbon   London   Madrid   Mexico City
Milan   New Delhi   San Juan   Seoul   Singapore   Sydney   Toronto

The *McGraw·Hill* Companies

Library of Congress Cataloging-in-Publication Data

Streetwise Italian dictionary/thesaurus : the user-friendly guide to Italian slang and
   idioms / Nicholas Albanese . . . [et al.].
      p.   cm.
   Includes index.
   ISBN 0-07-143070-9
      1. Italian language—Slang—Dictionaries—English.   2. Italian language—Idioms—
Dictionaries—English.   3. Italian language—Conversation and phrase books—English.
I. Albanese, Nicholas.

PC1971.S77   2005
   453'.21—dc22   2004061110

1 2 3 4 5 6 7 8 9 0   DOC/DOC   0 9 8 7 6 5

ISBN 0-07-143070-9

Interior design by Village Typographers, Inc.
Interior illustrations by Luc Nisset

Other titles in the Streetwise series:
Streetwise Spanish, Mary McVey Gill and Brenda Wegmann
Streetwise Spanish Dictionary/Thesaurus, Mary McVey Gill and Brenda Wegmann
Streetwise French, Isabelle Rodrigues and Ted Neather
Streetwise French Dictionary/Thesaurus, Ian Pickup and Rod Hares
Streetwise German, Paul G. Graves

This book is printed on acid-free paper.

Contents

Introduction

Learning a foreign language is one of the most difficult tasks an adult can undertake. Vocabulary, grammar rules, verb tenses, and conjugations are all necessary components of a language, and mastering them can oftentimes be difficult and tedious. Even after these elements are mastered, there are still other challenges to overcome. One of the greatest of these challenges is that of bridging the gap between the standard language—the "official" language learned in textbooks and classrooms—and the spoken language—the "unofficial" language actually spoken "on the street," as it were. Even after years spent learning a foreign language, one may come to find the spoken target language incomprehensible in many instances or situations.

Another challenge closely linked to the difficulty of mastering the spoken language is that of distinguishing between *registers*—being able to choose the appropriate level of language for a given situation. One certainly would not want to speak to a person who commands respect—a professor, a policeman, a priest—with the jargon of a street thug. These subtleties of language can often lead to embarrassing or uncomfortable situations. It takes years to master a foreign language, and you know you're there when you are able to distinguish between high and low registers, between language acceptable for your term paper and language appropriate for informal conversation with friends and family. At that point you may say that you truly are near fluent in a foreign language, that you are, in fact, *streetwise*.

It would be improper to define all of the entries contained here as *slang*—nonstandard language used by a specific group or subculture—because many of these terms or expressions are widely used among both young and old, educated and uneducated, prostitutes and politicians. These terms would be more appropriately called *familiar*, although it is often difficult to distinguish between *slang* and *familiar*. What is clear, however, is that one must exercise some care in determining whether certain terms or expressions are appropriate in a given situation or context.

The goal of this book—*Streetwise Italian Dictionary/Thesaurus*—is to make you "streetwise" by providing Italian words, sayings, and expressions that are generally not found in textbooks or Italian-English dictionaries but are instead found only by *living the language*—participating firsthand in the linguistic interactions of everyday life. The primary function of language is oral communication, and therefore the spoken language is the most accurate form, the *true* language.

This volume is organized alphabetically by subject matter to allow the reader to quickly and easily find Italian expressions relating to a specific topic or category. Therefore we have chosen broad categories, which are in turn divided into subcategories. An example is the chapter titled "Entertainment," which is broken down into the sections "Bars," "Brothels/Prostitution," "Nightclubs/Discotheques," "Popular Music," "Theater," "Places and Sources of Entertainment," "Entertaining Oneself," and "Are We Having Fun?" This also allows the reader to focus on a specific subject area by reading through the Italian terms and expressions in the chapter of his or her choice.

For many of the entries, an example sentence or dialogue is provided, both in Italian and in English translation. These examples will help the reader to understand in what context(s) the terms or expressions may be appropriately used. There is also a literal English translation of the expression whenever possible. These literal translations are often quite humorous and can be of great interest to the linguist or linguaphile. They also help to further clarify the actual meaning of an idiomatic expression. In addition, a system has been provided for indicating the level of "offensiveness" of the entries in order to help the reader avoid **una figuraccia** (a *faux pas*, if you will). An entry followed by *(fam.)* means that the term or expression is familiar and therefore may not be suitable in some situations, though it is not terribly offensive. The appellative *(vulg.)* indicates that the term or expression is vulgar and is almost certainly offensive in most situations. If there is no indication of an entry's level of suitability, then the term or expression belongs to standard Italian and can be used in most situations without running the risk of offending anyone.

rompere i coglioni to break someone's balls, to nag the hell out of someone (fam.) ▪ **Perché mi devi rompere i coglioni ogni volta che esco con gli amici?** Why do you have to nag the hell out of me every time I go out with my friends?

The above is a typical entry that is considered to be *familiar*, and therefore some care needs to be exercised when using this expression. The reader may not want to use **rompere i coglioni** in front of a friend's grandmother; however, among young people it is a perfectly acceptable idiomatic expression. It is important to point out that the "Cursing" section in the "Emotions" chapter is especially vulgar. Great care must be taken when using these terms and expressions, as they are extremely offensive to most Italians.

At the end of each chapter, there are a number of exercises, which vary in format from chapter to chapter, for the reader to test his or her knowledge. An answer key is provided at the back of the book. Also at the back of the book, the reader will find an alphabetical dictionary/index, which is particularly useful for looking up expressions that the reader may have heard. The page reference refers the reader to the appropriate page on which the expression is used and translated into English.

It is important to remember that languages are never static—they are constantly changing and evolving. New terms and expressions are always entering into common usage while others fall out of fashion, perhaps to return again sometime in the future, perhaps not. This is especially true in this modern age of television, the Internet, and global communications. The reader, therefore, may encounter terms that have not yet found their way into this book, while other terms that are present may already be fading in use.

This dictionary/thesaurus is intended to be a starting point for all those who, after having studied standard Italian in school or on their own, are ready to learn the *true* Italian language, the spoken language. We hope this book will lead to many new and wonderful experiences of *living the language*. **In bocca al lupo!**

Thesaurus

Gestures: Speaking Without Words

BOREDOM

Ne ho fin qui!
I've had it up to here!

Che barba!
What a bore!

COST

Costa un occhio!
It's expensive!

DRINK AND DRUNKENNESS

Versami da bere!
Pour me a drink!

Giusto un goccio.
Just a drop.

FEAR

Ammettilo che c'hai strizza.
Admit that you're scared.

HOPE

Teniamo le dita incrociate.
Let's keep our fingers crossed.

INSULTS

Vaffanculo!
Fuck you!

Ma che sei scemo?
What are you, nuts?

Matto da legare!
A total nutcase!

LEAVING QUICKLY

Smammiamo!/Io scappo!/Filiamocela!
Let's jet!/I'm out of here!/Let's scram!

TELEPHONING

Ti faccio uno squillo.
I'll give you a call/ring/buzz.

Acronyms and Initials

The following list will give you a working knowledge of the most common abbreviations and acronyms used in Italian.

ACI [Automobile Club Italiano] Italian equivalent of AAA ▪ **Se vuoi informazioni sulle tasse automobilistiche devi rivolgerti all'ACI.** If you want to get information about automobile taxes you should contact ACI.

AN [Alleanza Nazionale] major right-wing party

APT [azienda promozione turistica] tourist office ▪ **Se vuoi informazioni sugli alberghi di questa zona rivolgiti all'apt.** If you need information about hotels in the area contact the APT.

CAP [codice avviamento postale] zip code ▪ **Mi raccomando signora, quando spedisce la Sua lettera non dimentichi il cap!** I advise you ma'am, when you mail your letter don't forget the zip code!

CC [carabinieri] police

> NOTE: **Polizia** and **carabinieri** are not the same thing, but even in Italy no one is really sure where the difference lies concerning their roles.

CF [Codice Fiscale] Social Security number

CGIL/CISL/UIL [Confederazione Generale Italiana Lavoro/Confederazione Italiana Sindacati Lavoratori/Unione Italiana dei Lavoratori] Italian trade union(s) ▪ **La CGIL/CISL/UIL ha proclamato lo sciopero per domani dalle otto alle undici.** The trade unions have called for a strike for tomorrow from eight to eleven.

CRI [Croce Rossa Italiana] Italian Red Cross

DOC [Denominazione di Origine Controllata] wine quality certification

> NOTE: **DOC** refers to wine quality but is used in everyday language to talk about something or someone of good quality. **Michele è veramente una persona DOC.** Michele is really a great person.

DS [Democratici di Sinistra] major left-wing party

ENEL [Ente Nazionale per l'Energia Elettrica] national electric company

FIAT [Fabbrica Italiana Automobili Torino] Major Italian car corporation

IVA [Imposta sul Valore Aggiunto]   sales tax

KO   KO, knockout   ■ **Quel whisky mi ha messo KO.** That whisky knocked me out.

OK   OK, okay

PPI [Partito Popolare Italiano]   major Catholic party

PS [pubblica sicurezza/polizia]   police

RAI [Radiotelevisione Italiana]   public broadcasting channel

TAC [tomografia assiale computerizzata]   CAT scan   ■ **Domani è un giorno importante per mia madre. Deve andare all'ospedale a fare la TAC per vedere se la sua malattia è grave.** Tomorrow is an important day for my mother. She has to go to the hospital and have a CAT scan in order to see if her disease is serious.

TG [telegiornale]   TV news   ■ **Hai visto il TG? Sembra che la guerra inizi presto.** Have you seen the news? It seems that a war is going to start soon.

VM 18 [vietato ai minori di 18 anni]   NC-17

EXERCISES
Adesso tocca a voi!

A *Match each acronym with the corresponding meaning:*

_____ 1. CGIL/CISL/UIL	a. police
_____ 2. ENEL	b. wine quality certification
_____ 3. ACI	c. Italian equivalent of AAA
_____ 4. CAP	d. national electric company
_____ 5. CF	e. Italian trade unions
_____ 6. VM 18	f. zip code
_____ 7. DS	g. Social Security number
_____ 8. PS	h. NC-17
_____ 9. DOC	i. left-wing party
_____ 10. AN	j. right-wing party

B *Choose the acronym that best fits each of the following hints:*

1. You want to be informed about what is happening in the world. You watch (TG/CRI/APT).

2. You want information on the most beautiful churches to visit in Florence. You go to the (IVA/APT/CC).

3. You want to make a donation to the major Italian Catholic party. You call the (PPI/RAI/VAT).

4. To express that you are exhausted, you would say that you are (OK/KO/TAC) 'd.

5. You want to watch a show on TV. You watch (FIAT/ACI/RAI).

Animals

BARNYARD ANIMALS
Familiar words used by children

l'agnellino (m)   little lamb (fam.)

il capretto   little goat (fam.)

il cavalluccio   horsey (fam.)

il porcellino   piggy (fam.)

Idiomatic expressions involving barnyard animals

Asino!/Pezzo d'asino!   (*lit.*, Donkey!/Piece of a donkey!) Dunce! (fam.)

Qui casca l'asino!   (*lit.*, Here the donkey falls!) There is the rub! (fam.)

Siete a cavallo!   (*lit.*, You all are on horseback!) You all have it in the bag! (fam.)

pisciare come un cavallo   to piss like a horse ▪ **Se bevo troppo piscio come un cavallo.** If I drink too much I piss like a horse. (vulg.)

Portami a cavalluccio!   (*lit.*, Take me "little horse style"!) Give me a piggy back ride! (fam.)

il cocco/la cocca (*lit.*, hen's egg) chick, chickadee, darling (fam.) ▪ **Beatrice è figlia unica. È la cocca di mamma.** Beatrice is an only child. She is mommy's darling.

Non essere un coniglio! (*lit.*, Don't be a rabbit!) Don't be a coward! (fam.)

La settimana scorsa ho trombato come un coniglio. Last week I fucked like a rabbit. (vulg.)

Non essere un coniglio!

Lui fa sempre il galletto. (*lit.*, He always plays the rooster.) He always plays the gallant. (fam.)

Abbiamo trovato una gallina dalle uova d'oro. (*lit.*, We found a hen with golden eggs.) We found a gold mine. (fam.)

Sei un cervello di gallina! (*lit.*, You're a hen's brain!) You're not smart! (fam.)

andare a letto con le galline e svegliarsi col gallo (*lit.*, to go to bed with the hens and wake up with the rooster) early to bed, early to rise. (fam.)

Mangi come un maiale! You eat like a pig! (fam.)

È carico come un mulo. He's loaded like a mule. (fam.)

Ho la pelle d'oca. (*lit.*, I've got goose's skin.) I've got goose bumps. (fam.)

Sono la pecora nera della famiglia. I am the black sheep of the family.

Io conosco i miei polli. (*lit.*, I know my chickens.) I'm nobody's fool. (fam.)

Lui è davvero un pollo. (*lit.*, He's really a chicken.) He's very easily fooled. (fam.)

Mi piace la storia dei tre porcellini. I like the story of the three little pigs.

Non fare il porco! Don't be a pig! (fam.)

Sei grasso come un porco! You're fat like a pig! (fam.)

Non fare la vacca! (*lit.*, Don't be a cow!) Don't be a slut! (vulg.)

CATS

il gattino (*lit.*, little cat) kitty (fam.)

il micio/micetto kitty (fam.)

Idiomatic expressions involving cats

Hanno nove vite come i gatti. They have nine lives like cats. (fam.)

Qui gatta ci cova. (*lit.*, Here the cat broods on it.) I smell a rat here. (fam.)

Luciano è un gatto. (*lit.*, Luciano is a cat.) Luciano is smart. (fam.)

Devo sgattaiolare via da qui. I have to steal away from here. (fam.)

Siamo quattro gatti. (*lit.*, We're four cats.) We're very few. (fam.)

Tanto va la gatta al lardo che ci lascia lo zampino. (*lit.*, The cat goes to the lard so much that she loses her paw.) Curiosity killed the cat. (fam.)

C'è una brutta gatta da pelare. (*lit.*, There's an ugly cat to skin.) There's a big problem to be solved. (fam.)

DOGS

il cagnolino   doggy (fam.)

il cucciolo/cucciolino   puppy (fam.)

Idiomatic expressions involving dogs

Tu hai sette vite come i cani.   You have seven lives like dogs. (fam.)

Non temere, Mario, cane che abbaia non morde.   Don't worry, Mario, a barking dog does not bite. (fam.)

Cane non mangia cane. (*lit.*, Dog does not eat dog.) There's honor among thieves. (fam.)

Piove sempre, che tempo da cani! (*lit.*, It always rains, what dog's weather!) It always rains, what bad weather! (fam.)

Che vita da cani! (*lit.*, What a dog's life!) What a terrible life! (fam.)

Era solo come un cane. (*lit.*, He was alone like a dog.) He was all alone. (fam.)

Marco e Lucia sono come cani e gatti. (*lit.*, Marco and Lucia are like dogs and cats.) Marco and Lucia argue constantly. (fam.)

Ha fatto un lavoro da cani. (*lit.*, He/She did a dog's job.) He/She did a very poor job. (fam.)

Lavora come un cane. (*lit.*, He/She works like a dog.) He/She works a lot. (fam.)

Dai, smetti di menare il cane per l'aia e arriva al punto. (*lit.*, Come on, stop leading the dog around the barnyard and get to the point.) Come on, stop beating around the bush and get to the point. (fam.)

Mondo cane! (*lit.*, Dog world!) Damn it all! (fam.)

Non c'era un cane. (*lit.*, There was not a dog there.) There was no one there. (fam.)

Te l'ho detto di non svegliare il cane che dorme. (*lit.*, I told you not to wake the sleeping dog.) I told you to let sleeping dogs lie. (fam.)

Sei un cane! (*lit.*, You're a dog!) You're a despicable person! (fam.)

Lo tratti sempre come un cane! (*lit.*, You always treat him like a dog!) You always treat him poorly! (fam.)

WILD ANIMALS, BIRDS, FISH, AND INSECTS
Idiomatic expressions involving birds

Non essere un allocco! (*lit.*, Don't be a tawny owl!) Don't be stupid! (fam.)

Perché fai sempre la figura dell'allocco? (*lit.*, Why do you always make the impression of the tawny owl?) Why do you always come off as being stupid? (fam.)

Sono rimasti come un allocco. (*lit.*, They remained like a tawny owl.) They were left stunned.

È uno specchietto per allodole. (*lit.*, It is a little mirror for skylarks.) It is a lure/a decoy. (fam.)

Giorgio è un'aquila! (*lit.*, Giorgio is an eagle!) Giorgio is a genius! (fam.)

Non fare l'avvoltoio! (*lit.*, Don't be a vulture!) Don't be greedy! (fam.)

Devi smetterla di fare la civetta. (*lit.*, You've got to stop being the owl.) You've got to stop flirting. (fam.)

Smetti di civettare! (*lit.*, Stop playing the owl!) Stop flirting/playing the coquette! (fam.)

Sono un vero civettone. (*lit.*, I'm a real big male owl.) I'm a real fop. (fam.)

È sempre il solito corvo del malaugurio. (*lit.*, He's always the crow of ill omen.) He's always the person who brings bad luck. (fam.)

Vede come un falco. He/She has eyes like an eagle. (fam.)

Canta come un fringuellino. (*lit.*, He/She sings like a little finch.) He/She sings happily. (fam.)

Non mi gufare! (*lit.*, Don't "owl" me!) Don't bring me bad luck!/Don't jinx me! (fam.)

Sei un gufo. (*lit.*, You are an owl.) You're a person who brings bad luck. (fam.)

Ho preso due piccioni con una fava. (*lit.*, I caught two pigeons with one fava bean.) I killed two birds with one stone. (fam.)

Non ripetere a pappagallo! Do not repeat like a parrot! (fam.)

Ho l'uccello grande. (*lit.*, I have the big bird.) I have a big cock. (vulg.)

Idiomatic expressions involving fish and other aquatic creatures

Sono cotto come un'aragosta. (*lit.*, I'm cooked like a lobster.) I'm exhausted. (fam.)

Sei una balena! You're a whale! (fam.)

Se mangi così diventi grasso come una balena! If you eat like this you'll become big like a whale! (fam.)

«In culo alla balena!» «Speriamo non caghi!» "In the ass of the whale!" "Let's hope it does not shit!" (vulg.)

Temo di prendere un granchio. (*lit.*, I'm afraid to get a crab.) I'm afraid to make a mistake/to mess up. (fam.)

Lo studente è muto come un pesce. The student is mute like a fish. (fam.)

Mi sento come un pesce fuor d'acqua! I feel like a fish out of water! (fam.)

Pesce d'aprile! (*lit.*, fish of April) April fools! (fam.)

Chi dorme non piglia pesci. (*lit.*, Those who sleep get no fish.) The early bird gets the worm. (fam.)

Mi prendono a pesci in faccia. (*lit.*, They hit me with fish in the face.) They treat me very poorly. (fam.)

Non so che pesci prendere. (*lit.*, I don't know what fish to catch.) I don't know what to do. (fam.)

Vito è simpatico ma è una piovra! (*lit.*, Vito is nice but he is an octopus!) Vito is nice but he is clingy! (fam.)

Mi tocca sempre ingoiare il rospo! (*lit.*, I always have to swallow the toad!) I always have to swallow a bitter pill! (fam.)

Non sputare il rospo! (*lit.*, Don't spit out the toad!) Don't express a hidden thought! (fam.)

Rosanna è proprio un rospo. (*lit.*, Rosanna is definitely a toad.) Rosanna is rather ugly. (fam.)

Vattelapesca. (*lit.*, Go fish for it.) Goodness knows. (fam.)

Idiomatic expressions involving insects

Mi muovo a passo di formica. (*lit.*, I move at an ant's pace.) I move very slowly. (fam.)

Avete grilli per la testa. (*lit.*, You guys have crickets in the head.) You guys are full of fancy. (fam.)

Detesto fare la lucciola! (*lit.*, I hate being a firefly!) I hate being a prostitute! (fam.)

Tu prendi sempre lucciole per lanterne! (*lit.*, You always take fireflies for lanterns!) You always misunderstand! (fam.)

Sei lento come una lumaca! You're slow like a snail! (fam.)

Bobby è una mosca bianca. (*lit.*, Bobby is a white fly.) Bobby is a very rare person. (fam.)

Ermanno non farebbe male a una mosca. Ermanno would not hurt a fly. (fam.)

Non si sente volare una mosca. (*lit.*, You can't hear a fly flying.) There's absolute silence. (fam.)

Resterete con un pugno di mosche. (*lit.*, You all will be left with a fistful of flies.) You all will be left empty-handed. (fam.)

Dovresti sentirti un verme! (*lit.*, You should feel like a worm!) You should be ashamed! (fam.)

Sei un verme! (*lit.*, You are a worm!) You are despicable! (fam.)

Sono nudo come un verme. (*lit.*, I'm naked like a worm.) I'm stark naked. (fam.)

Idiomatic expressions involving wild animals

Lui lavora come una bestia. He works like a beast. (fam.)

Puzza come un cammello! He stinks like a camel! (fam.)

Sei una giraffa! (*lit.*, You're a giraffe!) You're super tall! (fam.)

Vedi quella ragazza alta come una giraffa? Do you see that girl who's tall like a giraffe? (fam.)

S'incazza come una iena. He/She gets pissed like a hyena. (vulg.)

Sei coraggioso come un leone. You're brave like a lion. (fam.)

Riccardo ha l'occhio di lince. (*lit.*, Riccardo has the eye of the lynx.) Riccardo is sharp-eyed. (fam.)

A forza di gridare al lupo prima o poi nessuno ti crederà! If you cry wolf so often, sooner or later no one will believe you! (fam.)

Il lupo perde il pelo ma non il vizio. (*lit.*, The wolf loses the fur but not the habit.) You can't teach an old dog new tricks. (fam.)

«In bocca al lupo!» «Crepi!/Crepi il lupo!» "In the mouth of the wolf!" "May it die!/May the wolf die!" (fam.)

> NOTE: The expressions **In bocca al lupo!** and **In culo alla balena!** (under "Idiomatic expressions involving fish and other aquatic creatures") are the Italian equivalent of the saying "break a leg," which is commonly used in the world of theater. There is no expression in English that could function as a proper response (as is the case for **Crepi!** and **Speriamo non caghi!** in Italian).

Abito in culo ai lupi. (*lit.*, I live in the ass of the wolves.) I live very far away. (fam.)

Lei ha una fame da lupi. (*lit.*, She has a wolf's hunger.) She's starving. (fam.)

Luigi è un mandrillo. (*lit.*, Luigi is a mandrill.) Luigi is a lecher/given to sexual indulgence. (fam.)

Mariano è tanto buono ma è proprio un orso! (*lit.*, Mariano is a real good guy but he really is a bear!) Mariano is a real good guy but he is really asocial! (fam.)

È peloso come una scimmia. He's as hairy as a monkey. (fam.)

Sono viscido come un serpente. I'm as slippery as a snake. (fam.)

Sei cieco come una talpa. (*lit.*, You're blind like a mole.) You're as blind as a bat. (fam.)

Quel ladro ha fatto la fine del topo! (*lit.*, That thief ended up like the mouse!) That thief ended up like a rat in a trap! (fam.)

Stefano è un topo di biblioteca. (*lit.*, Stefano is a library mouse.) Stefano is a person who spends all his time in the library. (fam.)

Mio marito è davvero un toro! (*lit.*, My husband is truly a bull!) My husband is truly a stud! (fam.)

Mia sorella è una vipera! (*lit.*, My sister is a viper!) My sister is a snake! (fam.)

Tommaso è furbo come una volpe. Tommaso is clever like a fox. (fam.)

Giù le zampe! (*lit.*, Paws down!) Hands off! (fam.)

EXERCISES

Adesso tocca a voi!

A *Match each of the following Italian terms with the English equivalent:*

_____ 1. formica		a. worm
_____ 2. verme		b. snake
_____ 3. topo		c. lobster
_____ 4. serpente		d. monkey
_____ 5. scimmia		e. whale
_____ 6. cavallo		f. bear
_____ 7. aragosta		g. wolf
_____ 8. orso		h. mouse
_____ 9. balena		i. ant
_____ 10. lupo		j. horse

B *Select the animal that is commonly associated with the adjective in question:*

1. muto: a. scimmia   b. allodola   c. pesce

2. grasso: a. orso   b. giraffa   c. balena

3. furbo: a. lupo   b. gatto   c. volpe

4. coraggioso: a. iena   b. leone   c. lince

5. cieco: a. talpa   b. coccodrillo   c. asino

C *Choose the correct adjective to translate the following expressions:*

1. «Peloso come una scimmia» means "_____ like a monkey."

    a. astute   b. hairy   c. slippery

2. «Carico come un mulo» means "_____ like a mule."

    a. stubborn   b. stupid   c. loaded

3. «Grasso come un porco» means "_____ like a pig."

    a. fat   b. smelly   c. dirty

Art

ART AND ARTISTIC PEOPLE

l'appassionato/a, il patito/la patita (*lit.*, sufferer) buff, lover (of the cinema, of the theater, etc.) ■ **Vai a vedere un'altra commedia? Sei proprio un patito del teatro!** You are going to see another play? You are quite a theater buff!

d'autore (*lit.*, of the author) artistic, artsy-fartsy ■ **In quel cinema fanno solamente film d'autore, non le solite cazzate.** In that movie theater they only show artsy-fartsy films, not the usual shitty commercial films.

il cinefilo film buff ■ **La sua collezione di film è enorme. È un vero cinefilo!** His film collection is enormous. He is a true film buff!

il divo/la diva the star ■ **Vedi quella signora? È una diva della lirica! L'ho vista in *La Traviata*!** Do you see that woman? She is an opera star! I saw her in *La Traviata!*

il gigolò, il donnaiolo gigolo, womanizer (fam.)

il grande schermo the silver screen, the big screen ■ **È la prima volta sul grande schermo per quell'attore.** It's the first time on the big screen for that star.

l'intenditore (m) /l'intenditrice (f) expert, critic ■ **Se vuoi sapere qualcosa del teatro, parla con Paolo, che è un grande intenditore.** If you want to know something about the theater, talk to Paolo, who's a real expert.

licenza poetica poetic license

il/la melomane opera lover

> NOTE: In Italian the opera is also called **melodramma**, from which the term **melomane** is derived.

il nome d'arte stage name, pen name

il paroliere/la paroliera lyricist (poet or even songwriter) ■ **Solo perché scrivi canzonette per la tua ragazza non significa che sei un buon paroliere.** Just because you write ditties for your girlfriend does not mean you are a good lyricist.

il prosatore/la prosatrice prose writer

il romanziere/la romanziera novelist

il verseggiatore/la verseggiatrice versifier, rhymester, versemonger ▪ **Quello scrittore cerca di scrivere poesie ma non è altro che un pessimo verseggiatore.** That writer tries to write poetry but he's nothing but an awful versifier.

DESCRIBING ARTISTIC PEOPLE AND TEMPERAMENTS

all'antica, di vecchio stampo old-fashioned ▪ **La nonna non ti può capire perché pensa ancora all'antica.** Grandma can't understand you because she's old-fashioned.

alzare una lira (*lit.*, to raise a penny) to make money ▪ **I ragazzi vanno a suonare in piazza per vedere se riescono ad alzare una lira.** The guys are going to play in the square to see if they can make some money.

avere il naso all'aria to have one's nose in the air

avere la testa per aria to have one's head in the clouds ▪ **Lei non ti ascolta perché ha la testa per aria.** She isn't listening to you because she has her head in the clouds.

avere pretese artistiche to have artistic pretentions, artsy-fartsy

calcare le scene (*lit.*, to tread the scenes) to be an actor, to tread the boards ▪ **Lei è andata a Roma perché vuole calcare le scene per campare.** She went to Rome because she wants to act for a living.

chi detta la moda, chi lancia una moda who dictates or launches a trend or fashion, trendsetter ▪ **Sarebbe bello essere chi detta la moda!** It would be nice to be a trendsetter!

darsi delle arie to put on airs

esibirsi to appear onstage ▪ **Quel cantautore si esibisce raramente.** That folk singer rarely appears onstage.

fare la primadonna to act like a spoiled superstar ▪ **Ha avuto un solo successo e ora fa la primadonna!** He had one successful show and now he's acting like a spoiled superstar.

fare scene to make a scene

farsi una cultura to acquire profound understanding or knowledge about something ▪ **La profa si è fatta un'incredibile cultura del teatro.** The (female) professor has acquired great knowledge about the theater.

girare un film to shoot or make a film ▪ **Hanno girato il nuovo film in esterni in Sicilia.** They shot the new film on location in Sicily.

guardare dall'alto in basso to look down upon

l'intellettuale (m/f) intellectual, highbrow

montarsi la testa   to get a big head   ▪ **Lei non parla più con noi ora che si è montata la testa.** She doesn't talk to us anymore now that she has a big head.

non avere né arte né parte   (*lit.*, to have neither art nor part) to be good for nothing

pretenzioso   pretentious

un temperamento d'artista   an artist's temperament   ▪ **Dobbiamo perdonarlo; si comporta così perché ha un temperamento d'artista.** We must forgive him; he acts like that because he has an artist's temperament.

tirarsela   to be on one's high horse, to think very highly of oneself (fam.)   ▪ **Lei potrebbe essere anche bellissima, ma non la sopporto perché se la tira troppo.** She might even be gorgeous, but I can't stand her because she thinks way too much of herself.

SUCCESS AND FAILURE

andare a ruba   to sell like crazy, to sell like hotcakes   ▪ **Lui fa un sacco di soldi perché il suo nuovo romanzo va a ruba.** He is making tons of money since his new novel is selling like hotcakes.

a regola d'arte   perfectly, in a masterly fashion   ▪ **Ha fatto il martini proprio a regola d'arte!** He made the martini absolutely perfectly!

barba   (*lit.*, beard), **palle** (*lit.*, balls) (vulg.) boredom, a drag   ▪ **Che barba!** How boring!   ▪ **Che palle!** What a fucking drag!

una bomba   (*lit.*, a bomb) hit, smash, great show   ▪ **«Com'è il nuovo spettacolo?» «È una bomba!»** "How is the new show?" "It's the bomb!"

una cazzata, una stronzata   load of crap, bullshit, something not serious (vulg.)   ▪ **Non sprecare il tuo tempo perché il film è una cazzata.** Don't waste your time because the movie is a load of crap.

chic   very stylish or fashionable, hip, "in"

il copione, lo scimmiotto   (*lit.*, a monkey) copycat, not original   ▪ **Il giovane cantante è un po' scimmiotto; mi ricorda di tutti gli altri.** The young singer isn't very original; he reminds me of all the others.

dimenticare le battute   to forget one's lines

di moda, alla moda   in fashion, all the rage   ▪ **Va molto di moda questi giorni!** It's all the rage these days!

essere da non perdere, un must   not to be missed   ▪ **Ho visto il film ieri sera. Guarda, è da non perdere!** I saw the movie last night. Look, it is not to be missed!

essere il colmo (dei colmi)   (*lit.*, to be the top or the height) to be the most (of the most), to be too much, to be the max

il fallito/la fallita   failure ▪ Come attrice è una fallita, ma come fotomodella è alla moda. She's a failure as an actress, but as a model she's all the rage.

far furore, furoreggiare   to be all the rage

fare cagare   (*lit.*, to make one shit) to suck ass (vulg.) ▪ Questo gruppo musicale fa cagare! This (musical) group sucks ass!

fare schifo   (*lit.*, to disgust) to be horrendous, to bite ▪ Quella cantante fa schifo! That singer bites!

farsi un nome   to make a name for oneself

il fiasco   a failure, a flop ▪ L'ultimo film di questo regista è stato un fiasco totale! The last film by this director was a total flop!

la fine del mondo   (*lit.*, the end of the world) awesome, out of this world

fuori moda   out of style or fashion

in gamba   (*lit.*, on one's feet) with it, hip, alert ▪ È un musicista veramente in gamba! He is a really hip musician!

il giallo   (*lit.*, the yellow) detective story

> NOTE: The name comes from the traditional color of the book cover of this popular genre, which is obviously yellow.

Che barba!

il grosso nome   a big name   ■ **Quello che manca a quel film è un grosso nome.** What that film is missing is a big name (actor or actress).

mitico   mythical, legendary, of godlike proportions   ■ **Ha vinto il campionato la mitica squadra della Juventus!** The legendary team of Juventus won the championship!

il mito   legend

il romanzo rosa   (*lit.*, pink novel) romance novel

la schifezza   (*lit.*, something disgusting or filthy) something horrendous or awful   ■ **Non mi è piaciuto per niente, e quell'attore è stato una schifezza!** I didn't like it at all, and that actor was horrendous!

scimmiottare   to ape, to mimic, to imitate

sexy   sexy, exciting   ■ **Il film di Pieraccioni ha un titolo molto sexy.** Pieraccioni's movie has a very sexy title.

sfondare   to make it, to break through   ■ **Non ha mai sfondato come attore, ma come regista è un grande successo.** He never made it big as an actor, but as a director he is a huge success.

strepitoso, clamoroso   roaring, smashing, clamorous, stunning   ■ **Quel film ha avuto un successo strepitoso!** That movie was a smashing success!

il terremoto   (*lit.*, an earthquake) something revolutionary or groundbreaking

trendy   trendy, hip   ■ **La discoteca in periferia è molto trendy!** The discotheque outside of town is very trendy.

il/la vip   a very important person, a VIP

EXERCISES

Adesso tocca a voi!

A   *Match each word or expression on the left with its correct definition on the right:*

_____ 1. **farsi una cultura**

_____ 2. **una schifezza**

_____ 3. **la diva**

a. something awful

b. stage name

c. to get a big head

_____ 4. tirarsela   d. the opera buff

_____ 5. il nome d'arte   e. the star

_____ 6. l'intenditrice   f. out of this world

_____ 7. montarsi la testa   g. to acquire great knowledge about something

_____ 8. a regola d'arte

_____ 9. il patito della lirica   h. an expert or critic

_____ 10. la fine del mondo   i. to be on one's high horse

                                        j. perfectly

B   *Choose from the following words or phrases to complete the Italian sentences:*

scene	vip	cinefilo	fuori moda
lira	giallo		

1. Your friend speaks to you about his love for the movies.

   Guarda, sono proprio un _____; vado al cinema ogni giorno!

2. Your Italian literature professor explains Eco's novel, *The Name of the Rose*.

   Il _____ medievale di Umberto Eco è un romanzo postmoderno.

3. Your sister tells you about the nightclub where the movie stars hang out.

   Il locale La Dolce Vita è dove vanno tutti i _____ del cinema.

4. An acquaintance talks about a restaurant that has fallen out of favor among young people.

   Quel ristorante è ormai _____ fra i giovani.

5. Your mother talks about your cousin's difficulties in making money as an actor.

   Sai, sono due anni che Andrea calca le _____, ma non riesce ad alzare una _____.

C *Reply in Italian slang to the following questions:*

1. Hai visto il nuovo film di Moretti?

   Say that the film is a load of crap.

   _____

2. È bello il nuovo spettacolo al teatro La Pergola?

   Say that the show was a fucking drag.

   _____

3. Tua madre è contenta che tu calchi le scene?

   Say that your mother is too old-fashioned to understand.

   _____

4. Cosa pensi dell'interpretazione di Roberto Benigni in *La Vita è Bella?*

   Say that he was awesome.

   _____

5. Hai mangiato al ristorante di Via Ghibellina?

   Say that the restaurant is very fashionable.

   _____

6. Hai sentito qualcosa della nuova produzione di *La Bohème?*

   Say that it's a production that is not to be missed.

   _____

Beauty

COSMETIC SURGERY

avere le tette siliconate   to have fake tits, to have silicone tits (vulg.) ▪ Sembra che oggi tutte le ragazze abbiano le tette enormi, ma io penso che abbiano le tette siliconate. These days it seems like every girl has huge tits, but I think they all have fake tits.

avere le labbra siliconate   to have silicone lips

avere il doppio mento   to have a double chin

avere le zampe di gallina   to have crow's feet (eye wrinkles)

avere le tette cadenti   to have sagging boobs (vulg.)

avere le tette finte   to have fake tits (vulg.)

avere le tette piccole   to have small tits (vulg.) ▪ Quella ragazza mi piace. Peccato che abbia le tette piccole! I like that girl. It's too bad she has small tits!

avere il naso aquilino   to have a beaklike nose

avere le borse sotto gli occhi   to have bags under one's eyes

darsi una ritoccatina   (*lit.*, to be touched up) to have cosmetic surgery ▪ Quella ragazza è molto diversa dall'ultima volta che l'ho vista. Sono sicuro che si è data una ritoccatina. That girl is completely different than the last time I saw her. I'm certain she has had some cosmetic surgery.

fare/farsi il lifting   to get a face-lift, cosmetic surgery ▪ Marcello si è fatto il lifting. Non sembra più giovane? Marcello got a face-lift. Doesn't he look younger?

fare/farsi la plastica al naso   to have plastic surgery on one's nose

fare/farsi la plastica al seno   to have plastic surgery on one's breasts

fare la liposuzione   to have liposuction

rifarsi il naso   to get a nose job ▪ Giulia ha un volto più delicato rispetto all'ultima volta che l'ho vista. Si è rifatta il naso? Giulia's face looks more delicate compared to the last time I saw her. Did she get a nose job?

rifarsi le tette   to get a boob job (vulg.) ▪ **Lo sai che cosa ha voluto mia moglie per il suo compleanno? Si è rifatta le tette e ha chiesto che io pagassi l'operazione.** Do you know what my wife asked for for her birthday? She got a boob job and she asked me to pay for the operation.

rifarsi le labbra   to get a silicone injection in one's lips

rifarsi il culo   to get one's ass lifted (vulg.)

togliere la cellulite   to get rid of cellulite

DIETING

essere una balena   to be a whale (fam.) ▪ **Guarda quella donna! È una balena! Non riesce neanche ad entrare nella porta di casa sua.** Look at that woman! She's a whale! She can't even get through the door of her house.

essere ciccione/a   to be obese (fam.)

essere grasso/a   to be fat ▪ **Devo smettere di mangiare. Il mio fidanzato mi dice sempre che sono grassa!** I should stop eating. My boyfriend always says I'm fat!

essere magro come un grissino/come un chiodo   (*lit.*, to be as skinny as a breadstick, as a nail) to be as skinny as a beanpole ▪ **Guarda Paolo! Da quando si è messo a dieta è magro come un grissino!** Look at Paolo! Since he went on a diet he's as skinny as a beanpole!

essere magro/a   to be thin

essere una mongolfiera   to be a balloon (fam.)

essere obeso/a   to be obese

essere una palla di lardo   to be a lardass (fam.)

essere pelle e ossa   to be skin and bones ▪ **Mangia di più! Non vedi che sei pelle e ossa?** Eat more! Don't you see that you are just skin and bones?

essere più largo che lungo   to be more wide than tall ▪ **Ho conosciuto il marito di Sara. È così grasso che è più largo che lungo!** I met Sara's husband. He's so fat that he's more wide than tall!

essere magro come un grissino

essere ridotto a uno scheletro   to be reduced to a skeleton ▪ **Mio figlio non mangia mai niente e adesso è ridotto a uno scheletro!** My son never eats anything and now he's been reduced to a skeleton!

ingrassare   to gain weight

mettere a stecchetto   to ration someone else's food ▪ **Mi dispiace, ma non posso mangiare questo bel piatto di pasta. Mia moglie dice che sono obeso e mi ha messo a stecchetto.** I'm sorry, but I can't eat this beautiful plate of pasta. My wife says I'm obese and she is rationing my food.

mettere su pancia   to put on weight ▪ **Durante le feste di Natale ho mangiato senza ritegno e ho messo su pancia.** During Christmas I ate with reckless abandon and put on weight.

mettersi a dieta   to go on a diet ▪ **Dalla prossima settimana mi metto a dieta. Lo prometto!** Starting next week I will go on a diet! I swear!

mettersi in forma   to get in shape

perdere peso/dimagrire   to lose weight

stare a digiuno   to fast

stare a stecchetto   to watch what one eats

il/la trippone/a   a person with a big belly (fam.) ▪ **Se continuerai a bere e mangiare così diventerai un trippone come tuo padre!** If you keep drinking and eating like that you'll get a big belly like your father!

EXERCISING

essere un armadio   (*lit.*, to be a wardrobe) to be built like a refrigerator ▪ **Guarda quello! È un armadio! Scommetto che va in palestra tutti giorni.** Look at that guy! He's built like a refrigerator! I'll bet he goes to the gym every day.

essere gonfiato   (*lit.*, to be blown up, like a balloon) to be overly muscular (fam.)

> NOTE: This expression usually refers to a person who is so muscular that it is naturally impossible. **Essere gonfiato** implies that the person described must be taking steroids or other similar drugs.

essere una montagna di muscoli   to be a mountain of muscles

essere palestrato/a   to be a powerhouse

fare aerobica   to do aerobics

fare bodybuilding/fare culturismo   to lift weights

fare fitness   to do a light workout ▪ **Vorrei tenermi in forma e andare in palestra, ma non voglio lavorare con i pesi; voglio fare fitness.** I want to get in shape and go to the gym, but I don't want to lift weights; I want to do a light workout.

fare palestra/andare in palestra   to go to the gym ■ **Negli ultimi mesi sono un po' ingrassato. Dovrei fare palestra.** In the last few months I've gotten a little bit fat. I should go to the gym.

rassodare le cosce/l'addome/il sedere   to tone one's legs/stomach/buttocks, butt ■ **Il mio corpo è proprio un disastro! Dovrei fare esercizi per rassodare le cosce e il sedere.** My body is a mess! I should exercise to tone my legs and my butt.

rassodare il culo   to tone one's ass (vulg.)

HAIR

le basette   sideburns

i basettoni   long sideburns, chops

il barbiere   barber ■ **Lorenzo è il mio barbiere preferito. È bravo e non è caro.** Lorenzo is my favorite barber. He does a good job and he's not expensive.

il codino   ponytail

il ciuffo   cowlick

le doppiepunte   split ends

farsi i colpi di sole   to get highlights in one's hair ■ **Pensi che sarò più affascinante se mi faccio i colpi di sole?** Do you think I will be more attractive if I get highlights?

farsi la messa in piega   to style one's hair, to "do" one's hair ■ **Domenica devo andare al matrimonio di mia sorella. Voglio farmi la messa in piega.** On Sunday I have to go to my sister's wedding. I want to do my hair.

farsi la permanente   to get a perm (permanent)

la forfora   dandruff

ossigenarsi i capelli   to bleach one's hair ■ **Marilisa fino a qualche giorno fa aveva i capelli neri, ma ora è biondissima. Penso proprio che si sia ossigenata i capelli.** Until a few days ago, Marilisa used to have black hair, but now it's really blonde. I really think that she bleached her hair.

il parrucchiere/la parrucchiera   hairdresser ■ **Vado dalla parrucchiera ogni sabato.** I go to the hairdresser every Saturday.

il pizzetto   goatee

il salone   salon

la shampista   shampooer

tingersi i capelli   to dye one's hair

HEALTH CENTERS/GYMS/BEAUTY SALONS

andare dall'estetista   to go to a beautician ■ **Da quando Catia ha iniziato ad andare dall'estetista la sua immagine è completamente cambiata.** Since Catia started going to the beautician she seems to have a completely new look.

andare dalla visagista   to go to a cosmetologist

il centro dimagrante   weight loss center, spa

il centro estetico/la clinica di bellezza/il salone di bellezza   beauty parlor, salon

l'immagine (f)   style, image, look ■ **Avere una buona immagine è importante nel tuo lavoro. Dovresti quindi frequentare un centro dimagrante e un salone di bellezza.** Looking good is important to your job. You need to go to a spa and salon quite often.

il look   style, image, look ■ **Giovanna ci tiene molto al look. Va al salone di bellezza tutte le settimane.** Giovanna really cares about her image. She goes to the salon every week.

MAKEUP/MANICURE/PEDICURE

avere il trucco pesante   to wear thick/heavy makeup ■ **Quella ragazza ha il trucco pesante. Potrei disegnare sulla sua faccia con le mie dita.** That girl is wearing thick makeup. I could draw on her face with my fingers.

dare lo smalto alle unghie   to paint one's nails

fare la pulizia del viso   to clean one's face

farsi le unghie   to get a manicure ■ **Ogni volta che vado al salone di bellezza mi faccio le unghie e la pulizia del viso.** Every time I go to the salon I have a manicure and a facial.

farsi le unghie dei piedi   to get a pedicure

mettersi il rossetto   to put on lipstick

il rimmel   mascara

l'ombretto (m)   eye shadow

rifarsi il trucco   to reapply makeup

ritoccarsi le labbra   to reapply makeup to one's lips

tagliarsi le unghie   to cut one's nails

tagliarsi le unghie dei piedi   to cut one's toenails

truccarsi   to put on makeup   ▪ **Quando vado al lavoro non mi trucco mai, mi trucco solo quando vado alle feste.** When I go to work, I never put on makeup; I only do it when I go to parties.

PIERCING AND TATTOOS

fare/farsi il piercing   to get a piercing

fare/farsi un tatuaggio   to get a tattoo

EXERCISES

Adesso tocca a voi!

A   *Write the Italian slang equivalents for the following expressions:*

1. to have fake tits _____

2. to have silicone lips _____

3. to have small tits _____

4. to get one's ass lifted _____

5. to get a nose job _____

6. to get a boob job _____

7. to get a silicone injection (in one's lips) _____

8. to have sagging tits _____

9. to have bags under one's eyes _____

10. to have a double chin _____

B   *Choose from the following words or phrases to complete the sentences:*

parrucchiera	balena	tenerti in forma	armadio
mettere su	metta	fitness	colpi
gonfiato	peso		

1. Ieri ho visto Maria. Ha perso molto _____ negli ultimi tempi.
   Prima era così grossa che sembrava una _____.

2. Penso che Marco prenda degli steroidi. Guarda com'è _____!
   Sembra un _____.

3. Se continuo a mangiare così tanto rischio di _____ pancia. È ora
   che mi _____ a dieta.

4. Se vuoi _____, vai in palestra un'ora tutti giorni, ma non fare
   bodybuilding, fai _____.

5. Stasera vado dalla _____ a farmi i _____ di sole.

C *Complete the following sentences:*

1. Quel ragazzo è proprio una montagna _____.

2. Marco non mangia mai nulla ed è magro come _____.

3. Tuo fratello è veramente obeso. Sembra una palla _____.

4. Se continui a mangiare così tanto diventerai più largo _____.

5. Hai perso troppo peso con la tua dieta! Ora sei pelle e _____.

Business

BANKING AND MONEY MATTERS

agevolare le difficoltà   to grease the wheels, to facilitate ▪ **Gli ho dato una bustarella per agevolare le difficoltà.** I gave him a bribe to grease the wheels.

arricchirsi   to get rich

l'assegno a vuoto   bad check

il bancomat   ATM (automated teller machine)

il codice fiscale   Social Security number ▪ **Si deve ottenere un codice fiscale per essere pagati.** One must have a Social Security number in order to get paid.

il codice segreto   PIN (personal identification number)

il conto corrente   bank account

costare un occhio della testa   (*lit.*, to cost an eye from the head) to cost an arm and a leg

la carta   buck, bill ▪ **«Quanto ti è costato l'albergo?» «Settanta carte.»** "How much did the room cost?" "Seventy bucks."

essere al verde   (*lit.*, to be in the green) to be broke ▪ **Non posso uscire stasera perché sono al verde!** I can't go out tonight because I'm broke!

essere ricco sfondato   (*lit.*, to be bottomless rich) to be filthy rich ▪ **Lei viene da una famiglia ricca sfondata.** She comes from a filthy rich family.

fare quattrini   to make some money ▪ **Dobbiamo fare quattrini se vogliamo andare in vacanza quest'anno.** We have to make some money if we want to go on vacation this year.

fare una barca di soldi   to make a boatload of money

la grana, i quattrini, il denaro   dough, money

guadagnarsi il pane   (*lit.*, to earn one's bread) to earn one's living, to earn one's keep ▪ **Loro suonano in piazza per guadagnarsi il pane.** They play (music) in the square to earn their living.

i guadagni   earnings

essere ricco sfondato

il numero verde   (*lit.*, green number) toll-free number

prelevare   to withdraw ▪ **Devo prelevare dal bancomat prima di andare a cena, ma ho dimenticato il mio codice segreto.** I have to withdraw some money from the ATM before going to dinner, but I forgot my PIN.

riscuotere   to collect, to get paid ▪ **Purtroppo, il mio lavoro è stagionale e quindi non riscuoto in inverno.** Unfortunately, my job is seasonal and therefore I don't get paid in the winter.

i risparmi   savings

versare   (*lit.*, to pour) to deposit ▪ **Faccio un salto in banca per versare dei soldi nel mio conto corrente.** I'm going to run by the bank to deposit some money in my account.

>   NOTE: The following expressions originally referred to **lire**, the Italian currency prior to the introduction of the **Euro**. They are all numerical abbreviations, which were most useful inasmuch as they allowed one to avoid referring to money in the thousands, as was almost always necessary in the case of the **lira**.

il cinquino   (*lit.*, little five) a five (fam.) ▪ **Mi devi un cinquino da un mese, e adesso mi paghi gli interessi.** You've owed me a five for a month, and now you're going to pay interest on it.

il decino   (*lit.*, little ten) a ten (fam.)

il deca   a ten (fam.) ▪ **Ho scommesso un deca e ho perso.** I bet a ten and I lost.

dieci sacchi   (*lit.*, ten bags) ten bucks (fam.)

il ventino   (*lit.*, little twenty) a twenty (fam.)

il cinquantino   (*lit.*, little fifty) a fifty (fam.) ■ **Se mi presti un cinquantino ora, te lo rendo martedì.** If you loan me a fifty now, I'll give it back to you on Tuesday.

il centino   (*lit.*, little hundred) a hundred (fam.)

BUILDING TRADES

il cantiere edile   building site

il caposquadra, il capomastro   foreman

il carpentiere   carpenter

l'edile (m)   construction worker

l'elettricista (m)   electrician

il falegname   woodworker

l'idraulico (m)   plumber

l'imbianchino (m)   painter

l'industria edilizia (f)   building industry

il manovale, il bracciante   laborer, unskilled worker

il muratore   bricklayer

il palazzinaro   builder, constructor

> NOTE: The standard terms for "builder" or "constructor" are **l'impresario** (m) and **il costruttore**. The term **palazzinaro** is derogatory.

il subappaltatore   subcontractor

BUSINESS TITLES/JOB DESCRIPTIONS

gli alti ufficiali   top brass, high officials

il boss, il capo   boss

il capitano d'industria   tycoon, mogul

il capoccia   (*lit.*, the big head) boss (fam.) ■ **Il capoccia dice di no, quindi non lo faremo.** The boss says no, so we won't do it.

il direttore generale   chief executive officer, CEO

il galoppino   gofer, errand boy (fam.)

> NOTE: This term has a slightly negative connotation.

il grande capo   (*lit.*, the big chief) boss (fam.)

l'impiegato/a, il colletto bianco   office worker, white-collar worker

il magnate   mogul

il/la manager   manager

il negriero, il caporale   slave driver

il padrone/la padrona   owner

il personale   personnel

il pezzo grosso   (*lit.*, the big piece) bigwig

il/la responsabile   person in charge, manager

il subalterno, il tirapiedi (fam.)   underling

> NOTE: The term **tirapiedi** is derogatory, something like "peon" in the English language.

il/la VIP   a very important person, a VIP

BUYING AND SELLING/WHEELING AND DEALING

l'affarista (m), il faccendiere, l'intrallazzatore, il trafficone   wheeler-dealer

le cianfrusaglie, la roba inutile   junk, worthless goods

darsi da fare, trafficare, intrallazzare   to wheel and deal ■ **Vedi che gli affaristi trafficano sempre!** You see that the wheeler-dealers wheel and deal all the time!

> NOTE: **Intrallazzare** means to be involved in shady deals, while **darsi da fare** and **trafficare** can mean to wheel and deal in either legitimate or shady deals. **Non trattare con quella gente perché intrallazzano solo fra di loro.** Don't deal with those people because they only wheel and deal among themselves.

fregare   to rip off, to steal ■ **Quel venditore ambulante mi ha fregato! Questa radio non funziona!** That mobile vendor ripped me off! This radio doesn't work!

la fregatura   a rip-off

imbrogliare, truffare, raggirare   to swindle, to con ■ **Cerchiamo di imbrogliare questi turisti!** Let's try to swindle these tourists!

liquidare, svendere   to sell off (stolen goods) ■ **Ho una valanga di roba elettronica da svendere. Ti interessa?** I have a ton of electronic goods to sell off. Are you interested?

il racket   racket

riciclare   to launder money

il riciclaggio (di soldi)   money laundering

rifilare, sbolognare   to palm off, to unload ■ **Hanno sbolognato quella roba a me, e ora la rifilo a te!** They palmed off this stuff to me, and now I'm palming it off to you!

spacciare   to peddle, to push

lo spacciatore   trafficker, (drug) pusher

la truffa, l'imbroglio (m), il raggiro   scam ■ **Non scommettere con quelli che giocano a carte alla stazione! È una truffa!** Don't bet with those guys that play cards at the train station! It's a scam!

il truffatore, l'imbroglione (m)   swindler, con artist

EMPLOYMENT (NORMAL/OCCASIONAL/ILLEGAL)

essere a spasso   (*lit.*, to be on vacation) to be unemployed ■ **Non va più al lavoro perché è a spasso!** He/She doesn't go to work anymore because he/she is unemployed!

essere pagato in nero   (*lit.*, to be paid in black) to be paid under the table/off the books ■ **Sono pagati in nero perché non hanno i documenti per lavorare regolarmente.** They are paid under the table because they don't have the papers to work legally.

ingaggiare, arruolare, assoldare   to engage, to enlist, to recruit, to sign someone up (for a job) ■ **Ti ingaggio, ma ti pago in nero per evitare le tasse!** I'll sign you up, but I'm paying you under the table to avoid paying taxes!

lavorare in nero   to work illegally ■ **Non ho un lavoro regolare, ma lavoro in nero.** I don't have a legal job, but I do work illegally.

i lavori occasionali   odd jobs, occasional employment

il lavoro a tempo pieno   full-time job

il lavoro nero   illegal job

il lavoro part-time   part-time job

il lavoro stagionale   seasonal work

licenziare su due piedi, mettere alla porta, mandare a spasso, dare gli otto giorni   to fire, to can, to sack ■ **Dopo tutto quello che ho fatto per loro, mi hanno messo alla porta!** After all I did for them, they canned me!

FACTORIES AND FACTORY WORK

la cosa da nulla, il gioco da ragazzi   child's play, a piece of cake ▪ **Questo lavoretto è un gioco da ragazzi!** This little job is child's play!

il coso/l'affare (m)   thingamabob (fam.)

la ditta, la azienda, l'impresa (f), la società   firm, company

fare i turni   to work in shifts ▪ **In questa fabbrica, gli operai fanno i turni.** In this factory the workers work in shifts.

il lavoro di tutto riposo   easy job ▪ **Beata lei che c'ha un lavoro di tutto riposo mentre noi ci siamo rotti la schiena dall'alba al tramonto!** Lucky her that she has an easy job while we break our backs from dawn to dusk!

il marchingegno/il trabiccolo/l'aggeggio (m)   contraption (fam.) ▪ **Metti giù quel dannato aggeggio e dammi una mano!** Put down that darn contraption and give me a hand!

il metalmeccanico   steelworker

l'operaio/a, il lavoratore/la lavoratrice, il colletto blu   factory worker, blue-collar worker

sgobbare, lavorare sodo   to work hard ▪ **Dai, sgobbiamo ancora un paio d'ore così finiamo questo lavoraccio stasera.** Come on, let's work hard another couple of hours so that we finish this awful job tonight.

timbrare il cartellino all'entrata/all'uscita   to clock in/out ▪ **Non dimenticare di timbrare il cartellino all'entrata e all'uscita!** Don't forget to clock in and clock out!

il/la turnista   shiftworker

EXERCISES

Adesso tocca a voi!

A   *Give the slang equivalent for the following standard Italian terms or expressions:*

1. l'impresario _____

2. il subalterno _____

3. i soldi _____

4. lavorare sodo _____

5. l'euro _____

6. licenziare _____

7. non avere soldi _____

8. essere disoccupato _____

9. guadagnare _____

B *Translate into English the slang words and phrases that are in italics.*

1. Quel tipo (a) *spaccia la droga* per (b) *guadagnarsi il pane.*

   a. _____ b. _____

2. Questi vestiti (a) *costano un occhio della testa* ma in realtà sono (b) *una fregatura.*

   a. _____ b. _____

3. (a) *I colletti blu* si comportano bene quando (b) *gli alti ufficiali* sono in giro.

   a. _____ b. _____

4. (a) *Un bravo truffatore* sa che (b) *imbrogliare* gli stranieri è (c) *un gioco da ragazzi.*

   a. _____ b. _____

   c. _____

Cars and Driving

ACCIDENTS

l'incidente stradale (m)   car accident

lo schianto   crash ▪ **Siamo arrivati in ritardo a causa di uno schianto in autostrada.** We arrived late because of a crash on the highway.

il tamponamento (a catena)   (*lit.*, chain crash) pileup ▪ **La nebbia ha causato un tamponamento a catena!** The fog caused a pileup!

tamponare, schiantare   to crash

Damaging a car

andare a sbattere contro . . .   to bump or smash into . . . ▪ **Antonio ha fracassato la macchina! È andato a sbattere contro un albero!** Antonio wrecked the car! He smashed into a tree!

fracassare la macchina   to wreck or smash up the car

sfasciare/distruggere la macchina   to total one's car ▪ **Mi dispiace, ma ha sfasciato completamente la macchina.** I'm sorry, but he totaled the car.

Sustaining injuries

il colpo di frusta/della strega   (*lit.*, the whip of the witch) whiplash injury

il tamponamento a catena

CARS

il bolide hotrod

la cabriolet/la cabrio/la decappottabile convertible

la carcassa (*lit.*, a carcass) wreck (*fam.*) ■ **La macchina di Fabio è una carcassa.** Fabio's car is a wreck.

la Cinquecento Fiat 500 ■ **Non comprerò mai un'altra macchina perché amo la mia Cinquecento!** I will never buy another car because I love my Fiat 500!

> NOTE: The Fiat 500 has an almost cultlike following in Italy. There are a number of clubs (like the Fiat 500 Club Italia) that celebrate this much-loved classic automobile.

la famigliare station wagon

il fuoristrada, il 4 per 4 off-road or 4 x 4 vehicle

il gippone sport utility vehicle

scassato (adj) beat up, junky ■ **Questa macchina è un po' scassata, ma funziona bene.** This car is a little beat up, but it runs well.

il macinino (*lit.*, grinder for coffee or mill for pepper), **la carretta** (*lit.*, cart) jalopy, old clunker ■ **Se andiamo con la tua carretta, non ci arriveremo mai!** If we take your old clunker, we'll never get there!

il maggiolone/maggiolino (*lit.*, maybug) Volkswagen Beetle

DRIVING

la prova del palloncino (*lit.*, the test of the little balloon) Breathalyzer test ■ **Lo sbirro mi ha fatto fare la prova del palloncino ma l'ho fregato!** The cop made me do the Breathalyzer test, but I beat the rap!

allacciare/mettere la cintura to buckle/put on the seat belt

andare adagio to be careful

andare a tutto gas/a tutta birra/a tavoletta to go full throttle

andare piano to go slow ■ **Vai piano, Elisabetta, non andare a tutta birra!** Go slow, Elisabetta, don't go full throttle!

andare sparato, andare come una scheggia (*lit.*, to go like a piece of shrapnel) to bomb or shoot along

arrestarsi con uno stridio di gomme to screech to a halt ■ **Quando abbiamo visto il tamponamento, ci siamo arrestati con uno stridio di gomme!** When we saw the pileup, we screeched to a halt!

avere il piede pesante to have a heavy foot

correre (*lit.*, to run), **viaggiare** (*lit.*, to travel) to speed ■ **Adriano ha il piede pesante, ma non lasciarlo correre!** Adriano has a heavy foot, but don't let him speed!

effettuare un sorpasso azzardato to daringly pass someone

essere motorizzato to have wheels

fare l'autostop to hitchhike ■ **Non sono motorizzati, e quindi i ragazzi dovranno fare l'autostop per arrivare in montagna.** They don't have wheels, therefore the boys will have to hitchhike to get to the mountains.

in coda serrata in bumper-to-bumper traffic ■ **È da due ore che siamo in coda serrata! Che palle!** It's two hours that we've been in bumper-to-bumper traffic! How fucking annoying!

l'inversione a U/di marcia U-turn ■ **Non è lecito fare un'inversione a U qui, ma falla comunque!** It's not legal to do a U-turn here, but do it anyway!

le marce (*lit.*, the gears), **il cambio manuale** stick shift, manual transmission ■ **Non so guidare una macchina con le marce perché ho sempre guidato con il cambio automatico.** I don't know how to drive a stick shift because I've always driven with an automatic transmission.

la lumaca (*lit.*, the snail), **l'autista della domenica** (*lit.*, Sunday driver) slow driver

la marcia indietro reverse gear ■ **C'è poco spazio e quindi è meglio entrarci a marcia indietro.** There's not much room so it's better to get in there in reverse.

mettere in marcia to start the car

> NOTE: The expression **mettersi in marcia** is a figurative expression that means "to start doing something." **Sono sei settimane che voglio rifare la cucina, e finalmente oggi mi metto in marcia.** It's six weeks that I've been wanting to redo the kitchen, and finally today I'm getting started.

mettersi al volante to get behind the wheel

il passaggio, lo strappo ride ■ **Mi dai uno strappo a casa dato che parti ora?** Will you give me a ride home since you are leaving now?

passare col rosso to run a red light

il/la pilota (race car) driver ■ **Chi vuole guidare? Tu sei il pilota e io sono il secondo pilota!** Who wants to drive? You be the race car driver and I'll be the copilot!

pilotare to drive (in a race)

il pirata della strada road hog

scaricare (*lit.*, to unload) to drop off ▪ **Ti devo scaricare qui perché ho un appuntamento con una ciccia.** I have to drop you off here because I'm meeting a chick.

scivolare, slittare, sbandare to skid, to slide

schiacciare/premere/affondare l'acceleratore to put the pedal to the metal ▪ **Ecco gli sbirri! Sgommiamo! Affonda l'acceleratore!** The cops are here! Let's burn rubber! Put the pedal to the metal!

la scorribanda su un'automobile rubata joyride

sgommare to get a wheel, to burn rubber, to leave rapidly

smacchinare, fare un giro, andare in giro (in macchina) to cruise (in the car), to drive around

stare alle calcagne di . . . , stare incollato a . . . , tallonare, pedinare to tailgate, to be hot on someone's tail ▪ **Quello stronzo dietro mi sta incollato!** That shithead back there is tailgating me!

lo stridio di gomme screech

tagliare la strada (*lit.*, to cut the road) to cut off ▪ **Quello stronzo mi ha tagliato la strada!** That shithead cut me off!

EXERCISES
Adesso tocca a voi!

A *Supply the answers to the following:*

1. Give three different ways to indicate a car accident.

   _____   _____

   _____

2. How does one say "to smash into" in Italian? _____

3. Give two ways of saying "to total the car."

   _____   _____

4. Give three ways of saying "to go full throttle."

   _____   _____

   _____

B *Match each word or expression on the left with its correct definition on the right:*

——— 1.	il fuoristrada	a.	ride
——— 2.	la cinquecento	b.	to cut someone off
——— 3.	correre	c.	to run a red light
——— 4.	sgommare	d.	whiplash injury
——— 5.	fare l'autostop	e.	off-road or 4 x 4 vehicle
——— 6.	tagliare la strada	f.	to burn rubber
——— 7.	il macinino	g.	Fiat 500
——— 8.	passare col rosso	h.	to hitchhike
——— 9.	lo strappo	i.	to speed
——— 10.	il colpo di frusta	j.	jalopy

City

BUSES

l'abbonamento   bus pass

l'autista (m/f), il/la conducente   driver ▪ **Non devi parlare all'autista mentre guida il pullman.** You must not talk to the driver while he is operating the bus.

il biglietto   ticket

il borseggiatore   pickpocket ▪ **State attenti ai borseggiatori quando siete sul pullman!** Be careful of pickpockets when you are on the bus!

il bus, l'autobus, il pullman, la corriera   city bus

il capolinea   end of the line ▪ **I signori passeggeri sono pregati di scendere perché siamo al capolinea.** The kind passengers are asked to get off the bus because this is the end of the line.

il controllore   ticket police ▪ **Se sale il controllore, devi timbrare il biglietto subito!** If the ticket police get on, you must stamp your ticket right away!

convalidare, timbrare, obliterare   to validate or stamp (your ticket)

> NOTE: In Italy, as in most other European countries, you cannot pay the fare once aboard the bus. Tickets must be purchased in advance and are sold at most newsstands (called **edicole**) or in tobacco shops (called **tabacchi**). When you get on the bus you must stamp your ticket with the time and date. You generally have sixty minutes to complete your travel with that ticket, depending on the type of ticket you purchase. If a **controllore** asks you for your ticket, he will check the time and date stamp, and you will receive a hefty fine if you have an old ticket or if you haven't had it stamped. Pretending not to understand that you were supposed to stamp it often gets you out of paying the fine, but if you see a **controllore** get on the bus, stamp your ticket right away, or just speak in English as if you didn't know anything about tickets or stamping them.

la fermata   (bus) stop ▪ **I signori scendono alla fermata più vicina al Duomo.** The gentlemen are getting off at the stop closest to the Cathedral.

prendere, pigliare   to take (the bus) ▪ **Dobbiamo pigliare il numero 37 per andare in Via Garibaldi.** We must take the number 37 bus to go to Via Garibaldi.

NOTE: **Prendere** and **pigliare** are interchangeable. The verb **prendere** is used in central and northern Italy while **pigliare** is predominantly used in the south.

il tram   cable car ▪ **La sera, i ragazzi tornano a casa in tram.** At night the kids return home by the tram.

NOTE: **Il tram** is found only in larger cities like Milano, Roma, and Napoli.

SHOPPING AND BUYING

a buon mercato   at a good price ▪ **Al mercato di San Lorenzo si trovano giubotti di cuoio a buon mercato.** At the San Lorenzo market one can find leather jackets at a good price.

l'abbigliamento (m), i vestiti, gli indumenti   clothes, garments

un affare   (*lit.*, transaction) deal ▪ **Per venti euro questa camicia è un affare da non perdere!** For twenty euros this shirt is a deal not to miss!

allungarsi   (*lit.*, to lengthen, to stretch) to buy ▪ **I tuoi amici non si allungano mai più di una bottiglia di vino!** Your friends never buy more than one bottle of wine!

andare a ruba   to sell like hotcakes

la bancarella   (outdoor) market stand

la bottega   workshop ▪ **Alle otto in punto il mercante chiude bottega e va a casa a cenare.** At exactly eight o'clock the merchant closes up shop and goes home for dinner.

NOTE: **Chiudere bottega** is frequently used figuratively as if to mean "to call it a day" or "to finish up for the day." **Gli studenti studiano fino alle undici di sera ma poi chiudono bottega e vanno a bere una birra.** The students study until eleven o'clock at night, but then they call it a day and go for a beer.

la cassa   cash register ▪ **Prima si paga alla cassa e poi porta lo scontrino al banco.** First pay at the cash register and then bring the receipt to the bar.

il centro commerciale   (*lit.*, commercial center) shopping mall

la commessa   saleswoman ▪ **Quel negozio cerca una nuova commessa.** That store is looking for a new saleswoman.

comprarsi   buy oneself something ▪ **Sono contentissima! Mi sono comprata un elegante vestito nero!** I am so happy! I bought myself a very stylish black dress!

costare un occhio della testa   (*lit.*, to cost an eye from the head) to cost an arm and a leg ▪ **La macchina è bella, ma mi è costata un occhio della testa!** The car is beautiful but it cost an arm and a leg!

43

di seconda mano, usato   secondhand, used

l'emporio (m), i grandi magazzini   department store

fare lo shopping, fare acquisti   (*lit.*, to make acquisitions), **fare compere** to shop ■ **La mia amica fa lo shopping ogni sabato. Beata lei!** My (female) friend shops every Saturday. Lucky her!

una fregatura   rip-off ■ **Non compriamo nulla da quella bancarella perché tutto è una fregatura!** Let's not buy anything from that stand because everything is a rip-off!

fregare   to rip off ■ **Mi hanno fregato! Questa giacca non è di cuoio!** They ripped me off! This jacket isn't made of real leather!

guardare le vetrine   to window shop ■ **Le nostre mogli escono ogni pomeriggio a guardare le vetrine.** Our wives go out every afternoon to window shop.

il mercato   (outdoor) market

il mercato delle pulci   flea market

il mercato nero   black market

la merce, la roba   merchandise, goods ■ **Oggi tutta la merce è in offerta!** Today all the merchandise is a bargain/is on sale!

il negozio   store, shop

l'offerta (f)   (*lit.*, offer), **l'occasione (f)** (*lit.*, occasion) bargain

picchiare   (*lit.*, to hit) to cost (fam.) ■ **Il nuovo ristorante picchia! Non ci andare!** The new restaurant costs a lot! Don't go there!

il prezzo speciale   special price ■ **Non ti preoccupare! Ti faccio un prezzo speciale!** Don't worry about it! I'll give you a special price!

il prezzo turistico   tourist price

regalarsi, concedersi   to treat oneself ■ **Per il mio compleanno, mi sono regalato un paio di scarpe.** For my birthday I treated myself to a new pair of shoes.

la ricevuta, lo scontrino   receipt, sales slip

il rimborso   refund ■ **Non sono soddisfatto con questo prodotto; voglio un rimborso!** I am not satisfied with this product; I want a refund!

i saldi   sales ■ **I saldi cominciano a fine gennaio.** The sales begin at the end of January.

spendere   to spend ■ **«Quanto spendo per la birra?» «Spendi otto euro, grazie.»** "How much am I spending for the beer?" "You are spending eight euros, thanks."

il supermercato   supermarket

taroccato (adj)   knock-off ▪ **Macché! Non è una vera Prada. È solo una borsa taroccata!** Are you kidding? It's not a real Prada. It's just a knock-off purse!

tirare sul prezzo   (*lit.*, to pull on the price) to haggle, to negotiate on the price ▪ **Il venditore è sempre disposto a tirare sul prezzo, soprattutto se paghi in contanti.** The seller is always willing to haggle on the price, especially if you are paying in cash.

> NOTE: When buying from an outdoor market (like San Lorenzo in Florence), it is customary to negotiate the price. In stores, however, the prices are fixed and there is no haggling to be done.

vendere sottobanco   to sell under the table

il venditore ambulante   mobile vendor

SUBWAY

la biglietteria   ticket office

i binari   tracks or rails (for both trains and subways) ▪ **È vietato attraversare i binari a piedi.** It is forbidden to cross the tracks on foot.

il corrimano   handrail

la direzione   direction ▪ **Mio fratello prende la linea rossa in direzione di Anagnina per tornare a casa dal lavoro.** My brother takes the red subway line in the direction of Anagnina to return home from work.

il distributore automatico   automatic ticket dispenser

l'entrata (f)   (subway) entrance

la fermata   (subway or bus) stop

la linea   (subway) line ▪ **Quale linea devo prendere per andare in centro?** Which subway line must I take to go downtown?

> NOTE: The subway systems in Italian cities (Milan, Rome) have more than one subway line, which are often named with colors as in **la linea gialla** or **la linea rossa**.

la metropolitana, la metro   the subway ▪ **Dov'è l'entrata della metro?** Where is the subway entrance?

le porte scorrevoli   sliding doors ▪ **Occhio alle porte scorrevoli quando sali e scendi!** Look out for the sliding doors when you enter and exit (the subway train).

il pulsante apriporta   button to open the doors

l'uscita (f)   the (subway) exit

WALKING

a due passi (*lit.*, at two steps) nearby ∎ **Il mercato è qui a due passi; ci puoi andare a piedi.** The market is right nearby; you can go on foot.

andare a piedi to go somewhere on foot

andare a spasso, andare a zonzo to go for a stroll ∎ **Vado a portare il cane a spasso.** I'm taking the dog for a stroll.

andare bel bello to go along one's merry way

l'area pedonale (f) pedestrian area

battere le strade (*lit.*, to hit the streets) to work the streets in prostitution ∎ **Non andare in quella zona di notte perché lì battono le strade e c'è gentaglia in giro.** Don't go to that part of town at night because there they (the prostitutes) work the streets and there are bad people around.

il centro storico the historic center of town

fare due passi (*lit.*, to take two steps) to take a little stroll ∎ **Dai, dopo cena facciamo due passi prima di tornare a casa.** Come on, after dinner let's take a little stroll before returning home.

fare il gran passo (*lit.*, to take the big step) to get married

fare il primo passo to take the first step, to make the first move ∎ **Io perdonerei tua sorella ma lei deve fare il primo passo.** I would forgive your sister but she has to make the first move.

fare un passo avanti (*lit.*, to take a step forward) to make progress

fare una passeggiata to take a walk

il marciapiede sidewalk

in fila indiana (*lit.*, in Indian line) in single file ∎ **Ehi, ragazzi, camminate in fila indiana; così nessuno si perde.** Hey kids, walk in single file; that way nobody will get lost.

non fare il passo più lungo della gamba (*lit.*, don't take a step that is longer than your leg) don't bite off more than you can chew

i pedoni pedestrians ∎ **Sono cinquanta punti per ogni pedone che prendi!** Fifty points for every pedestrian that you hit!

la periferia suburbs, outskirts ∎ **Devo pigliare l'autobus ogni giorno per venire in centro perché abito in periferia.** I have to take the bus every day to come into town because I live in the outskirts of town.

il pirata della strada (*lit.*, the street pirate) road hog

lo smog smog

il pirata della strada

vagabondare   to wander about aimlessly ▪ **Devi andare a casa, amico; è pericoloso vagabondare a quest'ora!** You need to go home, friend; it is dangerous to wander about at this hour!

la zona di traffico limitato   limited traffic zone ▪ **Il centro storico è una zona di traffico limitato; i pedoni hanno sempre la precedenza.** The historic center of town is a limited traffic zone; pedestrians always have the right of way.

EXERCISES
Adesso tocca a voi!

A *Match each of the Italian words below with its English equivalent:*

il marciapiede	una fregatura	l'autista	la bancarella
un affare	lo scontrino		

1. a bargain _____

2. the driver _____

3. the receipt _____

4. a rip-off _____

5. the sidewalk _____

6. the market stand _____

B *Give the Italian equivalent for the following English words or phrases:*

1. sales _____

2. nearby _____

3. to shop _____

4. to haggle _____

5. road hog _____

C *Match each of the following Italian expressions with the English equivalent:*

battere le strade	concedersi	andare a spasso
convalidare il biglietto	costare un occhio della testa	

1. to go for a stroll _____

2. to work the streets (in prostitution) _____

3. to treat oneself (to something) _____

4. to cost an arm and a leg _____

5. to stamp the (bus) ticket _____

Clothing

DRESSES

il collant   tights (fam.) ■ **La mia ragazza si mette sempre il collant quando fa freddo.** My girlfriend always wears tights when it's cold.

degli stracci   (*lit.*, some rags) some clothes of poor quality (fam.) ■ **Non ti puoi mettere degli stracci per andare a teatro.** You can't put on rags to go to the theater.

mettersi in ghingheri   to get dressed up to the nines (fam.) ■ **Ci siamo messi in ghingheri per andare all'opera.** We got dressed up to the nines to go to the opera.

non ho uno straccio da mettermi   (*lit.*, I don't have a rag to wear) I haven't a thing to wear (fam.)

lo straccione   ragamuffin (fam.)

un vestito da quattro soldi   (*lit.*, a four-dollar outfit) a cheap outfit (fam.)

vestito di stracci   (*lit.*, dressed in rags) poorly dressed (fam.)

Expressions involving clothing

l'abito non fa il monaco   (*lit.*, the cloth does not make the monk) don't judge a book by its cover (fam.)

avere le borse agli occhi   (*lit.*, to have bags at the eyes) to have bags under the eyes (fam.) ■ **Tuo zio lavora troppo e non dorme mai. Vedi che borse agli occhi che ha?** Your uncle works too much and never sleeps. Do you see the bags he has under his eyes?

avere le tasche bucate   to have holes in one's pockets (fam.) ■ **Se tu non avessi le tasche bucate non saremmo nei guai.** If you didn't have holes in your pockets we would not be in trouble.

avere un asso nella manica   to have an ace up one's sleeve (fam.)

avere una scarpa e uno zoccolo   (*lit.*, to have one shoe and one clog) to dress poorly, to wear clothes that clash (fam.)

49

essere di manica larga

calare le brache (*lit.*, to pull one's trousers down) to surrender (fam.)

ciucciami il calzino (*lit.*, suck my sock) eat my shorts (fam.)

colletto bianco white-collar worker (fam.)

colletto blu blue-collar worker (fam.)

colpire sotto la cintura to hit below the belt (fam.)

essere di manica larga (*lit.*, to be wide in the sleeve) to be generous (fam.) ■ **Se fossi di manica larga ti avrei comprato un regalo per il tuo compleanno.** If I were generous I would have bought you a gift for your birthday.

essere nato con la camicia (*lit.*, to be born with a shirt) to be born with a silver spoon in one's mouth (fam.) ■ **Tu sei nato con la camicia, e non devi mai sforzarti per nessun motivo.** You were born with a silver spoon in your mouth, and you never have to exert yourself for any reason.

fare la scarpetta (*lit.*, to do the little shoe) to scoop up the leftover pasta sauce from the plate with a piece of bread (fam.)

fare le scarpe a qualcuno (*lit.*, to make shoes for somebody) to double-cross someone (fam.) ■ **Non ti fidare di loro, so che hanno intenzione di farti le scarpe.** Don't trust them, I know they plan on double-crossing you.

mettersi nei panni di qualcuno (*lit.*, to put oneself in someone else's clothes) to put oneself in someone else's shoes (fam.) ■ **Mettiti nei suoi panni. Tu a chi chiederesti aiuto?** Put yourself in his/her shoes. Who would you ask for help?

uno scarpone (*lit.*, big shoe) incompetent person (fam.)

stringere la cinghia (*lit.*, to tighten the belt) to be conservative with money (fam.)

sudare sette camice (*lit.*, to sweat seven shirts) to sweat profusely, to work very hard (fam.)

togliersi tanto di cappello   (*lit.*, to go as far as taking off one's hat) to take one's hat off (fam.) ▪ **Mi tolgo tanto di cappello di fronte ai giocatori della nazionale brasiliana.** I take my hat off to the player from the Brazilian national team.

trattare qualcuno con i guanti di velluto   (*lit.*, to treat someone with velvet gloves) to treat someone with kid gloves (fam.) ▪ **È venuto l'ambasciatore spagnolo e l'hanno trattato con i guanti di velluto.** The Spanish ambassador came and they treated him with kid gloves.

FASHION/FASHION ACCESSORIES

all'ultimo grido   (*lit.*, to the last cry) latest fashion (fam.) ▪ **Dicono che questo tipo di pellicce sia all'ultimo grido.** They say this kind of fur coat is the latest fashion.

il berretto   hat (fam.) ▪ **Io porto il berretto solamente d'inverno.** I only wear a hat in winter.

il bomber   flight jacket (fam.)

le brache   trousers (fam.) ▪ **Tirati su le brache, non ti rendi conto che ti si vedono le mutande?** Pull your trousers up. Can't you tell that your underwear is showing?

il chiodo   leather jacket (fam.)

la cinta   belt (fam.)

la giacchetta   (*lit.*, little jacket) jacket (fam.)

il gilè   vest ▪ **Con quel gilè Pierpaolo fa tanto il figo, ma a me pare un cretino.** With that vest Pierpaolo acts so cool, but he looks like a cretin to me.

i grandi stilisti   famous fashion designers (fam.)

il kappaway   windbreaker (fam.) ▪ **Portati il kappaway, dicono che pioverà stasera.** Bring your windbreaker with you; they say it will rain this evening.

la kefiah   traditional Palestinian scarf

il passamontagna   ski mask ▪ **Se vai a sciare, non dimenticare il passamontagna.** If you go skiing, don't forget the ski mask.

lo schiavo/la schiava della moda   slave to fashion (fam.) ▪ **Per fortuna non sono schiavo della moda.** Luckily I am not a slave to fashion.

lo spolverino   (*lit.*, dust coat) overcoat (fam.)

vestirsi alla moda   to dress in style (fam.)

vestirsi firmato   (*lit.*, to dress signed) to wear brand-name clothing (fam.)

vestirsi sbracato (*lit.*, to dress without pants) to dress poorly (fam.) ■ **Mi fai tanto ridere quando ti vesti sbracato.** You make me laugh a lot when you dress poorly.

il vestito firmato/di marca brand-name clothing (fam.) ■ **Non posso mai permettermi di comprare i vestiti firmati.** I can never afford to buy brand-name clothing.

FASHION SHOWS

fare la passerella (*lit.*, to do the catwalk) to walk the catwalk (fam.)

il modello/la modella fashion model

la passerella catwalk

la sfilata di moda fashion show ■ **Non sono mai stata a una sfilata di moda.** I have never been to a fashion show.

la top model supermodel ■ **Federico ha un appuntamento con una top model.** Federico has a date with a supermodel.

SHOES

gli anfibi (*lit.*, the amphibians) combat boots (fam.)

le babbucce slippers (fam.) ■ **Caro, mi porteresti le mie babbucce, per favore?** Dear, would you bring me my slippers, please?

le ciabatte slippers

gli infradito (*lit.*, the in-between finger) thong flip-flops (fam.)

> NOTE: The Italian word for "toe" is **dito del piede** (*lit.*, finger of the foot), which is why the name of these sandals seems to refer to the fingers of the hand.

i mocassini moccasins

i texani (*lit.*, the Texans) cowboy boots (fam.) ■ **Ho comprato i texani quando erano fuori moda da sei mesi.** I bought cowboy boots when they had been out of style for six months.

gli zoccoli clogs (fam.) ■ **Molti italiani portano gli zoccoli esclusivamente in casa.** Many Italians wear clogs exclusively in the house.

SPORTSWEAR

i dopo-sci (*lit.*, after-skis) après-ski boots (fam.)

fare il footing (*lit.*, to do the footing) to jog (fam.) ■ **Mia moglie fa il footing tre volte a settimana in estate.** My wife jogs three times a week in the summer.

la felpa   sweatshirt   ■ **Vorrei molto una felpa gialla come quella di Kobe Bryant.** I would really like a yellow sweatshirt like Kobe Bryant's.

i mammut   (*lit.*, mammoths) après-ski boots (fam.)

> NOTE: Many Italians commonly refer to **dopo-sci** as **mammut**. This name is presumably a mispronunciation of the brand name Moon Boots. These boots were large and cylinder shaped, and left elephantlike footprints in the snow.

i pantaloncini   (*lit.*, little pants) shorts (fam.)

il pile   fleece (fam.)

le scarpe da corsa   running shoes

le scarpe da ginnastica   gym shoes   ■ **Le mie scarpe da ginnastica sono consumate.** My gym shoes are worn out.

le scarpe da tennis   tennis shoes

le scarpe coi tacchetti/da calcio   shoes with cleats/soccer shoes   ■ **Ho comprato un nuovo paio di scarpe da calcio.** I bought a new pair of soccer shoes.

SUITS

l'abito (m)/il vestito   suit

il frac   tailcoat

lo smoking   tuxedo   ■ **Mi sono messo lo smoking per il matrimonio di mio fratello.** I put on a tuxedo for my brother's wedding.

UNDERWEAR

la biancheria intima   (*lit.*, intimate underwear) lingerie

i boxer   boxers (fam.)   ■ **Ti metti i boxer o gli slip?** Do you wear boxers or briefs?

le mutande   underwear

le mutandine   panties   ■ **Le mutandine vanno lavate a mano.** Panties must be washed by hand.

il reggipetto/reggiseno   (*lit.*, the breast holder) bra

gli slip   briefs

il tanga   thong (fam.)   ■ **In che anno andava di moda il tanga?** What year was the thong in style?

VACATION CLOTHES

i bermuda   bermuda shorts (fam.)

il bikini   bikini ▪ **Non mi sono mai messa in bikini.** I have never worn a bikini.

i calzettoni di lana   (*lit.*, big socks of wool) wool socks (fam.)

la camicia hawaiana   Hawaiian shirt (fam.)

il cappello da baseball   baseball cap (fam.) ▪ **Portami un cappello da baseball dall'America.** Bring me a baseball cap from America.

il costume da bagno   (*lit.*, the costume for bathing) bathing suit

essere in topless   to be topless

gli occhiali da sole   sunglasses ▪ **Ho perso i miei occhiali da sole in spiaggia.** I lost my sunglasses on the beach.

il paraorecchie   (*lit.*, ear blockers) earmuffs ▪ **Con questo vento avrò bisogno del paraorecchie.** With this wind I will need earmuffs.

la tuta da sci   ski suit ▪ **Quanto costa quella tuta da sci?** How much does that ski suit cost?

EXERCISES

Adesso tocca a voi!

A *Select the proper translation for each of the following terms and expressions:*

1. avere le tasche bucate:
   a. to surrender
   b. to have holes in one's pocket
   c. to hit below the belt

2. avere le borse agli occhi:
   a. to take one's hat off
   b. to be conservative with money
   c. to have bags under the eyes

3. fare la scarpetta:
   a. incompetent person
   b. to scoop up the leftover pasta sauce from the plate with a piece of bread
   c. to double-cross someone

4. **vestirsi firmato:**
   a. to wear brand-   b. to dress poorly   c. to dress in style
   name clothing

5. **gli zoccoli:**
   a. Moon Boots   b. gym shoes   c. clogs

B   *Translate the following expressions:*

1. I haven't a thing to wear _____

2. To get dressed up to the nines _____

3. To sweat profusely _____

4. To take one's hat off _____

5. To dress poorly _____

Coffee Shops

COFFEE DRINKS

il caffè   coffee

il caffè americano   American coffee

il caffè corretto   (*lit.*, corrected coffee) espresso coffee with a little bit of liquor ▪ **Il caffè corretto con un goccio di sambuca è veramente buono!** Espresso with a drop of Sambuca is absolutely delicious!

> NOTE: Usually when one asks for a **caffè corretto**, the bartender will add an anise liquor unless otherwise specified.

il caffè freddo   iced coffee ▪ **D'estate il caffè freddo è la mia bevanda preferita!** In the summer iced coffee is my favorite drink!

il caffè lungo   opposite of caffè ristretto; more water, less coffee, weak coffee

il caffè macchiato   espresso coffee with a touch of milk ▪ **Per favore, posso avere un caffè macchiato?** Can I please have an espresso with a little milk?

il caffè ristretto   (*lit.*, shrunk coffee) a small and dense espresso coffee, very creamy and strong ▪ **Sono così stanco stamattina! Mi ci vuole proprio un bel caffè ristretto per svegliarmi!** I am so tired this morning! I need a good strong coffee to wake me up!

il caffè shakerato   coffee shaken with ice

il caffellatte   part coffee, part milk

il cappuccino/cappuccio   cappuccino

la crema del caffè   crema, i.e., the white foam on top of an espresso shot

l'espresso (m)   espresso ▪ **L'espresso italiano è famoso in tutto il mondo!** Italian espresso is famous all over the world!

> NOTE: In Italy **espresso** and **caffè** are essentially the same thing. If one wants an American-style coffee, he/she must specifically ask for a **caffè americano**, which is very hard to find and is more like an espresso with a cup of water in it.

il latte macchiato   milk with a touch of coffee

il caffè ristretto

la schiuma   foam ▪ **Vorrei un cappuccino. Con tanta schiuma, per favore! I** would like a cappucino. With extra foam, please!

PASTRIES

il babà   Neopolitan sponge cake soaked in rum syrup

il bignè   cream puff

il bombolone   a fried pastry with cream inside

il cannolo   single cannoli ▪ **I cannoli siciliani sono i più buoni in assoluto!** Sicilian cannoli are the very best!

il cornetto/la brioche   croissant ▪ **Tutti i giorni faccio colazione con cornetto e cappuccino.** Every day I have a croissant and a cappucino for breakfast.

il diplomatico   small square layer pastry with liqueur

la pasta   pastry

la pasticceria   pastry shop

COFFEE SHOP CULTURE

il caffè/il bar   café/bar

> NOTE: **Caffès** are much more common than **caffetterias** that specialize specifically in breakfast foods and coffee products. Furthermore, **caffès** always serve alcohol as well as coffee (hence the **caffè corretto**).

la caffetteria   coffee shop and breakfast bar

fare colazione   to have breakfast

la macchina per il caffè   coffee/espresso machine

la macinazione   the process of grinding coffee

il macinino   coffee grinder

la moca   mocha

prendere un caffè   to have a coffee   ▪ **Perché non vieni con noi a prendere un caffè al bar?** Why don't you come with us to have a coffee at the bar?

prendere un cappuccino/un caffè al banco   to have a cappuccino/coffee at the counter   ▪ **Questa mattina non abbiamo tempo di fare colazione al tavolo come gli altri giorni. Prendiamo un caffè al banco e andiamo al lavoro.** This morning we don't have time to have breakfast at a table like most other days. Let's have our coffee at the counter and go to work.

prendere un cappuccino/un caffè al tavolo   to have a cappuccino/coffee at a table

> NOTE: Most Italians drink their coffee at the counter, because if you drink at a table you must usually pay more. Coffee to go is extremely uncommon.

EXERCISES

Adesso tocca a voi!

A   *Write the name of the described coffee drink below in Italian:*

1. You feel like having a small, thick coffee. You ask for _____.

2. You would like to have a little liquor in your coffee. You ask for

   _____.

3. You want an iced coffee. You ask for _____.

4. You want coffee shaken with ice. You ask for _____.

5. You want milk with a touch of coffee. You ask for _____.

B *Match each Italian word in the left column with an English word on the right:*

_____ 1. il cornetto   a. café/bar

_____ 2. il bombolone   b. sponge cake soaked in rum syrup

_____ 3. il cappuccio   c. fried pastry with cream inside

_____ 4. il caffè/bar   d. coffee grinder

_____ 5. il babà   e. croissant

_____ 6. il macinino   f. coffee shop

_____ 7. la caffetteria   g. foam

_____ 8. la schiuma   h. cappuccino

C *Choose the word in parentheses that best fits each sentence:*

1. Il cappuccino mi piace con molta (pasta/schiuma).

2. Tutti i giorni faccio colazione mangiando un (macinino/cornetto) e bevendo un caffè.

3. Andiamo (al bar/alla caffetteria) a bere un po' di whisky.

4. Molti italiani fanno colazione al (banco/diplomatico).

5. Andiamo alla (pasticceria/macinazione) a comprare babà, bignè, e cannoli.

Conversations and Invitations

BEING BORED/ANNOYED

dare fastidio   to bother ▪ C'era un tizio al bar che mi dava fastidio, ma il buttafuori l'ha mandato via. There was some guy at the bar who was bothering me, but the bouncer sent him away.

far girare le palle a qualcuno   (*lit.*, to make someone's balls turn) to piss somebody off (fam.)

levarsi di torno, levarsi dei coglioni   (*lit.*, to remove oneself from the balls) (vulg.), **smammare** to get out of there, to get lost ▪ Levati di torno, stronzo! Get lost, asshole!

rompere i coglioni   to break someone's balls, to nag the hell out of someone (fam.) ▪ Perché mi devi rompere i coglioni ogni volta che esco con gli amici? Why do you have to nag the hell out of me every time I go out with my friends?

rompere le palle a qualcuno   (*lit.*, to break someone's balls) to be a pain in the ass (fam.)

la rottura di palle a qualcuno   pain in the ass (fam.) ▪ È una rottura di palle spostare la macchina ogni volta che puliscono le strade. It's a pain in the ass to move the car every time they clean the streets.

stare alla larga   to stay away from, to avoid ▪ Ti consiglio di stare alla larga della gentaglia che c'è in giro. I advise you to stay away from the sketchy people that are around.

scocciare, seccare   (*lit.*, to dry) to annoy ▪ Mangiamo fuori stasera perché mi scoccia cucinare con questo caldo. Let's eat out tonight because it annoys me to cook when it's so hot.

scocciarsi   to be bored, to be annoyed

stare sul culo/sul cazzo/sulle palle a qualcuno   (*lit.*, to be on someone's ass/someone's dick/someone's balls) to bug or bother the shit out of someone (vulg.) ▪ Quel barrista mi sta sul cazzo! That bartender fucking bugs me!

COMPLAINING

fare storie   to make (up) excuses ▪ **Non fare storie! Finisci i compiti!** Don't make excuses! Finish your assignments!

frignare, piagnucolare   to whine

il frignone, il piagnucolone   a whiner, a crybaby ▪ **Non essere un frignone! Non serve a nulla!** Don't be a whiner! It doesn't help anything!

la lagna, la lamentela   whine, complaint

lagnarsi   to whine (fam.) ▪ **Ti lagni ogni volta che devi fare un po' di lavoro!** You whine every time that you have to do some work!

lamentarsi   to complain

DISCUSSING HOW THINGS ARE GOING

a posto   in place, all right (fam.) ▪ **«Tutto a posto?» «Sì, a postissimo!»** "Everything all right?" "Yep, everything's great!"

> NOTE: The question **«Tutto a posto?»** or more simply **«A posto?»** is very common in Italy, and especially so in southern Italy. One can respond by saying **«Tutto a posto.»** or more simply **«A posto.»**

tutto a posto e niente in ordine   (*lit.*, everything in place and nothing in order) life is crazy, as usual

essersi rotto i coglioni   (*lit.*, to have your balls broken) (vulg.), **averne le palle piene** (*lit.*, to have one's balls full of it) (vulg.), **non poterne più** to have had enough ▪ **Mi sono rotto i coglioni con quella ragazza! Ora la mollo!** I've had enough of that girl! I'm dumping her!

In forma!   (*lit.*, in shape) very well, in top condition

Insomma!   (*lit.*, in short) so-so

tenersi su   to keep one's spirits up ▪ **Dai, so che è una situazione difficile, ma cerca di tenerti su.** Come on, I know it'a a tough situation, but try to keep your spirits up.

tirare avanti   (*lit.*, to pull along) to get by ▪ **«Come va, Nonno?» «Eh, si tira avanti.»** "How's it going, Gramps?" "Eh, I'm getting by."

trovarsi   (*lit.*, to find oneself) to be doing ▪ **«Come ti trovi qui a Roma?» «Mi trovo benissimo!»** "How are you doing here in Rome?" "I am doing great!"

DISCUSSING THE WEATHER

fare bello   to have good/nice weather

fare brutto   to have bad/ugly weather ■ **Se fa brutto tempo, non vanno alla partita.** If the weather is bad, they aren't going to the game.

fare un caldo della Madonna   to be hot as hell (fam.)

> NOTE: The expression **della Madonna** is used with various nouns for exaggeration effect. It is difficult, if not impossible, to translate the expression, which means essentially "of Madonna-like proportions." The veneration of the Virgin Mary in the Catholic world (and especially in Italy) has for centuries given her a cultlike status, and thus all of her virtues are immeasurable. The expression does the same for the noun it is modifying. See also **avere una fame della Madonna** in "Food and Eating."

fare un freddo boia   (*lit.*, to be cold like an executioner) to be cold as hell ■ **Ha fatto un freddo boia stanotte! Ho dovuto mettere un'altra coperta!** It was cold as hell last night! I had to put another blanket on the bed!

fare un freddo cane   (*lit.*, to be dog cold) to be cold as hell

piovere a catinelle, piovere a secchie   to rain buckets ■ **Aspettiamo qui dentro un attimo perché piove a catinelle!** Let's wait here inside for a second because it's raining buckets!

piovere a dirotto   to pour

piovigginare   to drizzle ■ **Non piove fuori, ma pioviggina.** It's not raining out, but it's drizzling.

le previsioni (del tempo)   the weather forecast ■ **Avete sentito le previsioni?** Have you all heard the forecast?

il tempo da cani   (*lit.*, dog's weather) terrible weather

il tempo di merda   shitty weather (vulg.)

il temporale, la tempesta, la bufera   storm ■ **Oggi ha fatto un caldo della Madonna! Ci vorrebbe un bel temporale per rinfrescare un po' l'aria!** Today it was as hot as hell! We could use a nice rainstorm to cool things down a bit!

il tempo da cani

DISCUSSING YOUR HEALTH

alzarsi con la luna storta (*lit.*, to get up with the mood crooked) to get up on the wrong side of the bed ▪ **Che c'hai, ti sei alzato con la luna storta?** What's your problem, did you get up on the wrong side of the bed?

avere i giorni contati to have one's days numbered, to not be well

avere una brutta cera to not look well ▪ **Che brutta cera che hai oggi! Ti senti bene?** You don't look well at all today! Are you feeling okay?

avere visto/conosciuto giorni migliori to have seen/known better days

beccare un raffreddore to catch a cold ▪ **Mettiti il giubotto prima di uscire! Se no, becchi un brutto raffreddore!** Put your coat on before you go out! If not you'll catch a bad cold!

curarsi to take care of oneself ▪ **Sei malato? Allora vai a casa e curati!** You're sick? Then go home and take care of yourself!

essere a pezzi (*lit.*, to be in pieces) to be exhausted ▪ **Ho trombato tutta la notte! Sono a pezzi stamattina!** I boinked the entire night. This morning I'm exhausted!

essere fatto/a to be tired, to be done (but also drunk or high)

essere giù to be down or depressed ▪ **I ragazzi sono un po' giù oggi perché la loro squadra ha perso in finale.** The kids are a bit depressed today because their team lost the championship.

essere sano come un pesce (*lit.*, to be healthy as a fish) to be healthy as a horse

essere scazzato (*lit.*, to be without a dick) to be down in the dumps, to be without energy or emotion, to be depressed (vulg.)

essere stanco morto to be dead tired

fare male to hurt ▪ **Non posso mangiare perché mi fa male lo stomaco.** I can't eat because my stomach hurts.

girare la testa to spin ▪ **Mi gira la testa a mille.** My head is spinning like crazy.

lamentarsi to complain

rimettere/rimettersi in sesto to get back on one's feet, to make feel well ▪ **Non ti preoccupare. Vieni a casa mia e ti rimetto io in sesto.** Don't worry. Come over to my place and I'll get you back to feeling well.

sentirsi to feel

FLATTERY

Che elegante!   How elegantly dressed you are!

fare il ruffiano/la ruffiana   (*lit.*, to act like a pimp/madame) to butter someone up ■ **Non fare il ruffiano con me perché non funziona!** Don't try and butter me up because it's not going to work with me!

leccare il culo a qualcuno   (*lit.*, to lick someone's ass) to kiss someone's ass (fam.)

il leccaculo   (*lit.*, ass licker) ass kisser (fam.) ■ **La professoressa ha scelto quel leccaculo Simone per il premio!** The (female) professor chose that ass kisser, Simone, for the award!

il leccapiedi   (*lit.*, footlicker) brownnoser

lisciare il pelo a qualcuno   (*lit.*, to smooth someone's hair) to butter someone up

Quanto sei bello/bella!   How beautiful you look!

vedere bene   to see someone as being well ■ **Ti vedo bene!** You look great!

GREETINGS

Allora?   What's up? (fam.)

bello/bella   beautiful (person) (fam.)

> NOTE: It is as common for members of the same sex as it is for members of the opposite sex to greet each other with **Ciao, bello/bella!** It is not considered a come-on if you greet someone that you know in this way; it can be considered a come-on if you greet someone you don't know in this way.

Buondì!, Buongiorno!   Good day! Hello!

> NOTE: The old Italian word for "day" is **dì** (**giorno** is from the French *journée*), and in some parts of Italy, especially Tuscany, one will often hear **buondì** as well as the more common **buongiorno.**

Buonasera!   Good evening!

> NOTE: It changes from **buongiorno** to **buonasera** at different times, depending on where you are in Italy. In Tuscany, for example, after lunch (1:00 P.M.) it becomes **buonasera**. In most other places people say **buongiorno** until about 5:00 or 6:00 P.M. **Buonanotte** means "good night," and is only used at the end of the evening before retiring.

caro/cara, carissimo/carissima   dear or very dear (person) (fam.) ■ **Come stai, carissimo?** How are you, my very dear friend?

Che fai di bello?   What exciting/interesting things are you up to these days?

Che si dice?   What do you say?

Ciao!   Hi! (also Bye!) (fam.)

Com'è?   (*lit.*, How is it?), **Come te la passi?** (*lit.*, How are you spending it?) How's life? (fam.)

È una vita che non ci vediamo!   (*lit.*, It's a lifetime that we haven't seen each other!) Long time no see!

Ma chi si vede!   Look who's here!

Piacere!, Molto lieto!   It's a pleasure (to meet you)!

Salve!   Greetings!

> NOTE: **Salve** is a greeting that is appropriate in formal and semiformal situations, though it is less formal than **buongiorno. Ciao**, on the other hand, is much more informal and is generally used only among friends or between young people (even if they don't know each other).

tesoro   (*lit.*, treasure) dear (person) (fam.)

INTERRUPTING

Accidenti!   (*lit.*, Accidents!) Holy Cow! Holy Smokes!

Che cavolo dici?   What the heck are you saying? (fam.)

Che cazzo dici?   What the fuck are you saying? (vulg.)

Non ci posso credere!   I can't believe it!

Non dire cavolate!   Don't say stupid things! (fam.)

Non dire cazzate!   Don't say fucking stupid things! (vulg.)

Piantala!, Smettila!   Stop it!, Quit it!, Cut it out! (fam.)

prendere in giro   (*lit.*, to take someone for a ride), **pigliare/prendere per il culo** (*lit.*, to take someone by the ass) (vulg.) to pull someone's leg, to fuck with, to make fun of ■ **È un sempliciotto! Tutti lo pigliano per il culo!** He's so gullible! Everyone fucks with him!

stare zitto   to be quiet, to shut up ■ **Non è vero! Stai zitto!** That's not true! Shut up!

torniamo a Bomba   (*lit.*, let's return to Bomba) let's get back to the point (fam.)

INTRODUCING YOURSELF/A FRIEND

il compagno/la compagna, il/la partner, il/la complice buddy, pal, co-hort, partner in crime ■ **Vi faccio conoscere il mio compagno, Mario.** Let me introduce you to my buddy, Mario.

fare conoscere, presentare to introduce

Mi chiamo . . . , Io sono . . . My name is . . .

la banda, la compagnia band, gang, group of friends

Si chiama . . . , Lui/Lei è . . . His/Her name is . . . ■ **Ti presento una mia amica. Lei si chiama Giorgina.** Let me introduce you to a friend of mine. Her name is Giorgina.

INVITING A FRIEND/A STRANGER

andare da . . . to go to a drinking establishment or eatery or to someone's house ■ **Andiamo da Cabiria per una birra.** Let's go to Cabiria for a beer.

Ti va di . . . Are you up for . . . ■ **Ti va di vedere un bel film stasera?** Are you up for seeing a good flick tonight?

la birretta (small) beer

il boccone bite (to eat)

da qualche parte somewhere, someplace ■ **Andiamo a bere una birretta da qualche parte.** Let's go have a quick beer somewhere.

fare alla romana to go dutch, each person pays for his/her own food and/or drink

il locale drinking (or eating) establishment, bar ■ **Andiamo a vedere il nuovo locale in Via Faenza.** Let's go check out the new bar in Via Faenza.

offrire to offer to pay for something, to treat ■ **Ti offro io la cena stasera, ma domani offri tu!** I'll treat you to dinner tonight, but tomorrow it's on you!

piacere to like, to be pleasing ■ **Ti piacerebbe andare a ballare con me?** Would you like to go dancing with me?

volere to want ■ **Vuoi mangiare un boccone insieme?** Do you want to grab a bite together?

MEETING A FRIEND/A STRANGER

dare buca, tirare il bidone (*lit.*, to throw the tank or drum), **dare il pacco** (*lit.*, to give the package) to stand someone up ■ **Cesare ha aspettato per due ore, ma la sua ragazza gli ha dato buca.** Cesare waited for two hours, but his girl stood him up.

essere a corto di tempo, avere poco tempo   to be short of time

fissare un appuntamento   to establish a meeting time and place ▪ **Dai, fissiamo un appuntamento per domani sera in piazza.** Come on, let's set a meeting for tomorrow night in the square.

mollare   (*lit.*, to let go) to let go or get rid of someone or something, to dump ▪ **Ti voglio bene ma ti devo mollare perché non siamo fatti uno per l'altro.** I care about you but I have to let you go because we weren't made for each other.

il punto di incontro, il luogo di ritrovo   meeting place, appointment

rimanere   (*lit.*, to remain) to agree/settle on a plan ▪ **Come rimaniamo, che ci vediamo più tardi al bar?** So what's the plan—that we will see each other later at the bar?

sentirsi per telefono   to be in touch via telephone ▪ **Ci sentiamo per telefono stasera per parlare dei nostri progetti.** Let's be in touch by phone tonight to talk about our plans.

vedersi   to see or meet each other ▪ **Perché non ci vediamo in piazza alle 9:00?** Why don't we meet in the square at 9:00?

SAYING GOOD-BYE

A dopo!   See you later!

> NOTE: **A dopo** is used only if you are planning to see that person later on that same day.

Alla prossima!   Until the next time!

A presto!   See you soon!

Buonanotte!   Good night!

> NOTE: **Buonanotte** is used only when saying good-bye or goodnight for the last time that night, not as a greeting at the beginning of the evening, in which case one would say **buonasera**. Oftentimes, **buonanotte** is shortened to just **'notte**, especially among family and close friends.

Arrivederci!, ArrivederLa!   (*lit.*, until we see each other again) Good-bye!

> NOTE: **ArrivederLa** is more formal than **arrivederci**, which is often said even among friends. Although **arrivederci** is never wrong to say, in very formal situations it is more appropriate to use the more formal **arrivederLa**.

Ciao!   Bye! (also Hi!) (fam.)

sentirsi   to hear from each other, to be in touch ▪ **Ci sentiamo presto!** Let's be in touch soon!

farsi sentire (*lit.*, to make oneself heard), **farsi vivo** (*lit.*, to make oneself alive) to get in touch (generally by phone), to give someone a call ▪ **Non sparire! Fatti sentire ogni tanto!** Don't disappear! Give us a call every now and then!

In gamba! (*lit.*, On your feet!) On your toes! Stay sharp!

Stammi bene! Take care! (fam.)

EXERCISES
Adesso tocca a voi!

A *Choose the appropriate Italian word or expression for each of the following situations:*

1. You meet your Italian professor out for a walk in the main square of town after dinner.

   a. Ciao, Carissimo!   b. Buonasera, Professore!

2. You say good-bye to an elderly shopkeeper after making a purchase in his or her store.

   a. ArrivederLa!   b. Ciao, Tesoro!

3. You see a classmate having a coffee at the bar.

   a. Salve!   b. Che si dice?

4. You say good-bye to a close friend who you may not see for a few weeks.

   a. Stammi bene!   b. A dopo!

5. You see your boyfriend or girlfriend after a long day at work or school.

   a. Ciao, Tesoro!   b. Buondì!

B *Give the Italian slang equivalent for each of the English words or expressions below:*

1. to stand someone up _____

2. ass kisser _____

3. to catch a cold _____

4. to be dead tired _____

5. shitty weather_____

6. to make excuses _____

7. to piss somebody off _____

C *Give the equivalent English expression for each of the following Italian slang expressions below:*

1. fare alla romana _____

2. avere una brutta cera _____

3. essere sano come un pesce _____

4. fare un freddo boia _____

5. pigliare per il culo _____

6. farsi sentire _____

7. rompere i coglioni _____

8. stare sul cazzo _____

Disputes

BEING ANNOYING/BEING ANNOYED

fare il broncio   to pout   ■ **Se non la smettete di fare il broncio, io e Valeria ce ne andiamo.** If you guys don't stop pouting, Valeria and I are going to leave.

piantagrane   instigator, pain in the neck   ■ **La cugina di Valeria è una piantagrane insopportabile. Sarebbe meglio se stesse zitta.** Valeria's cousin is an intolerable instigator. It would be better if she kept quiet.

rompere/scassare le palle/i coglioni a qualcuno   to break (or bust) someone's balls/nuts (vulg.)

rompere/scassare il cazzo/la minchia a qualcuno   (*lit.*, to break/bust someone's dick/cock) to break someone's balls (vulg.)

rompere le scatole a qualcuno   to annoy or bother someone (fam.)   ■ **Se sono venuti solo per rompere le scatole, digli che smammino subito!** If they only came to be a bother, tell them to scram!

rompicazzo/scassaminchia/scassacazzo   (*lit.*, cock breaker) annoying, pain in the neck (vulg.)   ■ **Se non la smetti di fare lo scassaminchia te ne pentirai.** If you don't stop being a pain in the neck you will regret it.

> NOTE: This is similar to "he's a pain in the ass!" in English.

rompipalle/rompicoglioni   (*lit.*, ball breaker) annoying, pain in the neck (vulg.)   ■ **Ci sono quei tipi di rompicoglioni maleducati che ti insultano solo per divertimento.** There are those kinds of rude ball breakers that insult you just for amusement.

rompiscatole   (*lit.*, box breaker) annoying, pain in the neck (fam.)   ■ **Il tuo amico è un gran rompiscatole.** Your friend is a real pain in the neck.

CAUSING TROUBLE

arrabbiarsi   to get mad   ■ **Lo sapevo che si sarebbe arrabbiata.** I knew that she would get mad.

attaccare briga   to quarrel   ■ **Se sei venuto solo per attaccare briga puoi anche tornare a casa.** If you've only come to quarrel you can return home.

attaccabrighe   quarrelsome person

bisticciarsi bicker

cercare guai to look for trouble

È acqua passata! It's water under the bridge!

far arrabbiare qualcuno to make someone mad

far girare le palle/i coglioni a qualcuno (*lit.*, to make someone's balls spin) to cause someone to become irritated (vulg.)

far imbestalire qualcuno to make someone fly off into a rage

far incavolare qualcuno to make someone lose their temper

far incazzare qualcuno to piss someone off (vulg.) ▪ **Se mi fai incazzare ti spacco le ginocchia.** If you piss me off I will break your kneecaps.

fare pace to make peace ▪ **Facciamo pace e seppelliamo l'ascia.** Let's make peace and bury the hatchet.

far salire i nervi a qualcuno (*lit.*, to make someone's nerves go up) to get on someone's nerves ▪ **Quei ragazzini scatenati mi fanno sempre salire i nervi.** Those rowdy kids always get on my nerves.

fare una scenata to make a scene ▪ **L'altra sera mia moglie ha fatto una scenata al ristorante perché la sua bistecca era troppo cotta.** The other night my wife made a scene at the restaurant because her steak was overcooked.

far uscire di testa qualcuno (*lit.*, to make someone go out of their head) to make someone lose their head

ficcare il naso negli affari degli altri to stick one's nose in others' business

imbestialirsi to fly into a rage

impicciarsi degli affari degli altri to interfere in others' business ▪ **Non t'impicciare!** Don't interfere!

impiccione/a busybody

importunare qualcuno to bother someone

incavolarsi to lose one's temper (fam.) ▪ **Mia sorella si incavola per niente.** My sister loses her temper for no good reason.

incazzarsi to get pissed off (vulg.) ▪ **È un problema piccolo, Carlo. Non t'incazzare!** It's a small problem, Carlo. Don't get pissed off!

infastidire/dare fastidio a qualcuno to irritate someone

litigare to argue ▪ **Non ho nessuna intenzione di litigare. Sarà bene che ti calmi.** I have no intention of arguing. You'd better calm down.

mandare qualcuno a quel paese   (*lit.*, to send someone to that country) to tell someone where to go (fam.)

metterci una pietra sopra   (*lit.*, to put a rock on top of it) to let bygones be bygones

parlare male di qualcuno   to speak poorly of someone

perdere le staffe   to lose it

perdere la testa   to lose one's head ■ **Sta' tranquillo, non perdere la testa. Vedrai che tutto andrà bene.** Stay calm; don't lose your head. You'll see that everything will go well.

piantare grane   to make trouble ■ **Smettila di piantare grane e sta' zitto.** Stop making trouble and shut up.

scaldarsi   to get hot under the collar ■ **Mario si scalda facilmente e perde le staffe.** Mario gets hot under the collar easily and loses it.

scocciare qualcuno   to bother/annoy someone ■ **Dai, ti prego, non mi scocciare con queste storie.** Come on, please, don't bother me with these stories.

seppellire l'ascia   to bury the hatchet

spaccone/a   boaster ■ **L'amico di Paolo è uno spaccone insopportabile.** Paolo's friend is an intolerable boaster.

VERBAL ABUSE/INSULTS

Accidenti a te!   (*lit.*, Ailments to you!) Damn you!

Bastardo!   Bastard! (fam.)

bastonare   (*lit.*, to beat with a stick) to beat up ■ **Vorrei tanto bastonare quell'arbitro cornuto.** I would really like to beat up that cuckold referee.

cretino   cretin (fam.) ■ **Se tu non fossi così cretino non faresti così tanti errori.** If you were not such a cretin you would not make so many mistakes.

cornuto   cuckold (vulg.)

dare dello stronzo a qualcuno   (*lit.*, to give someone of the turd) to call someone a turd (vulg.) ■ **Lei non si deve permettere di dare della stronza a mia madre.** Don't you dare call my mother a turd.

> NOTE: The expression **dare** + contracted preposition (**di** + definite article) varies according to the insult or observation that is used, and the gender (and number) of the person(s) in question. For example: **Dare del cazzone/Dare dell'idiota/Dare della stronza/Dare dei bastardi** . . .

Disgraziato!   (*lit.*, Disgraced!) Scoundrel! (fam.)

Fanculo!/Vaffanculo!/Vai a fare in culo!/Vai affanculo! (*lit.*, Go do in the ass!) Fuck off! (vulg.) ▪ **Perché non te ne vai a fare in culo invece di romperci i coglioni?** Why don't you fuck off instead of breaking our balls?

farabutto person without scruples (fam.)

fare lo stronzo (*lit.*, to do the turd) to act like an asshole (vulg.)

fetente (*lit.*, stinking) rat (fam.) ▪ **Quel fetente di tuo zio mi ha preso in giro.** That rat of an uncle of yours made fun of me.

figlio di puttana (*lit.*, son of a whore) son of a bitch (vulg.) ▪ **Te l'ho detto che era un figlio di puttana.** I told you he was a son of a bitch.

fottersi (*lit.*, to fuck yourself) to fuck oneself (vulg.) ▪ **Se non ti sta bene, fottiti.** If you don't like it, fuck you.

idiota idiot (fam.) ▪ **Il tuo amico Matteo è un grande idiota!** Your friend Matteo is a big idiot.

Imbecille! Imbecile! (fam.)

Infame! Vile! (fam.)

levati/togliti di culo (*lit.*, get off the ass), **levati/togliti dal cazzo** (*lit.*, get off the dick) to get the fuck out of here (vulg.)

levati/togliti dalle palle/dai coglioni/dal cazzo (*lit.*, get off the balls/ nuts) to get the fuck out of here (vulg.) ▪ **Per favore, Tiziano, togliti dal cazzo e lasciami lavorare.** Please, Tiziano, get the fuck out of here and let me work.

menare to beat

merdaiolo shit vendor (vulg.)

mezza sega (*lit.*, half saw) wuss (vulg.) ▪ **Quella mezza sega di portiere non ha parato il rigore.** That wuss of a goalkeeper did not block the penalty kick.

minchione, cazzone, coglione (*lit.*, big prick, dick, testicle) idiot (vulg.)

Mortacci tua! (*lit.*, your nasty dead ones) fuck your dead ancestors (vulg.)

Morto di fame! a nobody (fam.)

pezzo di merda piece of shit (vulg.) ▪ **Il suo avvocato è un pezzo di merda.** His lawyer is a piece of shit.

speriamo che tu muoia let's hope you die (fam.)

stronzo turd (vulg.)

> NOTE: This insult is roughly the equivalent of the English "asshole" (**stronzo**) or "bitch" (**stronza**).

testa di cazzo (*lit.*, head of dick) dickhead (vulg.) ▪ **Non sei niente altro che una testa di cazzo.** You are nothing other than a dickhead.

Ti prendesse un colpo/un accidente! (*lit.*, may a blow/an accident get you) drop dead (fam.)

vai a farti fottere go get fucked (vulg.) ▪ **Perché non vai a farti fottere?** Why don't you go get fucked?

vai a pigliarlo/prenderlo nel culo go take it/get it in the ass (vulg.)

CAUSING AND SUFFERING VIOLENCE

beccare un monte di botte/cazzotti/schiaffi (*lit.*, to catch a mountain of blows/punches/slaps) to get a hell of a beating

beccare una valanga di schiaffoni (*lit.*, to catch an avalanche of big slaps) to get a hell of a beating ▪ **Preferisci beccare una valanga di schiaffoni adesso o più tardi stasera?** Do you prefer to get a hell of a beating now or later this evening?

cazzottare qualcuno to punch someone repeatedly

il cazzotto punch ▪ **Ho dato un cazzotto al muro e mi sono fatto un male boia.** I punched the wall and hurt myself big time.

beccare una valanga di schiaffoni

fare il danno   (*lit.*, to do the damage) to do some damage ■ **Sono molto incavolato. Sto per fare il danno.** I'm very pissed. I'm about to do some damage.

fare una strage/un macello   (*lit.*, to do a slaughter/massacre) to beat up or kill many people

darne   (*lit.*, to give some) to give a beating

dare un calcio   (*lit.*, to give a kick) to kick ■ **Mi hanno dato un calcio in faccia.** They kicked me in the face.

dare/prendere una sberla/botta   to give/receive a slap/blow

dare una spinta   (*lit.*, to give a push) to push

dare uno schiaffo a qualcuno   (*lit.*, to give someone a slap) to slap someone

dare uno spintone   (*lit.*, to give a big push) to push violently ■ **L'allenatore della squadra di pallacanestro ha dato uno spintone a un atleta durante la partita.** The coach of the basketball team violently pushed an athlete during the game.

distruggere   (*lit.*, to destroy), **rovinare** (*lit.*, to ruin), **disintegrare** (*lit.*, to disintegrate) to beat up severely ■ **Se mi graffi la macchina ti disintegro.** If you scratch my car I'll pound you.

graffiare   to scratch

mordere   to bite

picchiare   to beat ■ **Quando ero piccolo mio fratello mi picchiava sempre, e io non potevo farci niente.** When I was little my brother used to always beat me up, and I couldn't do anything about it.

picchiare/menare qualcuno a sangue   (*lit.*, to beat/thump someone to blood) to beat someone until they bleed

picchiarsi   to beat each other

prendere/dare un sacco di botte/cazzotti/schiaffi   (*lit.*, to get/give a bag of blows/punches/slaps) to get/give a hell of a beating

prendere a botte/a pugni qualcuno   (*lit.*, to get someone to blows/fists) to hit someone repeatedly

prendersi a schiaffi   to slap each other around

prendere a schiaffi qualcuno   to slap someone around ■ **A volte ho veramente voglia di prenderti a schiaffi.** Sometimes I really feel like smacking you around.

prenderne/buscarne (*lit.*, to take/get some), **prenderle/buscarle** (*lit.*, to take/get them) to receive a beating ■ **Vattene subito se non vuoi buscarle.** Leave immediately if you don't want to get a beating.

scassare la testa a qualcuno to break someone's head ■ **Stronzo di un coglione, se lo rifai io ti scasso la testa.** Turd of an idiot, if you do it again I'll break your head.

schiaffeggiare to slap ■ **Il professore ha schiaffeggiato uno studente drogato, e lo hanno licenziato.** The professor slapped a drugged-up student, and they fired him.

spaccare i denti a qualcuno to break someone's teeth ■ **Hanno minacciato di rompergli i denti.** They threatened to break his teeth.

spaccare la testa a qualcuno to break someone's head

spaccare qualcuno to break someone

POLICE AND OTHER INTERVENTIONS

il buttafuori (*lit.*, out-thrower) bouncer ■ **Mio cugino fa il buttafuori tre sere a settimana. Dice che guadagna bene.** My cousin is a bouncer three nights a week. He says he makes good money.

i carabinieri military police force ■ **I carabinieri hanno le uniformi nere.** The military police have black uniforms.

> NOTE: The **carabinieri** (also called **i caramba**) were once a part of the armed forces and now are police with civil and military duties.

la DIGOS/Divisione Investigazioni Generali e Operazioni Speciali (*lit.*, Division of General Investigations and Special Operations) police department dealing with political security

essere arrestato to be arrested ■ **Ci hanno arrestato senza motivo. Non stavamo facendo niente.** They arrested us for no reason. We were not doing anything.

essere beccato to be caught ■ **L'ho beccato, e adesso chiamo la pula.** I caught him, and now I'm calling the cops.

essere buttato fuori to be thrown out

essere fermato (*lit.*, to be stopped) to be pulled over

il piedipiatti (*lit.*, flat feet) cop

la polizia police ■ **Presto, chiamate la polizia!** Quick, call the police!

i pompieri/i vigili del fuoco firefighters

lo sbirro cop

gli sbirri/la pula the cops/the fuzz ■ **Gli sbirri mi hanno fermato e mi hanno dato una multa di cento euro.** The cops stopped me and gave me a one hundred euro ticket.

EXERCISES
Adesso tocca a voi!

A *Select the best way to describe each of the following terms and situations:*

1. **importunare qualcuno:**
   a. to irritate someone   b. to bother someone   c. to annoy someone

2. **piantare grane:**
   a. to quarrel   b. to speak poorly of someone   c. to make trouble

3. **ficcare il naso negli affari degli altri:**
   a. to interfere in other people's business   b. to stick your nose in others' business   c. to make a scene

4. **perdere la testa:**
   a. to lose one's head   b. to lose it   c. to look for trouble

5. **far arrabbiare qualcuno:**
   a. to piss someone off   b. to make someone fly into a rage   c. to make someone mad

6. **far incazzare qualcuno:**
   a. to piss someone off   b. to lose one's temper   c. to cause someone to become irritated

7. **Accidenti a te!:**
   a. Drop dead!   b. Damn you!   c. Fuck you!

8. **stronzo:**
   a. cretin   b. idiot   c. turd

9. **testa di cazzo:**
   a. cuckold   b. dickhead   c. wuss

10. **coglione:**
    a. idiot   b. bastard   c. shit vendor

B *Write the Italian equivalent for each of the following English expressions:*

1. to get pissed off _____

2. to let bygones be bygones _____

3. to call someone a turd _____

4. go get fucked _____

5. to beat _____

6. to break someone's head _____

7. to be caught _____

8. cop _____

9. boaster _____

10. scoundrel _____

Drinking and Smoking

DRINKING AND DRUNKENNESS

alcolizzato   alcoholic   ■ **Quei ragazzi finiranno alcolizzati.** Those guys will end up being alcoholics.

alzare il gomito   (*lit.*, to raise the elbow) to hit the bottle (fam.)   ■ **Dopo l'esame Giuseppe ha davvero alzato il gomito.** After the exam Giuseppe really hit the bottle.

l'amaro (m)   bitter

> NOTE: An **amaro** is a liquor usually made with some type of bark or root. It is commonly consumed as a cocktail before dinner or as an after-dinner drink to aid digestion.

alzare il gomito

l'aperitivo/l'happy hour (m) happy hour ▪ **Mi piace molto l'aperitivo che fanno al bar in piazza perché gli antipasti sono ottimi.** I really like the happy hour they have at the bar in the square, because the appetizers are excellent.

Alla salute! To our health!

avere la nausea to be nauseous ▪ **Mia cugina ha bevuto davvero troppo, e adesso ha la nausea.** My cousin drank way too much and now she's nauseous.

avere lo stomaco sottosopra (*lit.*, to have the stomach upside down) to have an upset stomach (fam.)

avere preso una bella sbornia/sbronza to have gotten very sloshed/plastered

avere la sbornia to be sloshed/plastered

il barbera barbera

> NOTE: This term denotes a dry red wine produced in the Asti region of Piedmont. Its popularity in the region is similar to **chianti** in Tuscany.

bere to drink

bere come una spugna (*lit.*, to drink like a sponge) to drink like a fish (fam.) ▪ **Da giovane mia madre beveva come una spugna.** When she was young, my mother drank like a fish.

bere alla salute di qualcuno to drink to someone's health

bere un bicchiere di troppo to drink one glass too many

il boccale di birra a mug of beer ▪ **Beviamo un boccale di birra per festeggiare.** Let's have ourselves a mug of beer to celebrate.

una bottiglia o lattina di . . . a bottle or can of . . .

il brandy brandy

birra alla spina beer on draft ▪ **Lapo beve solo birra economica alla spina.** Lapo only drinks cheap beer on draft.

brindare/fare un brindisi to toast/make a toast ▪ **Brindiamo alla vostra salute.** We're toasting to your health.

il caffè corretto con sambuca/grappa/crema al whisky coffee spiked with sambuca, grappa, cream of whisky ▪ **Per favore, mi dia un caffè corretto con la grappa.** Please, sir/miss, may I have a coffee spiked with grappa.

il caffè valdostano valdostano coffee

> NOTE: **Valdostano** coffee is from **Val d'Aosta**, one of the northern regions of Italy, which borders France and Switzerland. **Caffè valdostano** contains **grappa** and is typically set on fire when served, and allowed to burn briefly before consumption.

lo champagne   champagne

il cicchetto/il bicchierino   shot glass

ci vuole qualcosa di forte   we need something strong ▪ **Siamo tanto depressi. Ci vuole qualcosa di forte.** We're very depressed. We need something strong.

il cocktail   cocktail

con ghiaccio o liscio   on the rocks or straight up

il cognac   cognac

il cordiale   cordial

dare di stomaco   (*lit.*, to give of stomach) to throw up ▪ **Quando mi sono svegliato stavo malissimo, e temevo di dare di stomaco.** When I woke up I felt terrible, and I feared I would throw up.

distrutto   (*lit.*, destroyed) wrecked (fam.) ▪ **Ieri sera ero proprio distrutto.** Last night I was really wrecked.

il drink   drink

essere brillo/un po' brillo   to be tipsy/a little tipsy ▪ **Quelle ragazze dopo due birre erano brille.** Those girls were tipsy after two beers.

essere sbronzo   to be sloshed/plastered ▪ **Quando siete sbronzi vi comportate male.** When you guys are plastered you misbehave.

essere una spugna   (*lit.*, to be a sponge) to be a boozer (fam.)

farsi una bevuta   to have oneself a drink

farsi un bicchiere/un bicchierino   (*lit.*, to have oneself a glass/a little glass) to have oneself a drink ▪ **Fatti un bicchierino e rilassati.** Have yourself a drink and relax.

farsi una birra/un boccale di birra   to have oneself a beer/a mug of beer ▪ **Facciamoci una birra.** Let's have a beer.

il gin   gin

il marsala   marsala

metterlo sul conto   to put it on the tab

mettersi due dita in gola   to stick two fingers down one's throat

offrire una birra   to buy a beer

offrire un caffè   to buy a coffee

offrire un chinotto   to buy a chinotto

NOTE: **Chinotto** is a nonalcoholic, carbonated beverage similar in color to a cola.

offrire un giro di . . .   to buy a round of . . .   ■ **L'ultima volta ho pagato io, adesso offri un giro tu.** I paid last time, now you buy a round.

il poncetto   punch

il porto   port wine

proporre un brindisi   to propose a toast

il prosecco   (*lit.*, dry wine) sparkling dry white wine

rimettere   to throw up

il rum   rum

sboccare   to puke

sbronzarsi/prendere una sbronza   to get sloshed/plastered   ■ **Mi sono preso una sbronza micidiale.** I got totally sloshed/plastered.

lo scotch   scotch

lo shot/shottino   shot (fam.)   ■ **Una volta ogni tanto mi faccio uno shot di whisky.** Every once in a while I have myself a shot of whisky.

lo spumante dolce o secco   sweet or dry spumante

stare per vomitare   to be about to vomit   ■ **Ferma la macchina che sto per vomitare.** Stop the car; I'm going to vomit.

il superalcolico   hard liquor   ■ **Non possono bere superalcolici perché devono guidare.** They can't drink hard liquor because they have to drive.

trincare   to drink

ubriaco   drunk   ■ **Tu sei ubriaca, e io non ho intenzione di ascoltarti.** You're drunk, and I have no intention of listening to you.

ubriacone   drunkard

ubriacarsi   (*lit.*, to get oneself drunk) to get drunk   ■ **Dove vado? Vado dove vanno i becchi: a ubriacarmi!** Where am I going? I'm going where the cuckolds go: to get drunk!

vedere/vederci doppio   to see double   ■ **Dopo quel whisky vedevamo/ci vedevamo doppio.** After that whisky we were seeing double.

il vino rosso e bianco   red and white wine

il vinsanto   (*lit.*, holy wine) vinsanto

NOTE: **Vinsanto** is a sweet dessert wine produced in Tuscany. A regional specialty in Tuscany is **vinsanto** with **cantucci** or **cantuccini**, which are small **biscotti** made with almonds. The **cantucci** are dipped into the **vinsanto** to soak up the wine.

la vodka   vodka

vomitare   to vomit   ▪ **Avevano la nausea e hanno vomitato.** They were nauseous and they vomited.

il whisky   whisky

TOBACCO AND SMOKING

l'accendino (m)   lighter

accendersi una sigaretta   to light oneself a cigarette   ▪ **Senza un fiammifero o un accendino è molto difficile accendersi una sigaretta.** Without a match or a lighter it is very hard to light a cigarette.

andare il fumo di traverso   (*lit.*, to have the smoke go sideways) to choke on the smoke (fam.)   ▪ **Le è andato il fumo di traverso, e ha fatto una faccia stranissima!** She choked on the smoke, and made a very strange face!

aprire un pacchetto   to open a pack

avere il vizio   (*lit.*, to have the habit) to have a habit

aver voglia di una sigaretta   to feel like a cigarette   ▪ **Dopo il caffè ho sempre voglia di una sigaretta.** I always feel like having a cigarette after coffee.

il bocchino   cigarette holder

buttare fuori il fumo dal naso   to blow the smoke out of the nose

cartine lunghe/corte   long/short papers

C'hai il fuoco?   (*lit.*, Do you have fire?) Do you have a light?

centos   one hundreds

il cerino   match

comprare un pacchetto di sigarette   to buy a pack of cigarettes   ▪ **Per favore, Orlando, compra un pacchetto di sigarette per il nonno.** Please, Orlando, buy a pack of cigarettes for Grandpa.

comprare una stecca   to buy a carton

dure   hardpack

fare gli anelli di fumo   to blow smoke rings   ▪ **Non mi riesce fare gli anelli di fumo.** I can't blow smoke rings.

fare un tiro   to have a drag   ▪ **Mi fai fare un tiro?** Will you let me have a drag?

farsi una cicca   to have oneself a smoke (fam.)

farsi una sigaretta   to have oneself a cigarette (fam.) ▪ **Dopo un buon pasto una sigaretta è sempre un'ottima idea.** After a good meal a cigarette is always a good idea.

farsi un canna   to have oneself a joint (fam.) ▪ **Mi stavo facendo una canna quando mi ha fermato la polizia.** I was having a joint when the police stopped me.

farsi/fumarsi uno spinello   to have oneself/smoke oneself a joint (fam.)

il fiammifero   match

i filtrini   filters

il filtro   filter ▪ **Attento! Non accendere la sigaretta dal filtro!** Careful! Don't light your cigarette from the filter!

fumare   to smoke

fumare come un turco/come una ciminiera   (*lit.*, to smoke like a Turk/like a smokestack) to smoke constantly (fam.)

fumare una volta ogni morte di papa   (*lit.*, to smoke once every death of a pope) to smoke very rarely

fumare poco   to smoke a little

fumare troppo   to smoke too much ▪ **Mio zio fuma troppo; quasi tre pacchetti al giorno.** My uncle smokes too much, almost three packs a day.

fumare un pacchetto al giorno   to smoke a pack a day

fumatore abituale   habitual smoker

fumatore incallito   inveterate smoker ▪ **Tua zia è una fumatrice incallita, le puzzano sempre i capelli di fumo.** Your aunt is an inveterate smoker; her hair always stinks of smoke.

fumatore occasionale   occasional smoker ▪ **Detesto i fumatori occasionali che scroccano sempre le sigarette invece di comprarle.** I hate occasional smokers who always bum cigarettes instead of buying them.

fumo negli occhi   smoke in the eyes ▪ **Non vedevo perché avevo il fumo negli occhi.** I couldn't see because I had smoke in my eyes.

Hai da accendere?   Do you have a light?

Hai l'accendino?   Do you have a lighter?

iniziare a fumare   to start smoking

leccare la cartina   to lick the paper

Mi fai accendere?   Will you light me?

morbide   softpack

il mozzicone   cigarette butt

la nicotina   nicotine

offrire una cicca   to give a smoke (fam.)

un pacchetto da dieci   a pack of ten

passare lo spinello/la canna   to pass the joint (fam.)

la pipa   pipe

posacenere/portacenere   ashtray

puzzare di fumo   to stink of smoke

rovesciare il posacenere   to knock over the ashtray ■ **Quella cretina di tua sorella ha rovesciato il posacenere tre volte ieri sera.** That cretin sister of yours knocked over the ashtray three times last night.

rullarsi una sigaretta   to roll oneself a cigarette

sbattere le cicche   to pack the smokes (fam.) ■ **Non capiamo perché la gente sbatte le cicche.** We don't understand why people pack their smokes.

scroccare una cicca   to bum a smoke (fam.) ■ **Se non la smettete di scroccarmi sempre le cicce non ve ne do più.** If you guys don't quit bumming smokes off me I won't give you anymore.

rullarsi uno spinello   to roll oneself a joint (fam.)

il sigaro   cigar

smettere di fumare   to quit smoking ■ **Loro smettono di fumare una volta al mese.** They quit smoking once a month.

spegnere una sigaretta   to put out a cigarette

il tabacco da pipa   pipe tabacco

tabacco da sigarette   cigarette tabacco

il Toscano/Toscanello   Tuscan cigar

vorrei un pacchetto di . . .   I would like a pack of . . .

lo Zippo   Zippo

Vuoi una cicca/una sigaretta?   Do you want a smoke/a cigarette?

EXERCISES
Adesso tocca a voi!

A *Write the English equivalent for each of the following expressions:*

1. farsi uno spinello _____

2. scroccare una cicca _____

3. fumare come un turco _____

4. mettersi due dita in gola _____

5. alzare il gomito _____

6. sboccare _____

7. Vuoi una cicca? _____

8. fare un tiro _____

9. C'hai il fuoco? _____

10. il cerino _____

B *Choose the ending in parentheses that completes each of the following sentences:*

1. Graziano, non dovresti (fumare troppo/fumatore poco)!

2. Mi puzzano sempre i vestiti di fumo perché sono un (fumatore abituale/fumatore occasionale).

3. Maria e Geppina (fumano un pacchetto al giorno/un accendino).

4. Vorrei comprare (un pacchetto da dieci/rovesciare il posacenere).

5. Scusa, (mi fai accendere/iniziare a fumare)?

C *Select the best way to describe the following situations:*

1. avere il vizio:
   a. to have oneself   b. to have a habit   c. to give a smoke
      a cigarette

2. scroccare una cicca:
   a. to have oneself   b. to buy a pack of   c. to bum a smoke
      a smoke   cigarettes

3. **farsi un bicchierino:**
   - a. to have oneself a drink
   - b. to drink to someone's health
   - c. to our health

4. **offrire un giro di . . . :**
   - a. a bottle or can of . . .
   - b. to put it on the tab
   - c. to buy a round of . . .

5. **bere come una spugna:**
   - a. to drink
   - b. to drink like a fish
   - c. to be a boozer

Education

SCHOOL

il banco   desk

il bidello/la bidella   janitor

la campanella   school bell   ▪ **È suonata la campanella.** The school bell rang.

la cattedra   teacher's desk

il consiglio di classe   staff meeting

la lavagna   chalkboard

il preside/la preside   principal/headmaster

la ricreazione   break, recess   ▪ **Sono stanca e ho fame! Non vedo l'ora che arrivi la ricreazione!** I'm tired and hungry! I can't wait for recess!

la sospensione   suspension

il supplente/la supplente   substitute teacher   ▪ **Il prof sta male. Domani verrà la supplente.** The teacher is sick. Tomorrow a substitute teacher is coming.

SCHOOLWORK

ammazzarsi di studio   to kill oneself studying   ▪ **Ammazzarsi di studio la sera prima dell'esame non serve a nulla!** Killing oneself with studying the night before the exam is worthless!

l'appello (m)   roll call

avere/non avere la giustificazione   to have/not to have an absent note

avere culo all'esame/nel compito in classe   (*lit.*, to have ass) to be lucky during a test (vulg.)   ▪ **Ho avuto culo nel compito in classe. C'erano solo le cose che sapevo benissimo.** I was so lucky during the test. There were only things I knew really well on it.

il compito in classe   test   ▪ **Domani c'è il compito in classe di matematica.** Tomorrow there is going to be a math test.

copiare   (*lit.*, to copy) to cheat   ▪ **Non è giusto! Ha preso un bel voto ma ha copiato tutto!** It's not fair! He got a good grade but he cheated on everything!

essere un asino/un somaro   to be a dunce, jackass

essere bocciato/a   to fail ▪ **Se non studi quest'anno, sarai bocciato per la terza volta consecutiva.** If you don't study this year, you are going to fail for the third time in a row.

essere/non essere una cima   (*lit.*, to be/not to be a mountain top) to be/not to be a genius ▪ **Mio figlio va abbastanza bene a scuola ma non è una cima.** My son does quite well at school but he's not a genius.

essere promosso/a   to pass

essere una secchia   to be a nerd (fam.)

essere un secchione/una secchiona   to be a nerd (fam.) ▪ **Filippo ha una media spaventosa a scuola, ma non si diverte mai. È proprio un secchione!** Philip has a frightening average at school, but he doesn't ever enjoy himself. He's a real nerd!

fare un figurone nell'interrogazione/all'orale   to make a good impression during an oral exam ▪ **Maria ha studiato tanto! Ha fatto un figurone all'orale.** Maria studied a lot! She made a good impression during the oral exam.

fare forca   to skip class (fam.) ▪ **Oggi non voglio andare a scuola. Faccio forca e vado al mare.** Today I don't want to go to school. I'll skip class and go to the beach.

fare sega   to skip class (vulg.) ▪ **Non ho studiato per l'interrogazione di domani. Penso di fare sega.** I didn't study for tomorrow's oral exam. I think I'll skip class.

la gita   field trip

l'insufficienza (f)   failing grade

l'interrogazione (f)   oral exam

marinare/bigiare la scuola   to skip class

la media   grade point average, abbr. GPA ▪ **Sto tenendo una buona media questo semestre.** I have a good GPA this semester.

l'ora buca (f)   (*lit.*, empty hour) when a class is unexpectedly cancelled (fam.) ▪ **Il professore d'italiano è malato e non può venire a scuola. Abbiamo un'ora buca dalle 10 alle 11!** The Italian teacher is sick and can't come to school. We have a empty hour from 10:00 to 11:00!

la pagella   report card ▪ **Se avrai una buona pagella io e tua madre ti regaleremo un motorino.** If you get a good report card, your mother and I will buy you a scooter.

scaldare il banco

prendere una nota sul registro   disciplinary note   ■ **Se non vi comportate bene prenderete tutti una nota sul registro!** If you don't behave you are going to get a disciplinary note!

il registro di classe   grade book

scaldare il banco   (*lit.*, to warm up the desk) to sit around   ■ **Non studi mai! Vai a scuola solo per scaldare il banco!** You never study! You go to school just to warm up the desk!

spremersi le meningi   to rack one's brain   ■ **Mi sono spremuto le meningi tutto il pomeriggio ma non sono riuscito a risolvere il problema di matematica.** I racked my brain for the whole afternoon but I couldn't solve the math problem.

la sufficienza   passing grade

il voto in condotta   conduct grade

il voto   grade

HIGH SCHOOL

l'istituto tecnico (m)   high school specializing in technical studies

l'istituto professionale (m)   vocational school

il liceo classico   high school specializing in classical studies

il liceo scientifico   high school specializing in scientific studies

il liceo linguistico   high school specializing in foreign languages

HOMEWORK

andare a ripetizione/prendere ripetizioni   to take private lessons, to be tutored ▪ **Non riesco a capire nulla di fisica. Devo iniziare ad andare a ripetizione.** I can't understand anything about physics. I have to start taking private lessons.

il compito a casa/i compiti per casa   homework ▪ **Oggi non posso venire a giocare a pallone. Devo fare i compiti per casa.** I can't come to play soccer today. I have to do homework.

PLAYGROUND

l'altalena (f)   swing

il bullo   bully

il cortile   playground ▪ **Nel cortile della nostra scuola vedo spesso alcuni spacciatori.** On our school playground I usually see a few drug pushers.

menarsi   to fight (fist fight) ▪ **Guarda quei ragazzi che si menano nel cortile della scuola.** Look at those kids that are fighting on the playground.

la rissa/la zuffa   scrap, scuffle

saltare alla corda   to skip rope

lo spacciatore   pusher

TEACHERS

montare in cattedra   to start pontificating, to get on one's high horse

il precario/la precaria   teacher without tenure ▪ **I precari protestano perché vogliono migliori condizioni di lavoro.** The teachers without tenure are protesting because they want better working conditions.

il prof/la prof di matematica   math teacher ▪ **La prof di matematica non mi piace proprio!** I don't like the math teacher at all!

il prof/la prof di lettere   literature teacher

il prof/la prof di ginnastica   gym teacher

il professore/la professoressa di ruolo   teacher with tenure ▪ **Finalmente dopo dieci anni sono riuscito a diventare professore di ruolo!** Finally after ten years I have received tenure!

UNIVERSITY

l'assistente (m/f)   teaching assistant

la borsa di studio   scholarship ▪ **Potrò continuare l'università solo se mi daranno una borsa di studio.** I can keep attending school only if they give me a scholarship.

il CEPU [Centro Europeo Studi Universitari]   commercial tutoring school

il collegio/la casa dello studente   dorm ▪ **Marco quest'anno va all'università. Penso che abiterà al collegio universitario.** This year Marco is going to college. I think he is going to live in a dorm.

dare gli esami   to take exams

il dipartimento/la facoltà   department

il dottorato di ricerca   PhD, doctorate

l'esame di ammissione (m)   admission exam ▪ **È molto difficile entrare nella facoltà di medicina. L'esame di ammissione è molto duro.** It is very difficult to get into medical school. The admission exam is really hard.

gli esami   exams

essere fuori corso   to be a second-/third-/fourth-, etc. year senior. ▪ **Spero di finire l'università quest'anno. Mi sono iscritto al quarto anno fuori corso e sto spendendo tanti soldi per le tasse!** I hope to finish school this year. I'm a fourth-year senior and I'm spending so much money for tuition!

frequentare l'università/non frequentare l'università   to attend/not attend college or university

> NOTE: Attending classes is not as common in Italy as it is in other places; often students will go only to take their exams.

immatricolarsi   to register for classes

l'istituto (m)   branch of the department, institute

il libretto   transcript ▪ **Non sto studiando molto per i miei esami; ho il libretto pieno di diciotto.** I'm not studying much for my exams; I have a transcript full of D−s.

> NOTE: The **libretto** is a grade book that students keep with them, into which their professors will write their exam grades. The highest grade is 30+ and the lowest is 18.

la matricola   freshman ▪ **All'università di Roma quest'anno ci sono tantissime matricole.** There are a ton of freshmen this year at the University of Rome.

la mensa cafeteria ■ **Alla fine della lezione vado a mangiare alla mensa.** After class I'm going to eat in the cafeteria.

prendere trenta e lode to receive the highest grade possible, A+

il quarto d'ora accademico fifteen-minute grace period before class starts

> NOTE: In Italian universities a class may be scheduled to start on the hour, but often the professor will arrive and begin class fifteen minutes late.

il rettore president of the university

la segreteria registrar

la SISS [Scuola Interuniversitaria di Specializzazione per l'Insegnamento Secondario] university specializing in teaching education methods

i sissini SISS students

studiare al CEPU to study at CEPU ■ **Quel tipo va all'università ma non sa niente. Penso che studi al CEPU.** That guy goes to college but he doesn't know anything. I think he studies at CEPU.

EXAMINATIONS/DISSERTATIONS

bucare/cannare lo scritto to fail, bomb a written test (fam.) ■ **Non mi aspettavo proprio di bucare lo scritto di italiano!** I wasn't expecting to bomb the Italian test!

il diploma high school diploma

l'esame di maturità (m) high school final exam

essere sotto esame to be taking/studying for an exam

fare scena muta all'orale (lit., to do a mute scene) to be speechless during an oral exam ■ **Stamattina mi ha interrogato la prof di lettere ma io ho fatto scena muta.** This morning I took the oral exam with the literature teacher, but I was completely speechless.

la laurea university graduation

l'orale (m) oral part of exam

il relatore thesis advisor

lo scritto written part of exam

la tesi di laurea graduation thesis

la tesi di dottorato doctoral disseration

EXERCISES
Adesso tocca a voi!

A *Choose from the following words or phrases to complete the sentences:*

scena muta	andare a ripetizione	secchione	voto
compito in classe	bucato	fare sega	copiare
si ammazza di studio	nota sul registro		

1. Giovedì c'è il _____ di matematica, penso che dovrò _____ da un buon insegnante se voglio fare bene.

2. Oggi proprio non voglio andare a lezione e prendere un brutto _____. Ho intenzione di _____ e di fare una passeggiata.

3. Dovete fare il compito in classe da soli! Non dovete _____! Se lo fate, prenderete una _____.

4. Tutti i giorni Francesco _____ e non si diverte mai. È proprio un gran _____.

5. L'esame di maturità è stato un disastro. Ho _____ lo scritto e ho fatto _____ all'orale.

B *Translate into Italian the following English expressions:*

1. To rack one's brain _____

2. To kill oneself studying _____

3. To sit around _____

4. To be a genius _____

5. To be a dunce _____

C *Choose the word in parentheses that best fits the sentence:*

1. Il professore d'italiano sta male. Domani verrà (la supplente/il preside) e rimarrà qui per dieci giorni.

2. Voglio andare all'università ma non ho i soldi. Spero di ottenere una (borsa di studio/segreteria).

3. Le lezioni iniziano sempre in ritardo. Lo sanno tutti che c'è (il quarto d'ora accademico/la casa dello studente) nelle università italiane.

4. Alla (facoltà/mensa) universitaria, si mangia molto bene. Sembra di essere al ristorante!

5. Mio figlio studia veramente molto per i suoi esami universitari. Ha il libretto pieno di (diciotto/trenta e lode).

Emotions

ANGER

alzarsi con la luna storta   (*lit.*, to get up with the moon crooked) to wake up on the wrong side of the bed

andare in bestia   to be angry as a beast ■ **Quando non obbedisco mio padre, lui va in bestia!** When I don't obey my father, he gets angry as a beast!

avercela con qualcuno   to be upset or angry with someone (fam.) ■ **Non ce l'ho con te, ma ce l'ho invece con tua sorella!** I'm not angry at you, but I am angry at your sister!

avere i cazzi girati   (*lit.*, to have your dicks twisted) to be irritable or angry (vulg.) ■ **Che c'hai? Sono tre giorni che hai i cazzi girati!** What's your problem? You've been irritable for the last three days!

avere la bava alla bocca   to be foaming at the mouth (with rage)

avere un caratterino   to have a temper ■ **Stai attento! Sai che lui ha un caratterino!** Be careful! You know that he has quite a temper!

crepare dalla bile   (*lit.*, to die from the bile) to be consumed with anger and envy ■ **Alessio crepa dalla bile ogni volta che vede la sua ex con il nuovo fidanzato.** Alessio is consumed with envy every time he sees his ex with her new boyfriend.

essere di cattivo umore/di malumore   to be in a bad mood

essere sfigato/a   to be unlucky (fam.) ■ **Paolo è stato mollato dalla fidanzata, è stato licenziato, e ora ha perso il suo migliore amico. È veramente sfigato!** Paolo was dumped by his girlfriend, he was fired, and now he lost his best friend. He is truly unlucky!

essere una testa calda   to be a hothead ■ **Non uscire più con Pippo. Menate le mani ogni volta perché lui è una testa calda e vi mette nei guai!** Don't go out with Pippo anymore. You all get into a fight every time because he is a hothead and he gets you all in trouble!

incavolarsi   to be angry

incazzarsi, essere (incazzato) nero   to be fucking pissed off (vulg.) ▪ **Mi sono incazzata nera quando l'ho saputo!** I got so fucking pissed off when I found out about it!

> NOTE: One can also just say simply «**Sono nero/a!**» to indicate being extremely pissed off.

perdere le staffe   (*lit.*, to lose the stirrups) to lose one's temper

perdere la testa   (*lit.*, to lose one's head) to flip out ▪ **So che tu sei incavolata, ma cerca di non perdere la testa.** I know you are angry, but try not to flip out.

la sfiga   misfortune, bad luck (fam.) ▪ **La tua macchina non parte? Che sfiga!** Your car won't start? What rotten luck!

COURAGE/ENCOURAGEMENT

Animo!, Dai!, Forza!   Come on!

avere il sangue freddo   (*lit.*, to have cold blood) to have ice water in your veins ▪ **All'esame orale, non devi essere nervosa. Devi avere il sangue freddo.** At the oral exam, you mustn't be nervous. You have to have ice water in your veins.

buttarsi, lanciarsi   to dive or throw oneself into something ▪ **So che tu hai paura, ma ti devi buttare per avere successo.** I know you are afraid, but you have to throw yourself in to be successful.

avere il sangue freddo

97

Coraggio!   Have courage!

farcela   to be able to do something ■ **«Ce la fai a portare la valigia per le scale?» «Non ti preoccupare!» «Ce la faccio.»** "Are you able to carry the suitcase up the stairs?" "Don't worry about it! I can do it."

perdersi d'animo   to lose heart ■ **Non perderti animo. È solo una piccola battuta d'arresto.** Don't lose heart. It's only a minor setback.

rimanere sulla breccia   to keep at it

tenere duro   (*lit.*, to stay tough) to hang in there, to be strong or tough ■ **Tieni duro! Ce la farai!** Hang in there! You can do it!

> NOTE: Be careful here with the verb **tenere**! If used reflexively, such as when saying **«tenersi duro»**, the expression means "to keep oneself hard," as in to keep an erection. **Dai, bello, tieniti duro perché non sono venuta ancora!** Come on, stud, stay hard because I haven't come yet!

CRYING

allungare il muso   to have a long face ■ **Ogni volta che ti dico di no, devi allungare il muso.** Every time I tell you no, you have to make a long face.

avere gli occhi bagnati   to have wet eyes

avere le lacrime in tasca   (*lit.*, to have tears in your pocket) to be easily moved to crying ■ **Non posso andare al cinema con Nicola perché ha le lacrime in tasca. Piange anche per i film comici!** I can't go to the movies with Nicola because he cries too easily, even for comic films!

commuoversi   to be moved, to be touched ■ **La lettera mi ha fatto commuovere.** The letter moved me.

piangere a dirotto   to blubber, to weep ■ **Lei piangeva a dirotto! Non sapevo cosa fare per calmarla!** She was weeping! I didn't know what to do to calm her down!

piangere sul latte versato   to cry over spilled milk

il/la piagnucolone/a   crybaby

scoppiare in pianto   to burst into tears ■ **Il professore è stato così severo che lei è scoppiata in pianto.** The professor was so severe with her that she burst into tears.

CURSING

In Italian there are two different types of cursing: **parolacce** (bad words) and **bestemmie** (blasphemous cursing). WARNING: All of the **bestemmie** are extremely offensive as they involve various Christian saints and/or religious figures, most often the Virgin Mary or God. It is virtually impossible to precisely translate most of these expressions into English, so we've provided the literal meaning along with, in some cases, possible English equivalents.

Accidenti! (*lit.*, Accidents!) Wow! Holy cow! My goodness!

NOTE: The expression **Accidenti!** is often used with blasphemous expressions. For example, **Accidenti alla Madonna troia!**

Cazzo!, Minchia! (*lit.*, Dick!) Damn!, Shit!, Fuck!

Dio bastardo! (*lit.*, Bastard God!) Goddammit!

Dio becco/cornuto! (*lit.*, Cuckold God!)

Dio boia! (*lit.*, Executioner God!)

Dio cane! (*lit.*, Dog God!)

Dio infame! (*lit.*, Vile God!)

Dio maiale! (*lit.*, Pig God!)

Dio zingaro! (*lit.*, Gypsy God!)

Madonna cane! (*lit.*, Dog Virgin Mary!)

Madonna Eva! (*lit.*, Eve Virgin Mary!)

Madonna maiala! (*lit.*, Pig Virgin Mary!)

Madonna Santa! Holy Mother of God!

Madonna troia! (*lit.*, Whore Virgin Mary!)

Madonna zoccola! (*lit.*, Clog Virgin Mary!)

NOTE: **Zoccola**, which is literally a clog, means "whore."

Mannaggia (la miseria)!

NOTE: **Mannaggia** comes from the old Italian expression «che malanno aggia», which when said to someone means "may you fall ill." This is a commonly used term and is not very offensive, even when directed at another person.

Porco Dio! (*lit.*, Dirty God!)

NOTE: The adjective **porco** (meaning "dirty") can be followed by numerous nouns to constitute a bad word or a swear. The very common «porca miseria», for example, while rather dramatic, is not particularly vulgar. «Porco Dio!», on the other hand, is very strong and surely offensive.

Porca Eva! (*lit.*, Dirty Eve!)

Porco Giuda! (*lit.*, Dirty Judas!)

Porca Madonna! (*lit.*, Dirty Virgin Mary!)

NOTE: Oftentimes the variations «**Porco Zio!**» and «**Porca Madosca!**» are used in place of «**Porco Dio!**» and «**Porca Madonna!**», to make these less offensive than taking the names of God and the Virgin Mary in vain. In fairy tales **Orco Zio** is the ogre chieftain while **Orca Madosca** is his female companion.

Porca miseria!   (*lit.*, Dirty misery!) Holy cow!, Rats!, Wow!, Darn it!

NOTE: This term can be used to express not only anger or disgust, but also surprise and marvel.

Porca puttana!   (*lit.*, Dirty whore!)

Puttana Eva!   (*lit.*, Eve the whore!)

Santo cielo!   Good heavens!

EMBARRASSMENT

arrossire   to blush

diventare rosso come un peperone   (*lit.*, to turn red as a pepper) to turn red as a beet ■ **Quando Alessandro le ha chiesto di uscire, è diventata tutta rossa come un peperone!** When Alessandro asked her out, she turned red as a beet!

fare una cavolata/una cazzata (vulg.)/una stronzata (vulg.)   to do something stupid or dumb

fare una figuraccia/una figura di merda   to make a fool of oneself, to commit a faux pas, to lose face (fam.) ■ **Franco ha fatto una figuraccia di merda dicendo una balla alla professoressa perché lei sapeva già la verità!** Franco made a fool of himself telling that story to the (female) professor because she already knew the truth!

mettere in imbarazzo   to embarrass ■ **Non voglio vederlo perché mi mette sempre in imbarazzo!** I don't want to see him because he always embarrasses me.

lo stronzo   (*lit.*, turd) shithead, asshole, dork (vulg.) ■ **Non posso credere di aver detto una cosa del genere! Che stronzo!** I can't believe I said such a thing! What a shithead I am!

la vergogna   embarrassment

vergognarsi   to be ashamed ■ **Mi vergogno di chiederti questo favore, ma non ho scelta.** I am ashamed to ask you this favor, but I have no choice.

FEAR

cagarsi adosso, cagarsi sotto   to shit oneself, to shit one's pants (vulg.) ■ **Piero non può parlare con il capo perché si caga adosso.** Piero can't talk to the boss because he'll shit his pants.

il/la cagasotto   a person who shits oneself, a person who shits one's pants (for every little thing) (vulg.)

fare venire la pelle d'oca   (*lit.*, to get goose skin) to get goose bumps

farsela addosso, farsela sotto   to piss in one's pants (fam.) ▪ **Quando la polizia ci ha fermato, me la sono fatta addosso!** When the police stopped us, I pissed my pants!

la fifa   fear

il fifone/la fifona   scaredy-cat, fraidy-cat

spavaldo   cocksure

spaventarsi, prendere un colpo   (*lit.*, to take a hit) to become scared ▪ **Pensavo di essere solo! Mi hai fatto prendere un colpo!** I thought I was alone! You scared me!

il vigliacco/la vigliacca, il codardo/la codarda   coward

JOY

avere culo   (*lit.*, to have ass) to be a lucky son of a bitch (fam.) ▪ **Patrizio ha vinto la lotteria! Che culo che ha!** Patrizio won the lottery! What a lucky son of a bitch!

andare in brodo di giuggiole   (*lit.*, to be in **giuggiola** broth) to be overjoyed

> NOTE: A **giuggiola** is the sweet fruit from a small tree brought to Europe from China.

avere qualche santo dalla propria parte   to have some saints on your side ▪ **Ha avuto un bruttissimo incidente ma non si è fatto male per nulla. Deve avere qualche santo dalla sua parte!** He had a terrible accident but he didn't get hurt at all. He must have some saints on his side!

avere un colpo di fortuna   to have a stroke of good luck

beato   blessed, lucky ▪ **Vai a fare una vacanza al mare? Beato te!** You are going on a vacation at the beach? Lucky you!

crepare/schiantare dal ridere   to die laughing ▪ **Se fai questa battuta tutti schianteranno dal ridere!** If you tell that joke everyone will die laughing!

essere al settimo cielo   (*lit.*, to be in seventh heaven) to be on cloud nine

essere baciato dalla fortuna   to be kissed by fate ▪ **Sono stato baciato dalla fortuna per avere una ragazza così!** I've been kissed by fate to have such a girlfriend!

essere di buon umore   to be in a good mood

essere felice come una pasqua   to be happy as a lark

nascere sotto una buona stella   to be born under a good sign ▪ **Quella ragazza non deve mai lavorare se non vuole perché la sua famiglia è ricca sfondata. È nata proprio sotto una buona stella.** That girl doesn't ever have to work if she doesn't want to because her family is filthy rich. She really was born under a good sign.

non stare più nella pelle   to come out of one's skin ▪ **Sono così contenti che non stanno più nella pelle!** They are so excited that they are coming out of their skin!

ridere a crepapelle   to laugh until one's sides split

scoppiare dalla contentezza   to burst from happiness

scoppiare dalle risate, scoppiare in risata   to burst with laughter ▪ **Gli studenti sono scoppiati dalle risate quando il professore è entrato con la bottega aperta!** The students busted out laughing when the professor entered with his fly down!

spensierato/a   (*lit.*, one without thoughts) happy-go-lucky ▪ **Quella ragazza è sempre di buon umore! È una persona veramente spensierata!** That girl is always in a good mood! She is really happy-go-lucky!

toccare il cielo con un dito   (*lit.*, to touch heaven with your finger) to be in heaven

trovare l'America   (*lit.*, to find America) to find happiness, to have all one wants ▪ **È andato in Germania dove ha un buon lavoro, una bella macchina, e una fidanzata. Insomma, ha trovato l'America!** He went to Germany where he has a good job, a nice car, and a girlfriend. In short, he has all he wants!

THREATS AND VIOLENCE

allungare un dritto   to punch

azzuffarsi   to scrap ▪ **C'è stata una baruffa a scuola; ci siamo azzuffati e mi sono fatto male.** There was a scuffle at school; we scrapped and I got hurt.

la baruffa, la zuffa, la rissa   scrap, scuffle

bisticciare   to squabble, to bicker ▪ **Ieri sera ho bisticciato con la mia donna quindi stasera non mi vuole vedere.** Last night I squabbled with my woman and therefore she doesn't want to see me tonight.

cercare dei guai   to look for trouble

fare una faccia così   (*lit.*, to make someone's face swell up a large size from the beating) to beat someone's face (fam.) ▪ **Se non chiudi la bocca, io ti faccio una faccia così!** If you don't shut your mouth, I'll beat your face in!

fare un culo così   to beat someone's ass (vulg.)

NOTE: These expressions are accompanied with a gesture in most cases. The hands are held open and apart, with the fingers closed in a fist except for the thumbs and index fingers, which form an L, indicating the size of something, as if to say "I'll make your face/ass swell up to this size from the beating I'm going to give you!"

menare le mani   to punch someone, to fistfight with someone

mettersi nei guai   to get into trouble

minacciare   to threaten   ▪ **Se minacci la gente non fai altro che metterti nei guai.** If you threaten people, you don't do anything but get yourself into trouble.

picchiare   to hit

prendere a cazzotti   to sock someone (fam.)   ▪ **Se quello continua a darci fastidio lo prendo a cazzotti.** If he continues to bother us, I'm going to sock it to him.

spaccare la faccia   to break someone's face (fam.)   ▪ **Dammi i soldi o ti spacco la faccia!** Give me the money or I'll break your face!

spaccare la testa   to break someone's head (fam.)

venire alle mani   to get into a fight with someone   ▪ **Smammiamo prima di venire alle mani!** Let's scram before we get into a fight!

Murder

cavare le budella a qualcuno   to dig someone's guts out (fam.)

fare fuori   to take someone out   ▪ **Hanno fatto fuori il capo mafioso stanotte.** They took out the mafia boss last night.

fare la festa a qualcuno   to kill someone

fare sparire   to make someone disappear   ▪ **Basta che tu mi dica chi ti rompe le palle e io lo faccio sparire.** All you need to do is tell me who is bothering you and I'll make him disappear.

impiombare   to fill someone with lead

WISHES/DELUSIONS

chiudere bottega   (*lit.*, to close up shop) to give up   ▪ **È importante seguire i propri sogni, ma è anche importante capire quando il momento di chiudere bottega è arrivato.** It is important to follow your dreams, but it is also important to realize when it's time to give up.

farsi illusioni   to be under the illusion of something

illudersi to deceive oneself ▪ **Non illuderti, caro amico. Quella ragazza non ti ama.** Don't deceive yourself, my dear friend. That girl doesn't love you.

morire dal desiderio/dalla voglia di fare qualcosa to be dying to do something ▪ **Muoio dalla voglia di sapere com'è andato con Monica e Antonio ieri sera!** I'm dying to know how it went with Monica and Antonio last night!

non vedere l'ora di fare qualcosa to not be able to wait to do something ▪ **Non vedo l'ora di andare al mare per l'estate!** I can't wait to go to the beach for the summer!

rimanerci male to be disappointed ▪ **Ci rimango male se mi dai buca!** I'll be disappointed if you stand me up!

rimanere con la bocca amara (*lit.*, to be left with a bitter taste in the mouth) to be disappointed

sognare a occhi aperti, fantasticare to daydream

EXERCISES

Adesso tocca a voi!

A *Choose from the following words or phrases to complete the statements:*

le mani	culo	la bocca amara
tasca	girati	le staffe

1. Your friend's car was about to be towed but he arrived just in time to move it.

   Mario, che _____ che hai!

2. Your sister has been angry at the world since she was dumped by her boyfriend.

   Sto alla larga di Susanna perché c'ha i cazzi _____ da una settimana.

3. Your cousin lost control and started yelling at her boyfriend during a discussion.

   É importante non perdere _____ quando discuti con lui.

4. You are babysitting your little nephew whose feelings are hurt very easily.

Devi essere molto gentile con lui perché ha le lacrime in

_____.

5. You and your buddy get into a fistfight because some jerks are bothering your friends.

Stronzi, se non smettete di rompere i coglioni dovremo menare

_____.

6. Your boss let you go but kept a colleague who has been there less time than you have.

Cazzo! Sono rimasto con _____.

B *Match the following Italian expressions with the equivalent English translation on the right.*

_____ 1. Diventare rosso come un peperone

_____ 2. Fare la festa a qualcuno

_____ 3. Essere al settimo cielo

_____ 4. Non vedere l'ora di fare qualcosa

_____ 5. alzarsi con la luna storta

_____ 6. Fare venire la pelle d'oca

a. to get up on the wrong side of the bed

b. to get goose bumps

c. to not be able to wait to do something

d. to turn red as a beet

e. to kill someone

f. to be on cloud nine

C *Give the English equivalent for each of the following Italian expressions:*

1. allungare il muso _____

2. fare una faccia così _____

3. fare una figuraccia di merda _____

4. nascere sotto una buona stella _____

5. rimanere sulla breccia _____

6. cagarsi sotto _____

Entertainment

BARS

l'alcolizzato, l'ubriacone (m)   lush, drunkard, alcoholic

buttare giù, tracannare   to throw down (a drink), to have a drink ▪ **Andiamo a buttare giù qualcosa prima di tornare a casa.** Let's go throw down a drink before going home.

il caffè corretto   (*lit.*, corrected coffee) spiked coffee (usually with grappa)

l'enoteca (f), la vinoteca   wine bar

fare il giro dei pub/dei bar   to go bar hopping, to have a pub crawl ▪ **Per il mio compleanno voglio fare il giro dei pub e ubriacarmi!** For my birthday I want to go bar hopping and get drunk!

il pub, il locale   bar, drinking establishment, watering hole

BROTHELS/PROSTITUTION

il bordello, il casino, la casa chiusa   brothel, whorehouse

> NOTE: The terms **bordello** and **casino**, which are familiar but not vulgar, are commonly used in spoken Italian to mean "a mess," "a disaster," or even "a lot of noise or commotion." **È un casino guidare in questa città a causa del traffico.** It's a mess driving in this city because of the traffic. **Ragazzi, non fate casino perché Paolo dorme.** Kids, don't make a racket, because Paolo is sleeping.

la mezzana, la madame, la ruffiana   madame

la puttana, la mignotta, la troia, la battona, la zoccola, la sorcia, la bagascia, la sgualdrina, la donnaccia, la lucciola, la squillo   (*lit.*, call girl) whore, hooker (vulg.)

il ruffiano, il magnaccia, il protettore, il pappone   pimp

NIGHTCLUBS/DISCOTHEQUES

l'after (m)   after-hours club

il buttafuori   bouncer

la consumazione obbligatoria   consumption mandatory

> NOTE: Many nightclubs don't charge a cover, but you are required to buy at least one drink from the bar. Otherwise, you will have to pay a cover charge to get out of the club.

la cubista   professional dancer who dances onstage or often in cages at nightclubs

la discoteca   discotheque

il guardaroba   coat check

il night   nightclub

pagare l'ingresso   to pay a cover charge

il PR   person who advertises for the nightclubs during the day, usually handing out flyers or business cards on the street

il privé   private nightclub

la tessera   membership card

> NOTE: Some clubs are private and thus require you to be a card-carrying member to get in.

POPULAR MUSIC

la musica leggera   pop/Top 40 music

il rap   rap

il rock   rock and roll

il rock duro   hard rock

il reggae   reggae

la techno   techno

THEATER

Bis!   Encore!

il camerino   dressing room

il divo/la diva, il/la star   star

esaurito   sold out ■ **Volevamo andare a vedere il concerto di Ligabue ma è esaurito!** We wanted to go see Ligabue's concert, but it is sold out!

la messinscena   production, performance

mettere in scena to produce or to put on (a play) ▪ **Alla Pergola mettono in scena una commedia di Pirandello.** At the Pergola Theater they are putting on a play by Pirandello.

il posto in platea/in galleria seat in the orchestra/in the balcony

la spalla (*lit.,* the shoulder) supporting actor

OTHER PLACES AND SOURCES OF ENTERTAINMENT

la bettola, il buco dive, hole in the wall

le giostre park rides

il luna park carnival

le montagne russe roller coaster

l'orgia (f) orgy, sex party

il party party

il party scatenato wild party

il pornazzo, il film hard porno flick

il sexy shop sex shop, adult store

la/lo spogliarellista stripper

lo strip-club strip club

lo strip-tease, lo spogliarello striptease

la tele TV, tube

ENTERTAINING ONESELF

dare un party to throw a party ▪ **Massimo dà un party domani sera da non perdere!** Massimo is throwing a party tomorrow night that is not to be missed!

fare due salti (*lit.,* to do two jumps) to dance, to bop ▪ **Cerchiamo un locale dove possiamo fare due salti.** Let's look for a place where we can dance a bit.

fare una jam session to have a jam session

fare una nuotata, fare un tuffo to take a dip ▪ **I ragazzi amano fare una nuotata in mare prima di andare a scuola.** The kids love to take a dip in the sea before going off to school.

godersi la vita, darsi alla pazza gioia to live it up ▪ **Nicola esce quasi ogni sera! E un tipo che sa godersi la vita!** Nicola goes out almost every night! He is the type of person who knows how to live it up!

pogare   to mosh

lo scacciapensieri   (*lit.*, thought expeller) pastime

tirar fuori, sganciare   (*lit.*, to unhook), **cacciare** to cough up, or fork out (money)   ■ **Non posso venire con voi al mare per il fine settimana perché ho dovuto sganciare ottocento carte per riparare la macchina!** I can't come with you all to the beach for the weekend because I had to cough up eight hundred bucks to fix my car!

ARE WE HAVING FUN?

la barba   (*lit.*, beard), **le palle** (*lit.*, balls) (fam.) drag, boring

il casino   (*lit.*, whorehouse) mess, utter shambles

il colmo, il massimo   top, best, most

divertirsi un sacco/da morire   to have a great time   ■ **Che party scatenato! Tutti si sono divertiti da morire!** What a wild party! Everyone had a great time!

esagerato   over-the-top

essere annoiato a morte   to be bored to death   ■ **Che palle quella festa! Mi sono annoiata a morte!** What a drag that party was! I was bored to death!

favoloso   super, fab(ulous)

losco, dubbioso   shady, sketchy

mega, iper   mega   ■ **Che festa megagalattica!** What a megagalactic party!

il must, da non perdere   must, must-see

pacchiano, di cattivo gusto   tacky

la pacchianeria   tackiness

piegarsi in due (dal ridere)   to double up (from laughter)   ■ **Il film è stato divertentissimo! Mi sono piegato in due dal ridere!** The film was very entertaining! I doubled up with laughter!

simpatico   nice

> NOTE: The term **simpatico** is often used out of politeness when the show/person/event is not very entertaining. **E ora vi presento la simpatica Sandy che canterà per noi!** And now I introduce the nice Sandy who will sing for us!

strappare gli applausi   (*lit.*, to pull out ovations) to bring the house down   ■ **Quell'ultima scena ha strappato gli applausi!** That last scene brought the house down!

super   super

una vera pizza   (*lit.*, a real pizza) as dull as dishwater

Uffa!   Oh! I can't take this (because it's boring, annoying, etc.)!

EXERCISES
Adesso tocca a voi!

A *Give the Italian expression for each of the following English words or phrases:*

1. porno flick _____

2. to cough up/fork out money _____

3. bouncer _____

4. to bring the house down _____

5. to live it up _____

6. dive/hole in the wall _____

7. to throw down a drink _____

8. must/must-see _____

9. after-hours club _____

10. to dance, to bop _____

B *You are at a party in Milan where people are discussing what they think of various types of entertainment. Give an English equivalent for each comment:*

1. Che palle! _____

2. Ci siamo annoiati a morte! _____

3. Uffa! _____

4. È stata una vera pizza! _____

5. Ci si diverte un sacco! _____

6. È il colmo! _____

Food and Eating

TYPES OF FOOD

gli affettati   sliced salami and/or lunch meat, cold cuts ▪ **Per un antipasto, prendiamo degli affettati.** As an appetizer, let's get a nice plate of salami.

l'antipasto   appetizer

gli avanzi   leftovers ▪ **Stasera mangiamo gli avanzi di ieri sera.** Tonight we're eating the leftovers from last night.

il banchetto   feast, big meal

il boccone   a bite, chow ▪ **Andiamo a mangiare un boccone prima di andare a casa.** Let's go grab a bite to eat before going home.

la bruschetta   bruschetta (toasted bread, garlic, fresh tomatoes, basil, and olive oil)

la carne tritata   ground or minced meat

il cibo leggero   light food

il cibo pesante   heavy food ▪ **Non voglio mangiare pesante stasera; prendo invece qualcosa di leggero. Un'insalata forse.** I don't want to eat heavy food tonight; I'm having something light, like a salad perhaps.

la ciccia   (*lit.*, meat or fat) meat (fam.) ▪ **Stasera ho voglia di mangiare la ciccia.** Tonight I want to eat some meat.

> NOTE: This term can also be used for "tail," as in girls or women. **Non vado alla festa se non c'è la ciccia.** I'm not going to the party if there isn't any tail there.

la colazione   breakfast

il contorno   side dish (usually vegetables)

i crostini   toasted bread served with various spreads ▪ **I crostini toscani vengono con il paté di fegato.** Tuscan crostini are served with liver paté.

il dolce   dessert, sweet food

il formaggio affumicato   smoked cheese

il formaggio fresco   soft cheese

il formaggio stagionato/invecchiato   aged or hard cheese

la merenda   afternoon snack   ■ **Dopo scuola, i ragazzi fanno una piccolo merenda.** After school, the kids have a little snack.

la pasta asciutta   (*lit.*, dry pasta) pasta with sauce   ■ **Stasera mi va un bel piatto di pasta asciutta!** Tonight I would like a nice plate of pasta with sauce!

> NOTE: The term includes any pasta dish served with any kind of sauce (red or white), or even pasta with nothing on it but olive oil, as opposed to **pasta al brodo** (pasta in broth).

il pasto   meal

le porcherie, le schifezze, il cibo spazzatura   junk food

il primo   first course (usually some type of pasta dish or soup)

il secondo   second course (usually meat or fish)   ■ **Non voglio un primo, ma prendo volentieri un secondo.** I don't want a first course, but I will willingly have a second course.

lo spuntino   snack

gli stuzzichini   appetizers, bar snacks   ■ **Non mangiare troppi stuzzichini al bar! Ti rovini l'appetito!** Don't eat too many snacks at the bar! You'll ruin your appetite!

NAMES FOR THE QUALITIES OF FOOD

al dente   (*lit.*, to the tooth) al dente, slightly undercooked (pasta)   ■ **La pasta va mangiata al dente.** Pasta must be eaten slightly undercooked.

> NOTE: Italian pasta is almost always served **al dente**. Pasta that is not **al dente** is not considered pasta, and for Italians is not edible. Thus when someone asks if the pasta is **al dente**, he or she is really asking if it is good pasta. **La pasta scotta** is overcooked pasta.

al sangue   rare   ■ **La bistecca fiorentina viene servita al sangue.** The Florentine steak is served rare.

cotto   medium well

ben cotto   well done

> NOTE: The three terms above refer to how red meat is cooked.

la brodaglia, la risciaquatura di piatti   (*lit.*, dirty dishwater) slop, nasty food (fam.)   ■ **Questo cibo fa schifo! Non è che la brodaglia!** This food sucks! It's nothing but slop/dirty dishwater!

duro   tough   ■ **Questa carne è troppo dura perché è incenerita!** This meat is too tough because it's burned to a crisp!

salato   salty food   ■ **Cosa preferisci per lo spuntino, dolce o salato?** What do you prefer for your snack, something sweet or something salty?

sapere di niente   to be bland   ■ **Questi prodotti surgelati non sanno di niente!** These frozen foods are bland!

la sboba/sbobba   bad food, slop (fam.)

stracotto   overcooked   ■ **Questa cotoletta è stracotta!** This cutlet is overcooked!

tenero   tender   ■ **La carne in quel ristorante è sempre molto tenera.** The meat in that restaurant is always very tender.

STAGES OF HUNGER

l'acquolina in bocca   to have one's mouth water   ■ **I dolci della pasticceria mi fanno venire l'acquolina in bocca!** The desserts in the pastry shop make my mouth water!

avere una fame da lupi   (*lit.*, to be hungry as a wolf) to be hungry as a horse

avere una fame della Madonna   (*lit.*, to be hungry like the Virgin Mary) to be starving (fam.)

essere pieno   to be full

fare gola   to tempt   ■ **Quella torta fa gola, ma non la posso mangiare perché sto a dieta.** That pie is tempting, but I can't eat it because I am on a diet.

la fame chimica   (*lit.*, chemical hunger) the munchies   ■ **Ogni volta che fumiamo la maria ci viene la fame chimica.** Every time that we smoke weed, we get the munchies.

morire di fame   to die of hunger

stare a dieta   to be on a diet

svenire per la fame   to faint from hunger

Expressions involving hunger

essere lento come la fame   (*lit.*, to be as slow as hunger) to be as slow as molasses   ■ **Guido, sbrigati! Sei lento come la fame!** Guido, hurry it up! You are as slow as molasses!

essere brutto come la fame   to be as ugly as hunger

essere un morto di fame   (*lit.*, to be dying of hunger) to be a nobody or a nothing (fam.)

NAMING THE EATERS

avere un verme/il verme solitario   to have a (tape)worm (because one eats so much)

buttare giù tutto come un lavandino   (*lit.*, to throw everything down like a sink) to eat everything in sight/within reach

essere a pane e acqua   to eat hardly anything

essere bene in carne/grassoccio/a, grassotello/a, paffuto/a   to be plump (fam.)

essere difficile nel mangiare   to be a picky eater

essere sciupato   to have gotten skinnier (fam.) ■ **Ma quanto sei sciupato! Non mangi più?** How skinny you have become! Don't you eat anymore?

essere secco/magro   to be skinny (fam.) ■ **Non ti ingrassi mai! Sei secco come un chiodo!** You'll never get fat! You're as skinny as a nail!

essere una buona forchetta   (*lit.*, to be a good fork) to be a hearty eater ■ **Alla mamma piace quando Enzo viene a cena perché è una buona forchetta.** Mom likes it when Enzo comes to dinner because he is a hearty eater.

buttare giù tutto come un lavandino

ghiotto gluttonous, greedy ▪ **Hai mangiato tre dolci?! Quanto sei ghiotto!** You ate three desserts?! How gluttonous you are!

mangiare svogliatamente to eat without interest or without much enthusiasm

restare a bocca asciutta (*lit.*, to be left with a dry mouth) to be left empty-handed

lo sbafatore/la sbafatrice, il ghiottone/la ghiottona glutton (fam.)

THE ACT OF EATING

abbuffarsi to stuff oneself, to gorge oneself, to pig out ▪ **Che bella cena! Ci siamo abbuffati come maiali!** What a great dinner! We gorged ourselves like pigs!

l'abbuffata (f), la sbafata big meal, blow out, binge

andare su e giù (*lit.*, to go up and down) to give indigestion ▪ **Non posso mangiare i peperoni perché vanno su e giù tutta la notte!** I can't eat peppers because they'll give me indigestion all night!

A tavola! Time to eat!, Dinner/Lunch is served!

essere arrivato (*lit.*, to have arrived) to be full ▪ **Sono arrivato. Non posso mangiare un altro morso.** I'm full. I can't eat another bite.

essere sazio to be full or satisfied

farsi la bocca to clean the palate

fare la scarpetta (*lit.*, to do the little shoe) clean the plate ▪ **Si fa la scarpetta con un pezzo di pane.** Cleaning the plate is done with a piece of bread.

mangiare alle spalle di qualcuno, mangiare alla busca di qualcuno to sponge off of someone ▪ **Non voglio invitare Salvatore alla cena perché lui mangia sempre alle spalle nostre.** I don't want to invite Salvatore to the dinner because he always sponges off of us.

mangiare come un bufalo/un maiale (*lit.*, to eat like a buffalo/a pig) to eat like a horse or pig

mangiucchiare to nibble at food ▪ **Non ho fame ancora perché ho mangiucchiato a casa.** I'm not hungry yet because I nibbled some food at home.

pappare to eat up, to gobble up (fam.)

riempirsi le budella (*lit.*, to fill one's guts) to stuff oneself, to overeat (fam.)

rimanere sullo stomaco (*lit.*, to remain in the stomach) to give indigestion

NOTE: This term can also be used figuratively for something that is bothering someone. **Il fatto che hanno dato il nuovo lavoro a lui mi rimane sullo stomaco.** The fact that they gave the new job to him bothers me.

ruttare   to burp ■ **Ragazzi, non dovete mai ruttare davanti agli altri. È molto scortese!** Kids, you mustn't ever burp in front of others. It is very impolite!

sbafare   to gobble up, to polish off

scoppiare   to explode ■ **Basta, mamma! Sto scoppiando!** That's enough, Mom! I'm going to explode!

sfamarsi   to get rid of the hunger ■ **Prima di uscire, mi devo sfamare perché se no, spenderò troppi soldi per il cibo.** Before going out, I have to get rid of my hunger because if not I'll spend too much money on food.

sgranocchiare   to munch, to nibble

stuzzicare   to pick at food

togliersi lo sfizio   to satisfy a craving ■ **Mangiamo un po' di cioccolata giusto per toglierci lo sfizio.** Let's eat a little bit of chocolate, just enough to satisfy our craving.

EXPRESSIONS INVOLVING FOOD

avere troppa carne al fuoco   (*lit.*, to have too much meat on the fire) too many irons in the fire ■ **Amanda non ha tempo per fare nulla perché ha troppa carne al fuoco.** Amanda doesn't have time for anything because she has too many irons in the fire.

essere buono come il pane   (*lit.*, to be as good as bread) as good as gold ■ **È una persona buona come il pane.** He/She is a person as good as gold.

essere della stessa pasta   (*lit.*, to be from the same dough) to be cast from the same mold

essere di buona pasta   (*lit.*, to be from good dough) to be good-natured or kindhearted

la gallina vecchia fa buon brodo   (*lit.*, the old hen makes a good broth) there's many a good tune played on an old fiddle ■ **«Quella donna è troppo vecchia per me!» «La gallina vecchia fa buon brodo!»** "That woman is too old for me." "There's many a good tune played on an old fiddle!"

lasciare cuocere nel suo brodo   (*lit.*, to let someone cook in his own broth) to let someone stew in his own juice ■ **Non rispondere alle sue telefonate. Lascialo cuocere nel suo brodo per un po'!** Don't answer his phone calls. Let him stew in his own juice for a while!

una minestra riscaldata (*lit.*, warmed soup) old hat ▪ **Per pubblicare, devi scrivere qualcosa di sorprendente, non una minestra riscaldata.** To get published, you must write something shocking, not something that's old hat.

non c'è fumo senza arrosto (*lit.*, there can't be smoke without a roast) where there's smoke, there's fire

non essere né carne né pesce (*lit.*, to be neither meat nor fish) neither fish nor fowl

non sputare nel piatto dove si mangia (*lit.*, to not spit in the plate you eat from) to not bite the hand that feeds you ▪ **Dobbiamo imparare a non sputare nel piatto dove si mangia.** We must learn to not bite the hand that feeds us.

qualcosa bolle in pentola (*lit.*, something is boiling in the pot) something's up or brewing ▪ **Mimmo si comporta in modo strano. Ci deve essere qualcosa che bolle in pentola.** Mimmo is acting strange. There must be something brewing.

tanto fumo e poco arrosto (*lit.*, a lot of smoke, not much roast) a lot of show and little substance ▪ **Quel professore parla molto, ma c'è tanto fumo e poco arrosto.** That professor talks a lot, but he's all talk and no show.

trovare la minestra bell'e pronta (*lit.*, to find the soup ready to eat) to find something on a silver platter

EXERCISES

Adesso tocca a voi!

A *Place a +, −, or an X after each of the following food words or expressions to show whether the food is good (+), bad (−), or neutral (X):*

1. la pasta asciutta _____

2. la bistecca incenerita _____

3. la ciccia _____

4. il boccone _____

5. la risciacquatura di piatti _____

6. la sboba _____

7. la carne tenera _____

8. la brodaglia _____

B *You have just come from a **banchetto**, and you explain to your room-mates what kind of eaters the other guests were. Translate the following sentences into Italian slang:*

1. Mario and Giulia ate everything in sight!

   _____

2. Riccardo, on the other hand, is a very picky eater.

   _____

3. Carlo ate like a horse, while Geppina nibbled at the food just a little bit.

   _____

4. Gianni is a hearty eater.

   _____

5. Massimo must have a tapeworm!

   _____

6. Pietro and Stefano scarfed down food all night long.

   _____

7. Monica just picked at food here and there.

   _____

8. I totally pigged out! I overate!

   _____

C *Match each of the following Italian expressions involving food on the left with the English equivalent on the right:*

_____ 1. **qualcosa bolle in pentola**

_____ 2. **non essere né carne né pesce**

_____ 3. **trovare la minestra bell'e pronta**

_____ 4. **tanto fumo e poco arrosto**

_____ 5. **la fame chimica**

_____ 6. **avere troppa carne al fuoco**

_____ 7. **essere di buona pasta**

_____ 8. **la gallina vecchia fa un buon brodo**

a. to have too many irons in the fire

b. to be kindhearted

c. a lot of show and little substance

d. something is brewing

e. there's many a good tune played on an old fiddle

f. the munchies

g. to be neither fish nor fowl

h. to find something on a silver platter

Geography

Many Italian names of regions, cities, and rivers do not have an English equivalent. This also means that there is often no specific English word to describe a person's place of origin. For example, a person from **Basilicata** is described as **lucano**, but in English the only option is to say "from Basilicata."

CARDINAL DIRECTIONS

il Settentrione   the North ▪ **A settentrione fa sempre più freddo.** In the North it is always colder.

NOTE: The word **Settentrione** derives from the Latin term *septemtrionalis*, used to indicate the seven stars of the constellation Ursa minor, which include the North Star. The term **Settentrione** has come to indicate the North.

settentrionale   northern

il Mezzogiorno, il Meridione   the South

NOTE: The South is indicated with the terms **Mezzogiorno** and **Meridione** because at noon (**mezzogiorno**) in the Eastern hemisphere, the sun is found on that side of the equator. **Meridione** comes from the Latin *meridianus*, meaning "of the (after)noon."

meridionale   southern ▪ **Mio padre è meridionale.** My father is southern.

il Ponente   the West

NOTE: In the Middle Ages, the verb **porre** (to put) was used to indicate the setting of the sun (**sole ponente**), and thus the term **ponente** has come to signify the direction in which the sun sets.

il Levante   the East

NOTE: **Levante** is derived from the verb **levare** (to rise). The direction of the rising sun (**sole levante**) is the east.

PRINCIPAL ITALIAN CITIES

Ancona

anconetano   from Ancona

L'Aquila

aquilano   from l'Aquila

Bari ■ **Da Bari si può andare in Grecia con la nave in dodici ore.** It is possible to go to Greece from Bari in twelve hours by ship.

barese   from Bari

Bologna ■ **A Bologna si può visitare la torre degli Asinelli.** In Bologna one may visit the tower of Asinelli.

bolognese   from Bologna

Cagliari ■ **Non sapevo che Manuela studiasse a Cagliari.** I didn't know that Manuela studies in Cagliari.

cagliaritano   from Cagliari

Campobasso ■ **I turisti non visitano mai Campobasso.** Tourists never visit Campobasso.

campobassano   from Campobasso

Firenze   Florence ■ **Firenze d'estate è piena di turisti americani.** In the summer Florence is crowed with American tourists.

fiorentino   Florentine

Genova   Genoa ■ **Il porto di Genova è pieno di brutta gente.** The port of Genoa is full of bad people.

genovese   Genovese

Milano   Milan ■ **Milano è la città della moda.** Milan is the city of fashion.

milanese   Milanese

Napoli   Naples ■ **Oggi Gianmario va a Napoli per vedere la partita di calcio.** Today Gianmario is going to Naples to see the soccer match.

napoletano   Neapolitan

Padova   Padua ■ **L'università di Padova è una delle più antiche d'Italia.** The University of Padua is one of the oldest in Italy.

padovano   from Padua

Palermo ■ **A Palermo fa sempre molto caldo.** In Palermo it is always very warm.

palermitano   from Palermo

Parma

parmigiano   Parmese

Perugia ■ **I miei nonni abitano a Perugia.** My grandparents live in Perugia.

perugino   from Perugia

Pisa ▪ **Pisa è famosa per la Torre Pendente.** Pisa is famous for the Leaning Tower.

pisano   from Pisa ▪ **Meglio un morto in casa che un pisano all'uscio.** Better to have a dead person in the house than someone from Pisa at the door.

Potenza ▪ **Pare che Potenza sia la città più fredda d'Italia.** It seems that Potenza is the coldest city in Italy.

potentino   from Potenza

Reggio Calabria

reggino   from Reggio Calabria

Roma   Rome ▪ **Tutte le strade portano a Roma.** All roads lead to Rome.

romano   Roman

Torino   Turin ▪ **I miei genitori vivono a Torino.** My parents live in Turin.

torinese   from Turin

Trento

trentino   from Trento

Treviso ▪ **Da Treviso a Venezia ci vogliono venti minuti in treno.** It takes twenty minutes from Treviso to Venice by train.

trevigiano   from Treviso

Trieste ▪ **Il prossimo mese andrò a Trieste a trovare il mio amico Dino.** Next month I'll go to Trieste to see my friend Dino.

triestino   from Trieste

Venezia   Venice ▪ **Dario lavora a Venezia da due anni.** Dario has been working in Venice for two years.

veneziano   Venetian

REGIONS

l'Abruzzo

abruzzese   from Abruzzo

la Basilicata ▪ **La Basilicata è una regione molto povera.** Basilicata is a very poor region.

lucano   from Basilicata

la Calabria

calabrese from Calabria

la Campania

campano from Campania

l'Emilia Romagna

emiliano from Emilia

romagnolo from Romagna

il Friuli Venezia Giulia

friulano from Friuli

giuliano from Venezia Giulia

la Liguria

ligure Ligurian

il Lazio

laziale from Lazio

la Lombardia Lombardy

lombardo Lombard

le Marche ▪ **Il mio amico Aldo è nato nelle Marche.** My friend Aldo was born in the Marche region.

marchigiano from Marche

il Molise

molisano from Molise

il Piemonte Piedmont

piemontese from Piedmont

la Puglia

pugliese from Puglia

la Sardegna Sardinia

sardo Sardinian

la Sicilia Sicily

siciliano Sicilian

la Toscana   Tuscany   ▪ **La Toscana è ricca di luoghi interessanti da visitare.** Tuscany is full of interesting places to visit.

toscano   Tuscan

il Trentino Alto Adige

trentino   from Trentino

altoatesino   from Alto Adige

l'Umbria

umbro   from Umbria

la Valle d'Aosta

valdostano   from Valle d'Aosta

il Veneto ▪ **Per bere del buon prosecco bisogna andare in Veneto.** To drink a good prosecco one must go to Veneto.

veneto   from Veneto

EXERCISES
Adesso tocca a voi!

A   *Write the Italian word for what you would call the people from the following Italian cities. Make sure the adjective agrees with the subject!*

1. Katia è di Firenze. Lei è _____.

2. Fabrizio e Luigi vengono da Genova. Sono _____.

3. Franco è di Potenza. Lui è _____.

4. Monica e Giorgio sono di Bologna. Sono _____.

5. Mario e Angelo vengono da Napoli. Sono _____.

6. Silvia è di Treviso. Lei è _____.

7. Francesca e Lucia sono di Parma. Sono _____.

8. Gianni viene da Bari. Lui è _____.

9. Paolo è di Campobasso. Lui è _____.

10. Claudio e Elisabetta vengono da Trieste. Sono _____.

B *Write the Italian word for what you would call the people from the following Italian cities. Make sure the adjective agrees with the subject!*

1. Franco è nato in Piemonte. Lui è _____.

2. Anna torna in Calabria per Natale perché lei è _____.

3. Roberta e Massimo vengono dalla Sardegna. Loro sono

   _____.

4. Michele è della Basilicata. Lui è _____.

5. Ermanno viene dalle Marche. Lui è _____.

6. Fabiana parla con un tipico accento della Puglia. Lei è

   _____.

7. Luisa è della Liguria. Lei è _____.

8. Gli amici di Carlo vengono dal Molise. Sono _____.

9. Mia madre è nata in Valle d'Aosta. Lei è _____.

10. Rosa e Carmine sono del Lazio. Loro sono _____.

C **Montagna, mare, lago o fiume?** *Identify each geographical body in the space provided:*

1. Le Alpi _____

2. Il Brenta _____

3. Il Monte Bianco _____

4. Il Tevere _____

5. Il Gran Sasso _____

6. Lago di Garda _____

7. L'Arno _____

8. Mar Adriatico _____

9. Le Dolomiti _____

10. Mar Tirreno _____

11. Lago di Como _____

12. Il Piave _____

13. Gli Appennini _____

Health

HOW ARE YOU FEELING?

andare abbastanza bene   to go rather well (fam.) ■ **Va tutto abbastanza bene.** Everything is going rather well.

avere un brutta cera   (*lit.*, to have a bad wax) to look ill (fam.)

> NOTE: The word **cera**, which means "wax" in English, is commonly used to refer to a person's appearance.

avere un piede nella tomba/fossa   to have one foot in the grave (fam.)

beccarsi un raffreddore   (*lit.*, to catch oneself a cold) to catch a cold (fam.) ■ **Ho giocato a calcio quando pioveva e mi sono beccato un raffreddore.** I played soccer in the rain and caught a cold.

così così   (*lit.*, like this like this) so-so (fam.)

essere in fin di vita   (*lit.*, to be at the end of life) to be at death's door (fam.)

essere in forma   (*lit.*, to be in form) to be in shape ■ **Non sono affatto in forma.** I'm not in shape at all.

essere in piena forma   (*lit.*, to be in full form) to be in perfect shape

essere messo male   (*lit.*, to be poorly placed) to be in bad shape (fam.)

essere sano come un pesce   (*lit.*, to be healthy like a fish) to be in perfect health (fam.) ■ **Il nonno è sempre stato sano come un pesce.** Grandpa has always been in perfect health.

essere spacciato   to be done for (fam.) ■ **I medici lo danno per spacciato.** The doctors say he's done for.

essere sul letto di morte   (*lit.*, to be on one's deathbed) to be about to die (fam.)

essere tra la vita e la morte   to be between life and death (fam.) ■ **Hanno avuto un incidente molto grave, e sono tra la vita e la morte.** They were in a very serious accident, and they're between life and death.

essere tutta salute   (*lit.*, to be all health) to be in perfect health (fam.) ■ **Il mio istruttore di yoga è tutta salute.** My yoga instructor is in perfect health.

reggere l'anima coi denti

guardare la morte in faccia   to look death in the face (fam.)

non sentirsi molto in forma   (*lit.*, to not feel in very good shape) to be under the weather (fam.)   ■ **Penso che non andrò in ufficio oggi; non mi sento molto in forma.** I think I won't go to the office today; I'm feeling under the weather.

prendersi un malanno   (*lit.*, to get oneself an illness) to get sick (fam.)

reggere l'anima coi denti   (*lit.*, to hold on to the soul with your teeth) to be at death's door (fam.)   ■ **Non ho mai visto una persona tanto anziana. Reggeva l'anima coi denti.** I've never seen such an elderly person. He was at death's door.

ritrovare la forma   (*lit.*, to find the form again) to get back in shape (fam.)

scoppiare di salute   (*lit.*, to burst with health) to be bursting with health (fam.)

sentirsi __ anni di meno   (*lit.*, to feel oneself __ years less) to feel __ years younger (fam.)

sentirsi rinati   (*lit.*, to feel oneself reborn) to feel reborn (fam.)   ■ **Dopo questo massaggio mi sento rinato.** After this massage I feel reborn.

sprizzare salute da tutti i pori (*lit.*, to be squirting health from all pores) to be bursting with health (fam.)

stare attenti alla linea (*lit.*, to be careful of the line) to watch one's figure (fam.) ▪ **Da un paio d'anni sta molto attenta alla linea.** She has watched her figure very carefully for two years.

stare di merda/cazzo to feel like shit/dick (vulg.) ▪ **Oggi sto di merda, e non ho voglia di fare niente.** Today I feel like shit, and I don't feel like doing anything.

stare più di là che di qua (*lit.*, to be more there than here) to be more dead than alive (fam.)

tenersi in forma (*lit.*, to keep oneself in shape) to stay in shape ▪ **Vedo con piacere che ti tieni in forma.** I'm happy to see that you're staying in shape.

ti facevo più giovane/vecchio (*lit.*, I made you younger/older) I thought you were younger/older (fam.)

SPECIFIC SYMPTOMS AND COMPLAINTS

la bua boo-boo (fam.)

dare di stomaco/gozzare to throw up/to puke (fam.)

farsi la bua (*lit.*, to make oneself a boo-boo) to get hurt (fam.) ▪ **Ti sei fatto la bua, piccino?** Did you get hurt, little boy?

un malessere indisposition

perdere conoscenza to lose consciousness ▪ **Sono caduto dalle scale e ho perso conoscenza.** I fell down the stairs and lost consciousness.

pigliarsi un accidente (*lit.*, to catch oneself an accident) to catch a serious illness (fam.) ▪ **Se non ti copri ti piglierai un accidente.** If you don't cover up you will catch a serious illness.

rovinarsi to ruin oneself (fam.) ▪ **Se continui a bere ti rovinerai.** If you keep on drinking you will ruin yourself.

rovinarsi la salute (*lit.*, to ruin oneself the health) to ruin one's health (fam.)

venire meno (*lit.*, to come less) to faint

voltare gli occhi (*lit.*, to flip one's eyes) to pass out (fam.)

PSEUDOMEDICAL VOCABULARY

il body-building   bodybuilding (fam.) ▪ **Da giovane facevo spesso il body-building, ma adesso non ne ho mai il tempo.** When I was young I often did bodybuilding, but now I never have the time.

bucarsi   (*lit.*, to hole oneself) to shoot up (fam.)

chiamare il 118   to call 911 ▪ **Aiuto! Qualcuno chiama il 118!** Help! Someone call 911!

la croce rossa   Red Cross

crepare/schiantare   to croak/kick the bucket (fam.) ▪ **Se crepasse domani sarei tanto contento.** If he/she died tomorrow I would be very happy.

passare a miglior vita/spegnersi   (*lit.*, to pass on to a better life, to extinguish oneself) to pass away (fam.)

la ricetta   prescription ▪ **Il medico mi ha fatto la ricetta per un antistaminico molto forte.** The doctor wrote me a prescription for an antihistamine.

un sieropositivo   HIV-positive person

un tossicodipendente/tossicomane   drug addict

EXERCISES

Adesso tocca a voi!

A *Match each term with the proper translation:*

_____ 1. conoscenza	a. to croak
_____ 2. salute	b. cold
_____ 3. rinato	c. indisposition
_____ 4. giovane	d. reborn
_____ 5. accidente	e. consciousness
_____ 6. crepare	f. health
_____ 7. malessere	g. young
_____ 8. raffreddore	h. serious illness

B *Select the best translation for each of the following expressions:*

1. reggere l'anima con i denti:
   a. to be in shape
   b. to faint
   c. to be at death's door

2. sprizzare salute da tutti i pori:
   a. to catch a cold
   b. to be bursting with health
   c. to stay in shape

3. pigliarsi un accidente:
   a. to catch a serious illness
   b. to pass away
   c. to croak

4. dare di stomaco:
   a. to give of stomach
   b. to puke
   c. to throw up

C *Select the best translation for each of the following nouns:*

1. ricetta:
   a. recipe
   b. reflex
   c. prescription

2. forma:
   a. form
   b. shape
   c. pharmacy

3. salute:
   a. health
   b. indisposition
   c. cold

Hobbies and Pastimes

HOBBIES AND PASTIMES

il fai da te   do-it-yourself ■ **In famiglia riusciamo a risparmiare molti soldi da quando mio marito si è appassionato al fai da te.** In our family we are able to save a lot of money since my husband is a huge fan of do-it-yourself.

la filatelia   stamp collecting

il giardinaggio   gardening ■ **Penso che dedicarsi al giardinaggio sia molto rilassante.** I think gardening as a hobby is very relaxing.

il modellismo   modeling (small cars, airplanes, etc.)

la numismatica   coin collecting ■ **Quand'ero piccolo ero un vero appassionato di filatelia e numismatica.** When I was a young boy I was really passionate about stamp collecting and coin collecting.

LETTING YOUR HAIR DOWN

andare a fare quattro salti in discoteca   (*lit.*, to go to do four jumps at the disco) to go dance in a disco ■ **Mi è venuta voglia di ballare! Perché non andiamo a fare quattro salti in discoteca?** I feel like dancing! Why don't we go dance at the disco?

andare fuori di testa/andare su di giri   to go out of one's mind

diventare matto/impazzire   to go crazy, to go wild ■ **Damiano è un ragazzo timido, ma quando va a ballare impazzisce.** Damiano is a timid guy, but when he goes out dancing he goes wild.

divertirsi da morire   (*lit.*, to enjoy oneself to death) to have tons of fun ■ **Ieri sera sono andato a vedere lo spettacolo di quel comico famoso e mi sono divertito da morire!** Last night I went to see a show by that famous comedian and I had tons of fun!

fare il giro dei locali   to go around town, to paint the town red, to have a night out

lasciarsi andare   to let oneself go

perdere la testa   to lose one's head

SHOWING YOUR TALENTS OR OTHERWISE

avere il pollice verde   to have a green thumb ▪ **Non so perché tutte le mie piante muoiano dopo pochi giorni dopo averle comprate! Forse non ho il pollice verde!** I don't know why all my plants die a few days after I buy them! Maybe I just don't have a green thumb!

avere le mani d'oro   to be good with one's hands ▪ **Giacomo è capace di aggiustare tutto! Ha proprio le mani d'oro!** Giacomo can fix anything! He's good with his hands!

avere talento per   to have a talent for something

cavarsela   to be able to manage ▪ **Devo aggiustare il tetto della casa. Lo voglio fare da solo; non sono un muratore ma spero di cavarmela.** I have to fix the roof of my house. I want to do it by myself; I'm not a carpenter but I hope I can manage.

essere negato/a per   to be terrible at something ▪ **Non provarci nemmeno! Lo sanno tutti che sei negato per cucinare!** Don't even try it! Everybody knows you're terrible at cooking!

essere ossessionato con/essere fissato con   to be obsessed with something

essere pazzo per/impazzire per   to be crazy for/to go crazy for something ▪ **Mio marito guarda sempre le partite alla TV. Impazzisce per il calcio!** My husband always watches games on TV. He's crazy for soccer!

essere portato/a per   (*lit.*, to be taken for) to have a talent for, to have a gift for ▪ **Francesca suona il piano molto bene. È proprio portata per la musica.** Francesca plays the piano very well. She has a real gift for music.

non avere la minima idea   to not have the slightest idea ▪ **Non ho la minima idea di come si aggiustino i freni della macchina. La porterò dal meccanico.** I don't have the slightest idea how to fix car brakes. I will take it to a mechanic.

saperci fare con   to really know how to do something, to be really good at something ▪ **Eric Clapton ci sa fare con la chitarra!** Eric Clapton really knows how to play guitar!

sapersi arrangiare   to get by

VARIOUS ENTHUSIASTS

l'amatore (m) / il dilettante   amateur

il bibliofilo   book lover, avid reader and collector ▪ **Non ho mai conosciuto un bibliofilo come Stefano! Pensa che ha una collezione di costosissimi libri an-**

tichi e li legge tutti! Stefano is the most avid reader I've ever known! Just think, he has a huge expensive collection of antique books and he reads them all!

il calciofilo   soccer lover

il cinefilo   cinema buff ▪ **Fabio è un vero cinefilo. Vede cinque film ogni settimana!** Fabio is such a cinema buff. He sees five films a week!

il fanatico/il patito   fanatic

il melomane   opera lover

il topo di biblioteca   bookworm

EXERCISES
Adesso tocca a voi!

A *Translate the following expressions into Italian:*

1. an opera lover _____

2. a bookworm _____

3. stamp collecting _____

4. coin collecting _____

5. do-it-yourself _____

6. modeling _____

7. cinema buff _____

B *Match each of the phrases in the following list with its equivalent below:*

essere ossessionato/a con	avere talento per
essere negato/a per	sapersi arrangiare

1. essere pazzo/a per _____

2. non avere la minima idea _____

3. cavarsela _____

4. essere portato/a per _____

C *Use the words in the box to complete the following sentences:*

le mani d'oro	melomane	impazzisce
dilettante	fai da te	

1. Giuseppe sa fare proprio tutto! Sa dipingere, sa aggiustare le cose, ha

   _____.

2. Mio fratello va sempre a vedere l'opera. È proprio un

   _____.

3. Quando va ai concerti rock, Michela _____.

4. Suono la chitarra ma non sono una professionista. Sono un buon

   _____.

5. Con il _____ si risparmiano molti soldi!

The Human Body

PARTS OF THE BODY

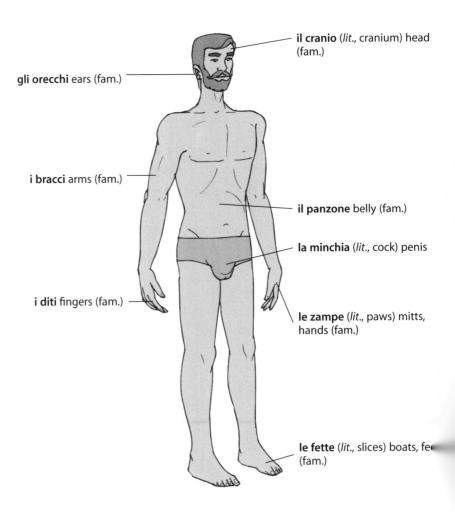

il cranio (*lit.*, cranium) head (fam.)

gli orecchi ears (fam.)

i bracci arms (fam.)

il panzone belly (fam.)

la minchia (*lit.*, cock) penis

i diti fingers (fam.)

le zampe (*lit.*, paws) mitts, hands (fam.)

le fette (*lit.*, slices) boats, fee (fam.)

i bracci   arms (fam.)

i diti   fingers (fam.)   ■ **Non ti mettere i diti nel naso!** Don't put your fingers in your nose!

i ginocchi   knees (fam)   ■ **Se non la smetti ti spacco i ginocchi!** If you don't stop it, I'll break your knees!

i labbri   lips (fam.)

gli orecchi   ears (fam.)

i dentoni   big teeth (fam.)   ■ **Guarda che dentoni che ha Marco!** Look at what big teeth Marco has!

le fette   (*lit.*, slices) boats, feet (fam.)   ■ **Con queste fette non riesco mai a trovare un paio di scarpe del mio numero!** With these boats I can't ever find a pair of shoes in my size!

le zampe   (*lit.*, paws) mitts, hands (fam.)   ■ **Luca ha due zampe grandi come quelle di un gorilla.** Luca has two mitts as big as a gorilla's!

Belly: **il pancione, la panza, il panzone** (fam.)

Bottom: **il fondoschiena** (*lit.*, end of back) backside, **il sedere** (*lit.*, sit) seat, **il deretano** (*lit.*, derriere) (fam.), **il posteriore** (*lit.*, posterior), **le mele** (*lit.*, apples), **le chiappe, il di dietro** (*lit.*, behind), **il culo** (*lit.*, ass) (fam.)

Breasts: **le tette** tits (fam.), **le poppe** boobs (fam.), **le mammelle** mammaries, **le zinne/i meloni** (*lit.*, melons) (fam.), **le noci di cocco** (*lit.*, coconuts) (fam.), **le bocce** (*lit.*, bocce balls) (fam.), **i pompelmi** (*lit.*, grapefruits) (fam.)

Hair: **il cestone** (*lit.*, big basket) (fam.), **la cesta** (*lit.*, basket) (fam.), **la chioma** (*lit.*, foliage)

Head: **il capo/la capa/la capoccia/la caveza/il cranio** (*lit.*, cranium) (fam.), **il testone** (*lit.*, big head) (fam.)

Nose: **il nappone, la nappa, la proboscide** (*lit.*, trunk) (fam.)

Penis: **il cazzo** (*lit.*, dick) (vulg.), **la minchia** (*lit.*, cock) (vulg.), **la mazza** (*lit.*, bat) (vulg.), **la verga** (*lit.*, shepard's staff) (vulg.), **l'uccello** (*lit.* bird) (vulg.), **la fava** (*lit.* fava bean) (vulg.), **il pisello** (*lit.* pea) (vulg.), **il bastone** (*lit.*, stick) (vulg.), **la salsiccia** (*lit.*, sausage) (vulg.), **il salame** (*lit.*, salami) (vulg.), **il membro** (*lit.*, member) (vulg.), **la terza gamba** (*lit.*, third leg) (vulg.), **il campanile** (*lit.*, belltower) (vulg.), **il manganello** (*lit.*, nightstick) (vulg.)

> NOTE: The term **cazzo** is used very frequently as a swearword, either by itself as an exclamation (**Cazzo!**, which might translate as "Shit!" or "Fuck!") or inserted

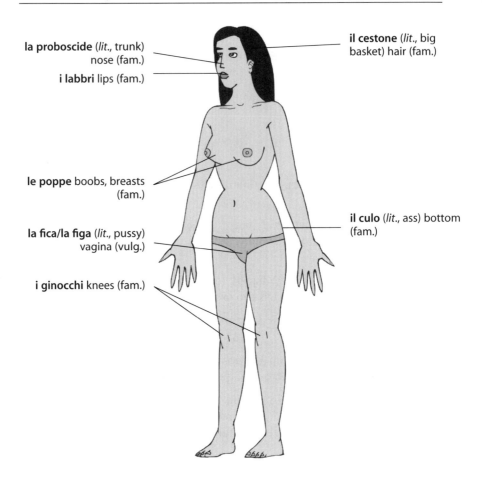

la proboscide (*lit.*, trunk) nose (*fam.*)

i labbri lips (*fam.*)

il cestone (*lit.*, big basket) hair (*fam.*)

le poppe boobs, breasts (*fam.*)

la fica/la figa (*lit.*, pussy) vagina (vulg.)

i ginocchi knees (*fam.*)

il culo (*lit.*, ass) bottom (*fam.*)

into a sentence. If one says, «**Che cazzo vuoi?**», for example, it could be translated as "What the fuck do you want?"

Vagina: **la fica/la figa** (*lit.*, pussy) (*vulg.*), **la passera** (*lit.*, female sparrow) (*vulg.*), **la fregna** cunt (*vulg.*), **la topa/la sorca** (*lit.*, female mouse)/**la sgnacchera** snatch (*vulg.*), **la ciccia** (*lit.*, fat) trim (*fam.*), **la vulva** (*lit.*, vulva), **la gnocca** (*lit.*, dumpling)

PASSING WIND

flatulento   farty, one who passes wind often

scoreggiare   to pass wind

la scoreggia   fart

la bronza, la loffa   smelly fart, asphyxiating fart

fare un profumino   (*lit.*, to make a little perfume) to make a smell, to fart
■ **Che profumino hai fatto!** What a smell you made!

EXERCISES

Adesso tocca a voi!

A *Match each of the following Italian words with its English equivalent:*

fregna	verga	topa	vulva	fava
passera	sorca	bastone	ciccia	cazzo
uccello	sgnacchera	mazza	pisello	

1. penis: _____

_____

2. vagina: _____

_____

B *Match the following Italian words:*

____ 1. cesta   a. pancione

____ 2. nappa   b. culo

____ 3. capo   c. zinne

____ 4. manganello   d. chioma

____ 5. sorca   e. testone

____ 6. sedere   f. proboscide

____ 7. panza   g. bastone

____ 8. tette   h. figa

Immigrants and Immigration

CLOTHING

il chador   chador (Islamic veil)

la kefiah   kaffiyeh

il turbante   turban

EXPRESSIONS INVOLVING NAMES OF FOREIGNERS

essere un beduino   (*lit.*, to be a Bedouin) to look unsophisticated (fam.)

fare il portoghese   (*lit.*, to do the Portuguese) to avoid paying for your ticket (vulg.)

fare l'ebreo   (*lit.*, to do the Jew) to be stingy (vulg.)

fare l'indiano   (*lit.*, to do the Indian) to be a thief (fam.)

lavorare come un negro   to work like a slave (vulg.)

per me questo è arabo   (*lit.*, for me this is Arabic) this is Greek to me (fam.)

HOUSING

la Caritas   Catholic humanitarian organization

il centro di prima accoglienza   temporary shelter

> NOTE: When immigrants land on the Italian coast, these shelters give them a place to sleep and food to eat for a few days.

IMMIGRANTS

le carrette del mare   old rusty boats (fam.)

> NOTE: Often immigrants will use broken-down boats and dinghies to emigrate, not always successfully.

il clandestino/la clandestina   illegal immigrant, stowaway ▪ **Migliaia di clandestini sbarcano ogni anno sulle coste italiane.** Thousands of stowaways land on Italy's shores every year.

la colf [collaboratrice familiare]   servant, nanny

NOTE: In the last few years most employed servants have been immigrants, most notably from the Philippines.

la convivenza   living together, cohabitation

l'emarginato/a   social outcast ■ **Nelle periferie delle grandi città italiane ci sono molti emarginati.** In the outskirts of large Italian cities there are many social outcasts.

entrare clandestinamente   to enter the country illegally ■ **Molti immigrati entrano clandestinamente attraverso il confine nord-orientale.** Many immigrants enter the country illegally through the northeast border.

l'espulsione (f)   expulsion ■ **Il ministero dell'Interno ha deciso l'espulsione di cinquecento immigrati clandestini arrivati in Italia dieci giorni fa.** The government has ordered the expulsion of five hundred illegal immigrants who arrived in Italy ten days ago.

essere in regola/essere a posto con i documenti   to have all of your documents (i.e., to live in a country legally with all the correct papers)

l'extracomunitario/a   a person from outside the European community

NOTE: This term usually refers to people emigrating from poorer countries.

il gommone   rubber dinghy

l'immigrato/a   immigrant

l'immigrato/a irregolare   illegal immigrant

l'immigrato/a regolare   legal immigrant

integrarsi   to integrate oneself ■ **Non è facile integrarsi subito nella società italiana per molti immigrati.** For many immigrants, it is not easy to integrate immediately into Italian society.

l'intolleranza (f)   intolerance

il lavavetri   window washer

lavorare in nero   to work illegally ■ **Molti immigrati non riescono a trovare un lavoro regolare e lavorano in nero.** Many immigrants are not successful in finding a regular job and work illegally.

le organizzazioni umanitarie   humanitarian organizations

il permesso di soggiorno   residence permit ■ **È molto difficile ottenere un permesso di soggiorno.** It is extremely difficult to obtain a residence permit.

la polizia di frontiera   border police

la prostituzione   prostitution

il pregiudizio   prejudice

il razzismo   racism

il rifugiato/la rifugiata   refugee ■ **L'Italia è un paese che ospita molti rifugiati politici.** Italy is a country that hosts many political refugees.

il rimpatrio forzato   deportation ■ **Per molti stranieri senza il permesso di soggiorno scatta il rimpatrio forzato.** Many foreigners without a residence permit receive automatic deportation.

sbarcare   to disembark, to land ■ **Il mese scorso sono sbarcati sulle coste della Sicilia quattrocento immigrati dai paesi dell'Africa Centrale.** Last month four hundred immigrants landed on the coast of Sicily from the countries of Central Africa.

lo scafista   navigator of ships carrying illegal immigrants ■ **Lo scafista del gommone sbarcato ieri sulle coste della Puglia è stato preso e arrestato.** The navigator of the rubber dinghy that landed yesterday on the coast of Puglia was caught and arrested.

il senzatetto   homeless person ■ **La percentuale dei senzatetto tra gli immigrati purtroppo è molto alta.** The percentage of homeless persons among immigrants is unfortunately quite high.

il vu cumprà   foreign street vendor (fam.)

> NOTE: This term refers to the accent of foreign street vendors. In Italian **Vuoi comprare?** means "Do you want to buy?" but from the mouth of an immigrant it may sound more like **vu cumprà. Il venditore ambulante** is the standard name.

NAMES FOR FOREIGNERS

un crucco   kraut (fam.)

un kiwi   kiwi

> NOTE: This term, which is also used in English, is used to denote a person from New Zealand. It is derived from the fruit and the bird (which are native to the island country), and has become the national emblem of New Zealand.

un vichingo   (*lit.*, Viking) Scandinavian (fam.)

uno yankee   yank (vulg.)

Names for races/foreigners (not country specific)

un magrebino   (*lit.*, a person from Maghreb, North Africa) a thief (vulg.)

un muso giallo   (*lit.*, yellow face) Asian (vulg.)

occhi a mandorla   almond-shaped eyes (vulg.)

un pellerossa   (*lit.*, redskin) Native American (vulg.)

uno zingaro   Gypsy (vulg.)

RELIGION

il fanatismo   fanaticism

il fondamentalismo   fundamentalism

l'integralismo (m)   extremism

la chiesa   church

la moschea (f)   mosque

EXERCISES

Adesso tocca a voi!

A *Match each of the words in the following list with its equivalent below:*

il clandestino	il rimpatrio forzato	il vu cumprà
le carrette del mare	il fondamentalismo	

1. il lavavetri _____

2. il gommone _____

3. l'integralismo _____

4. l'espulsione _____

5. l'immigrato irregolare _____

B *Put a +, −, or an X next to each word to indicate whether it is good (+), bad (−), or neutral (X):*

1. integrarsi _____

2. lavorare in nero _____

3. l'intolleranza _____

4. la convivenza _____

5. il fanatismo _____

6. l'emarginato ____

7. il senzatetto ____

8. il razzismo ____

9. il pregiudizio ____

10. il chador ____

11. le carrette del mare ____

12. la moschea ____

C *Create an expression by joining words from the two columns:*

____ 1. essere a posto   a. **di frontiera**

____ 2. il centro   b. **di soggiorno**

____ 3. il permesso   c. **con i documenti**

____ 4. la polizia   d. **di prima accoglienza**

____ 5. le organizzazioni   e. **umanitarie**

D *Select the best translation for each of the following terms and expressions:*

1. **lo zingaro:**
   a. kiwi   b. redskin   c. Gypsy

2. **un crucco:**
   a. yankee   b. kraut   c. Viking

3. **un magrebino:**
   a. Portuguese   b. Bedouin   c. thief

4. **Per me questo è arabo.**
   a. I think this   b. This is French   c. This is
      is Arabic.   to me.   Greek to me.

5. **fare il portoghese:**
   a. to be Portuguese   b. to drink port   c. to avoid paying for
                             wine   your ticket

142

Information Technology

COMPUTERS

bloccarsi, piantarsi to crash (fam.) ▪ **Il mio computer si è piantato, e ho perso tutti i miei documenti.** My computer crashed, and I lost all my documents.

il CD-ROM, il lettore CD/DVD CD-ROM/DVD-ROM ▪ **Il computer ha un CD-ROM interno.** The computer has an internal CD-ROM.

cliccare to click (fam.)

il computer computer ▪ **Accendi il computer.** Turn on the computer.

il dischetto floppy disk

essere un genio dei computer/dell'informatica to be a computer whiz

il file file (fam.) ▪ **Non trovo quel file che volevo farti vedere.** I can't find the file I wanted to show you.

il floppy disk drive (fam.) ▪ **Temo che il dischetto nel floppy abbia un virus.** I'm afraid the disk in the disk drive has a virus.

formattare to format (fam.) ▪ **Ho formattato il dischetto sbagliato, e adesso sono nei guai.** I formatted the wrong disk, and now I'm in trouble.

l'hard disk (m) hard drive (fam.)

l'informatica (f) computer science ▪ **La mia università non ha un programma di laurea in informatica.** My university does not have a degree program in computer science.

masterizzare to burn a CD or CD-ROM

il masterizzatore CD burner

il monitor monitor ▪ **I monitor a colori sono migliori.** Color monitors are better.

il mouse mouse ▪ **Questo è un mouse per mancini.** This is a mouse for left-handed people.

il PC personal computer (fam.)

piratare to burn a CD or CD-ROM ▪ **Ho piratato un CD di Eminem che a mia madre non piace.** I burned a CD by Eminem that my mother does not like.

143

il portatile   laptop ▪ **Marco ha un nuovo portatile.** Marco has a new laptop.

il programmatore   computer scientist/programmer

saperci fare con i computer   to be skilled with computers (fam.) ▪ **Mio fratello è un genio dell'informatica, lui ci sa fare con i computer!** My brother is a computer whiz; he is really skilled with computers!

lo scanner   scanner

scannerizzare   to scan

lo schermo   screen

la stampante   printer

stampare   to print ▪ **Devo stampare il mio curriculum vitae prima del colloquio di domani.** I have to print my resume before tomorrow's interview.

il tappetino   mouse pad (fam.)

la tastiera   keyboard

E-MAIL

allegare un documento/video/un'immagine ad un'e-mail   to attach a document/video/image to an e-mail ▪ **Ho allegato un video all'e-mail che le ho spedito ieri.** I attached a video to the e-mail I sent her yesterday.

l'e-mail (f) /la mail   e-mail (fam.)

l'indirizzo (m)   address

mandare/spedire un'e-mail a qualcuno   to e-mail someone ▪ **Mandare e-mail è uno dei mezzi di comunicazione più comuni in America.** Sending e-mails is one of the most common means of communication in America.

mandare un attachment   to send an attachment (fam.)

la posta elettronica   e-mail

INTERNET

l'antivirus (m)   virus protection software ▪ **Se non aggiorni l'anti-virus, è inutile averlo.** If you don't update your virus protection, it is useless to have it.

il browser   browser (fam.)

chattare   to chat online (fam.) ▪ **Quando chatto incontro sempre persone interessanti.** When I chat online, I always meet interesting people.

il collegamento   connection

fare ricerche sull'internet to do research on the Internet

l'indirizzo WEB (m) the Internet address

internet Internet

il link link (fam.) ▪ **Ho cliccato sul link, e tutto si è bloccato. Forse il sito è ancora in costruzione.** I clicked on the link, and everything froze up. Maybe the site is still under construction.

il modem modem ▪ **Magari avessi un modem cellulare!** If only I had a cellular modem!

il motore di ricerca search engine ▪ **Se non usi il motore di ricerca che ti ho suggerito, non lo troverai mai.** If you don't use the search engine I suggested, you will never find it.

navigare su internet to surf the Web (fam.) ▪ **Passi troppo tempo a navigare su internet!** You spend too much time surfing the Web!

la rete the Web

scaricare to download (fam.)

il servizio internet Internet service/access ▪ **C'è qualcosa che non va con il mio servizio internet. Non riesco a mandare e-mail. Forse non funziona il modem.** There's something wrong with my Internet service. I can't send e-mail. Maybe the modem isn't working.

il sito/la pagina web website/webpage

lo spyware spyware

il virus virus

> NOTE: **www.** is pronounced «**vu-vu-vu, punto. . .**» when dictating or reading an Internet address, even though the word for the letter **W** is «**doppia-vu.**» For example, **Ho usato la versione italiana di YAHOO!, l'indirizzo è vu-vu-vu, punto yahoo, punto it. Ho trovato un sito dove si può scaricare un video di Roberto Benigni.** I used the Italian version of YAHOO! The address is www.yahoo.it. I found a site where you can download a video of Roberto Benigni.

SOFTWARE

installare un programma to install a program

il pirataggio del software software piracy

il produttore di software software manufacturer

il programma the program ▪ **Il programma che hai scritto è pieno di errori.** The program you wrote is full of errors.

salvare un documento/file/programma to save a document/file/program (fam.) ■ **Non dimentichiamo di salvare questo documento prima di andare a casa!** Let's not forget to save this document before going home!

il software software ■ **Non ho il software necessario per far funzionare lo scanner.** I don't have the necessary software to make the scanner work.

EXERCISES
Adesso tocca a voi!

A *Choose from the following words or phrases to complete the sentences:*

collegamento	scaricare	dischetto	e-mail	Internet
stampante	modem	indirizzo	virus	sito

1. L'_____ è un risorsa incredibile! Ho trovato il
   _____ della RAI, e posso guardare molti video culturali e
   ascoltare la radio italiana.

2. C'è un _____ sul mio computer, e io non ho l'antivirus!
   Era sul tuo _____ ?

3. Tu conosci l'_____ di Cristina? Le voglio mandare un'
   _____ con una foto di noi due allegata.

4. Non ho ancora installato il software per la mia _____ e
   quindi non posso stampare il tuo documento.

5. Il suo _____ è molto buono perché il suo
   _____ è molto veloce. Lui può _____
   tutta la musica e i video che vuole!

B *Select the best translation for each of the following terms:*

1. **piratare:**   a. to print   b. to copy   c. to scan

2. **scaricare:**   a. to attach   b. to format   c. to download

3. **tastiera:**   a. mouse   b. keyboard   c. screen

Music

GENERAL VOCABULARY

l'assolo (m)   solo

il 33 giri   LP, long-playing record ■ **Peccato che non si trovino più i 33 giri. Io penso che abbiano un suono migliore dei CD.** It's too bad you can't find LPs anymore. I think they sound better than CDs.

la cassetta/il nastro   cassette tape

il CD/il compact disc   CD, compact disk

il deejay   DJ, deejay

il gruppo/la band   band

il gruppo spalla   (*lit.*, the shoulder group) opening act ■ **Il concerto di Eros Ramazzotti comincia alle nove e trenta. Prima suonerà un gruppo spalla.** The Eros Ramazzotti concert will start at 9:30. First there will be an opening act.

il jazzista   jazz player

il jazzofilo   jazz fanatic ■ **Andrea è un vero jazzofilo! Tutti gli anni va a Perugia per ascoltare tutti i concerti di Umbria Jazz.** Andrea is a real jazz fanatic! Every year he goes to Perugia to listen to every concert of the Umbria Jazz Festival.

il loggionista   operagoer who sits in the highest part of the theater (i.e., the cheapest seats)

> NOTE: Usually the **loggionisti** are the most critical and most knowledgeable. The success of an opera often depends on them.

il melomane   opera fan

il metallaro   metal head

il palasport   indoor stadium

> NOTE: Most pop-rock concerts take place in an indoor stadium, as it is usually the only place where so many concertgoers can gather at once.

la prima   the opening concert of a rock tour/opera ■ **Alla prima del concerto di Paolo Conte c'erano tutti i giornalisti delle più importanti riviste di musica italiane.** At the first concert of Paolo Conte, all the journalists of the important Italian music magazines showed up.

il rave party   rave

le repliche   all the shows after the opening concert

il rock duro   hard rock   ■ **Il rock mi piace, ma il rock duro non lo sopporto! I** like rock music, but I can't stand hard rock!

il rockettaro   rock 'n' roll fan

saltare   to skip   ■ **Questo CD salta sempre e non riesco a sentire neanche una canzone!** This CD skips all the time; I can't even hear a single song!

il singolo   single

il solista   soloist

lo strimpellatore   a less-than-average guitar/piano player   ■ **Da piccolo volevo diventare un chitarrista famoso, ma ora sono solo uno strimpellatore.** When I was little I wanted to become a famous guitar player, but now my playing is less than average.

il suono   sound system   ■ **Il concerto è stato bello ma il suono faceva schifo.** The concert was great but the sound system sucked.

la tecno   techno music

il turnista   touring musician   ■ **I cantanti più importanti e famosi quando vanno in tour vogliono essere accompagnati dai turnisti più bravi e affidabili.** When the most famous and important singers go on tour they want to be accompanied by the best and most reliable touring musicians.

il vinile   vinyl record

il veejay   VJ, veejay

GENERAL EXPRESSIONS

Buonanotte ai suonatori!   (*lit.*, Goodnight to the musicians!) That's that!

cambiare disco   (*lit.*, to change the record) to change the subject   ■ **Cambia disco! È da un'ora che ripeti sempre le stesse cose.** Change the subject! You've been repeating the same thing for an hour.

cantare/suonare dal vivo   to sing or play live

dare il la   (*lit.*, to give an A-note) to lead people by setting a standard/to be the first one to do something   ■ **Nella partita di ieri, Totti ha dato il la e i compagni hanno giocato benissimo./Nella partita di ieri, Totti ha dato il la alle marcature e i compagni hanno segnato altri tre gol.** In yesterday's game Totti set the standard and his teammates played well./In yesterday's game Totti was the first one to score and afterward his teammates made three more goals.

Buonanotte ai suonatori!

NOTE: The names for the seven musical notes in Italian are **do (C)**, **re (D)**, **mi (E)**, **fa (F)**, **sol (G)**, **la (A)**, **si (B)**. To make sure all instruments in a group are in tune, someone generally plays the **A**, and everyone else tunes their instrument to that note.

essere suonato   (*lit.*, to be played) to be out of one's mind   ■ **Continui a dire e fare delle cose prive di senso. Sei proprio suonato.** You keep saying and doing senseless things. You're really out of your mind.

essere stonato   to be out of tune   ■ **Mi hanno chiesto di far parte di un coro, ma ho detto di no perché sono stonato.** I was asked to be part of a choir, but I said no because I'm out of tune.

piano piano   softly, slowly

suonarle a qualcuno   to beat somebody up (fam.)

la stessa musica   the same old song, story, tune   ■ **Non si può parlare con Marco, con lui è sempre la stessa musica.** It's no use talking to Marco; with him it's always the same old story.

MUSICAL VENUES

l'Auditorium di Roma (m)   the major concert hall in Rome

la Scala di Milano   the major opera house in Italy

la Fenice di Venezia the major opera house in Venice

il teatro Ariston di Sanremo the Ariston Theater in Sanremo

NOTE: The Festival of Sanremo takes place in the Ariston Theater and is the most popular pop-music festival in Italy.

CHILDREN'S MUSIC

fare la conta, ambarabà ciccì coccò eeney meeney miney mo

la ninnananna lullaby

POPULAR MUSIC

l'agente (m/f) agent

l'album (m) album

la classifica billboard list

il cambio di etichetta label change

il/la cantante singer

cantare in playback to lip-synch, mime ■ **Quando i cantanti presentano le loro canzoni in televisione, spesso cantano in playback.** When singers perform their songs on TV, they usually lip-synch.

il cantautore/la cantautrice singer/songwriter ■ **Bob Dylan può essere considerato il padre di tutti i cantautori, anche di quelli italiani.** Bob Dylan can be considered the father of all singer/songwriters, even the Italian ones.

la canzone/il brano/il motivo/il pezzo song

il concerto concert

il disco d'oro gold record ■ **Si devono vendere moltissime copie per vincere il disco d'oro.** You need to sell a lot of CDs in order to get a gold record.

il disco di platino platinum record

fare una tournée/andare in tour to go on tour ■ **Sai per caso quando Claudio Baglioni farà la prossima tournée?** Do you happen to know when Claudio Baglioni is going on tour again?

il fiasco (*lit.*, flask) failure, disaster ■ **Quel CD è stato un fiasco.** That CD was a disaster.

il flop flop

la musica leggera (*lit.*, light music) pop music, easy-listening

il paroliere   lyricist ▪ **Penso che alcuni parolieri siano dei veri e propri poeti.** I think that some lyricists are real and true poets.

la prevendita   presale

sfondare   to make it, to break through

il successo   hit song ▪ **Quella allegra canzone brasiliana è stata il successo dell'estate in Italia.** That upbeat Brazilian song was the hit of the summer in Italy.

il video   music video

CLASSICAL MUSIC

l'auditorium (m)   auditorium

il bis   encore ▪ **Il concerto di ieri sera è stato un successo. Il pubblico ha chiesto a gran voce il bis.** Last night's concert was a success. The audience cheered for an encore.

il direttore d'orchestra/maestro   orchestra director

la musica classica   classical music

il podio   podium ▪ **Sul podio del Teatro alla Scala stasera ci sarà il Maestro Daniele Gatti.** On the podium of the Teatro alla Scala tonight will be Maestro Daniele Gatti.

il primo violino   first violin

il solista   soloist

il teatro   theater

ETHNIC MUSIC

l'afro-beat (f)   Afro-beat

il pop-rai   rai

> NOTE: **Pop-rai** is a form of popular Algerian music combining traditional Arabic vocal styles with various elements of popular Western music and featuring outspoken, often controversial, lyrics. This musical genre has achieved great popularity in France, Spain, and other parts of Europe, including Italy.

RAP

la musica rap   rap music

il rapper   rapper

REGIONAL MUSIC

Il liscio   (*lit.*, smooth) Italian folk music, waltz, polka

> NOTE: **Liscio** is very popular in Emilia-Romagna. In this sense it is a sort of regional music, but the dancing associated with **liscio** is done everywhere in Italy.

POPULAR DANCES

il saltarello   popular dance of central Italy

la tarantella   popular dance of Naples

EXERCISES

Adesso tocca a voi!

A   *Match each of the words or phrases in the following list with its equivalent below:*

il podio	cantare dal vivo	il vinile
il saltarello	il turnista	il paroliere

1. il brano _____

2. cantare in playback _____

3. il direttore d'orchestra _____

4. il 33 giri _____

5. andare in tour _____

6. la tarantella _____

B   *Write the English equivalent for each of the following Italian expressions:*

1. È sempre la stessa musica. _____

2. Cambia disco! _____

3. dare il la _____

4. essere suonato _____

5. essere stonato _____

C *Choose from the following words or phrases to complete the sentences:*

gruppo spalla	strimpellatore	suono	palasport
rock duro	fiasco	disco d'oro	loggionisti
ninnananna	jazzofilo		

1. Il concerto di Vasco Rossi inizia alle dieci ma prima suonerà un
   _____.

2. Giovanni pensa di suonare bene la chitarra ma è solo uno
   _____.

3. Questa sera vado a vedere il concerto di Laura Pausini al
   _____ di Milano.

4. Il concerto è stato bello ma il _____ era orribile!

5. Preferisco la musica leggera al _____.

6. L'ultimo disco di Eros Ramazzotti è stato un _____
   clamoroso.

7. Claudio Baglioni ha vinto per la decima volta il _____.

8. Camillo ha tutti i dischi di Miles Davis e Charlie Parker. È un vero
   _____!

9. Quando ero piccolo mia madre mi cantava spesso una
   _____.

10. Il successo di un'opera lirica dipende spesso dai _____.

Names

As in English, colloquial Italian uses proper names (for example, "John Doe" and "John Hancock"), often with a humorous intent. The following are some of the most common names of this sort.

l'amico Fritz (m)   (*lit.*, Fritz the friend) person you do not trust. (fam.) ■ **Sta' zitto che arriva l'amico Fritz che non si fa mai gli affari suoi.** Shut up, Fritz the friend who never minds his own business is coming.

> NOTE: The expression **amico Fritz** comes from inhabitants of northern Italy who did not trust German soldiers.

il Berlusca   Silvio Berlusconi, Italian prime minister (fam.)

il Bignami   *Cliff's Notes* ■ **Il Bignami di filosofia mi ha salvato!** The *Cliff's Notes* on philosophy saved me.

Ernesto, il coglione destro   Ernesto, the right nut (vulg.)

Evaristo, il coglione sinistro   Evaristo, the left nut (vulg.)

Minerva, il coglione di riserva   Minerva, the spare nut (vulg.)

Pasquale, il coglione artificiale   Pasquale, the artificial nut (vulg.) ■ **Mi fa male Evaristo, il coglione sinistro; e pure Ernesto il coglione destro. Per fortuna c'è Minerva, il coglione di riserva; e Pasquale il coglione artificiale.** Evaristo, the left nut, hurts, and so does Ernesto, the right nut. Luckily there is Minerva, the spare nut, and Pasquale, the artificial nut.

un Giuda   a Judas, a traitor (fam.) ■ **Sapevo che non dovevamo fidarci di quel Giuda!** I knew we should not have trusted that Judas!

un Lazzaro/Lazzarone   (*lit.*, Lazarus) lazybones (fam.) ■ **La mamma ha detto che Gianfilippo è un Lazzarone.** Mom said that Gianfilippo is a lazybones.

la Madama   (*lit.*, the My Lady) police (fam.)

un Matusa   person who understands nothing (fam.)

> NOTE: The term **Matusa** is an abbreviation of **Matusalemme**, and is used to denote a person who has an out-dated or old-fashioned way of looking at things.

un Matusalemme   (*lit.*, Methuselah) very old person (fam.) ■ **Questo Matusalemme avrà pure ragione, ma i suoi metodi sono troppo antiquati.** This very old person is even right, but his methods are too old.

il Paese dei Balocchi (*lit.*, the country of toys) toyland (fam.) ▪ **Non siamo mica nel Paese dei Balocchi!** We are not in toyland!

un povero Cristo (*lit.*, a poor Christ) a very unfortunate person (fam.) ▪ **C'è un povero Cristo che fa la carità in piazza.** There is a very unfortunate person who begs in the square.

Tizio, Caio, e Sempronio (*lit.*, Titus, Claudius, and Sempronius) Tom, Dick, and Harry

il Trap Giovanni Trapattoni, professional soccer coach who currently coaches the Italian national team (fam.)

un Vatusso very tall person (fam.)

> NOTE: The term **Vatusso** comes from an African population (**i Vatussi**) who are known for being extremely tall.

EXERCISES
Adesso tocca a voi!

A *Select the best translation for the following names:*

1. l'amico Fritz
   a. my friend Fritz
   b. Fritz the friend
   c. a person who cannot be trusted

2. il Bignami
   a. *Cliff's Notes*
   b. thingamabob
   c. devout Christian woman

3. La Madama
   a. My lady
   b. police
   c. a twenty

4. il Berlusca
   a. beggar
   b. redneck
   c. the Italian prime minister

5. un Vatusso
   a. fat person
   b. a bad soccer player
   c. a tall person

6. un Lazzaro
   a. a lazy person
   b. an old person
   c. a sick person

7. un Matusa
   a. an old person
   b. an old-fashioned person
   c. a wise person

People

GENERAL VOCABULARY

NOTE: The Italian names for people in the following section are all standard Italian.

l' accattone (m)   beggar (fam.)   ■ **Non ho nessuna simpatia per quell'accattone.** I have no sympathy for that beggar.

il burino   redneck (fam.)

NOTE: The term **burino** is specifically used as an insult toward rednecks who come from the area surrounding Rome.

il buzzurro   hillbilly, ignorant person

il fac totum   Jack of all trades   ■ **La prossima estate cercherò un lavoro come fac totum.** Next summer I'll look for a job as a Jack of all trades.

il giobba/giobbone/guapone   boaster (fam.)

il/la mendicante   beggar   ■ **A Padova, in Piazza Mazzini, ci sono molti mendicanti.** In Padua, in Mazzini's Square, there are a lot of beggars.

il polentone   (*lit.*, big polenta guy) polenta eater, northern Italian (fam.)

NOTE: This derogatory term is used by southern Italians to indicate a person from northern Italy, where **polenta** is a common dish.

la schiappa   klutz, clumsy or incapable person

il terrone   (*lit.*, big dirt guy) peasant, southern Italian (fam.)   ■ **Mio padre è di Caserta, e si arrabbia moltissimo se qualcuno gli dà del terrone.** My father is from Caserta, and he gets extremely mad when someone calls him a "terrone."

NOTE: Like the term **polentone**, this term is quite derogatory and is used to indicate a person from southern Italy, where agriculture is a major industry.

il tizio, il tipo   dude, guy (fam.)   ■ **È venuto un tizio a cercarti.** Some guy came looking for you.

la tizia, la tipa   chick, broad (fam.)

156

PHYSICAL CHARACTERISTICS

barbuto bearded

la befana ugly woman, hag (fam.) ▪ **La bibliotecaria sembra proprio una befana.** The librarian really looks like a hag.

> NOTE: **Befana** is the name of the old hag who traditionally brings gifts (or coal) to children on the sixth of January (Epiphany).

il biondo blond guy ▪ **Mi manda il biondo.** The blond guy sent me.

una botte (*lit.*, barrel) very fat (fam.) ▪ **Prima della dieta, la moglie di Guido era una botte.** Before the diet, Guido's wife was very fat.

il brufolo (*lit.*, pimple) person with acne

il capellone (*lit.*, big hair) a person with long hair (fam.)

il ciccione/la cicciona (*lit.*, big fat) fat, fatty (fam.)

la gobba hump

il gobbo hunchback ▪ **Il gobbo sa tutto di tutti.** The hunchback knows everything about everybody.

il grissino/lo stecchino/lo stuzzicadenti (*lit.*, breadstick/toothpick) a very thin person ▪ **É magro come uno stecchino.** He is as thin as a toothpick.

handicappato handicapped ▪ **Mi arrabbio sempre quando rubano i posti per gli handicappati.** I always get mad when they steal the handicapped-parking places.

mani di burro (*lit.*, hands of butter) butterfingers (fam.)

naso all'insù turned-up nose ▪ **Mi piacciono le ragazze con il naso all'insù.** I like girls with turned-up noses.

naso a maialino pig-nosed

naso a punta pointy-nosed

le orecchie a sventola floppy ears (fam.) ▪ **Luca si vergogna di avere le orecchie a sventola.** Luca is ashamed of having floppy ears.

il panzone/la panzona (*lit.*, big belly) fat person (fam.)

il paraplegico paraplegic

il quattrocchi four-eyes ▪ **Quel quattrocchi pensa di sapere tutto lui.** That four-eyes thinks that he knows everything.

rachitico rickety

lo smilzo skinny guy

lo stangone/la stangona (*lit.*, beanpole) very tall, thin person ▪ **Kareem Abdul Jabbar è veramente uno stangone.** Kareem Abdul Jabbar is really a very tall person.

lo stempiato man with receding hairline

lo strabico cross-eyed person

il tappo/il nano/lo gnomo (*lit.*, the cork/the dwarf/the gnome) shorty, very short person (fam.)

il tarchiato stocky guy ▪ **Il tarchiato è stato in prigione per due anni.** The stocky guy was in prison for two years.

testa a pinolo (*lit.*, pine-seed head) pinhead (fam.)

EXERCISES
Adesso tocca a voi!

A *Match each of the Italian words in the first column with the appropriate English word in the second column:*

_____ 1. il gobbo   a. peasant

_____ 2. il nano   b. old hag

_____ 3. il giobba   c. hillbilly

_____ 4. lo strabico   d. hunchback

_____ 5. il terrone   e. skinny person

_____ 6. il buzzurro   f. very short person, dwarf

_____ 7. la befana   g. boaster

_____ 8. lo smilzo   h. cross-eyed person

B *Complete the sentences with the appropriate Italian word using the clue in parentheses:*

1. Chiediamo una sigaretta a questa _____ (chick, broad) bionda.

2. Apri tu la bottiglia perché sono una _____ (klutz).

3. Roberto è quel _____ (long-haired person) che esce con mia sorella.

4. Non toccare il vaso perché c'hai _____ (butterfingers), te!

5. Se mi chiami _____ (polenta eater) un'altra volta, ti spacco la faccia!

6. Sarebbe un tizio molto bello se non fosse per quel _____ (pig's nose).

Politics

GENERAL VOCABULARY

la bustarella   (*lit.*, little envelope) bribe, kickback (fam.)

la mazzetta   (*lit.*, wad of banknotes) bribe, kickback (fam.)

il politichese   political language (fam.)

il politico   politician

la tangente   bribe, kickback

la tangentopoli   (*lit.*, city of bribes) kickback system (fam.)

l'uomo politico   (*lit.*, political man) man of politics, politician

> NOTE: The remaining portion of this chapter contains only standard Italian expressions.

la Camera dei Deputati   (*lit.*, the chamber of deputies) Congress

le camicie verdi   (*lit.*, green shirts) separatists

la campagna elettorale   electoral campaign

il Capo del Governo   head of government

il cattocomunista   Catholic Communist

il colpo di spugna   a political pardon, amnesty

Commissione d'inchiesta   (*lit.*, commission of inquiry) investigatory committee

Corte Costituzionale   Constitutional Court

Corte dei Conti   Court of Accounts

la Costituzione   the Constitution

il deputato/la deputata   congressman/congresswoman

essere un moderato   to be conservative

gli euroscettici   Euro-skepticals

l'exitpoll (m)   exit poll

il garantismo   guaranteeism

i girotondini   grass-roots reform movement

i gruppi parlamentari   parliamentary groups

l'inciucio (m)   when opposing majority parties come to an agreement (often for their own personal gain)

la legge   law

il ministro   minister

la par condicio   (*lit.*, same condition) equal time

il Parlamento   Parliament

il partito dei giudici   party of the judges

la poltrona   (*lit.*, armchair) position of power

post fascista/post comunista   post-Fascist/post-Communist

il Presidente della Repubblica   president of the republic

prodiano   pro-Prodi

> NOTE: Romano Prodi is an industrial economist and a university professor turned politician. He was the Italian prime minister (1996–1999) and was the president of the European Union (1999–2004).

il progetto di legge   bill

la quercia   (*lit.*, oak tree) democratic party of the left

il querciaiolo   oak treeist (fam.)

il referendum   referendum

la Repubblica Italiana   Italian Republic

il ribaltone   when a minority party allies itself with the opposition thereby putting the controlling party in the minority, which calls for new elections

il risultato elettorale   (*lit.*, electoral result) election result

scendere in campo   (*lit.*, to take the field) to enter the world of politics

il Senato   Senate

il senatore   senator

il sondaggio   poll

lo Stato   the State

la toga rossa   (*lit.*, red toga) magistrate

ulivista   olive treeist

il voto   vote

MINISTRIES

Ministero degli Affari Esteri   Ministry of Foreign Affairs

Ministero dell'Ambiente   Ministry of the Environment

Ministero per i Beni e le Attività Culturali   Ministry for Cultural Assets and Activities

Ministero del Commercio con l'Estero   Ministry of Foreign Trade

Ministero delle Comunicazioni   Ministry of Communications

Ministero della Difesa   Ministry of Defense

Ministero delle Finanze   Ministry of Finance

Ministero di Grazia e Giustizia   Ministry of Justice

Ministero dell'Industria, del Commercio e dell'Artigianato   Ministry of Industry, Commerce and Handicraft

Ministero dell'Interno   Ministry of the Interior

Ministero dei Lavori Pubblici   Ministry of Public Works

Ministero della Pubblica Istruzione   Ministry of Education

Ministero della Sanità   Ministry of Health

POLITICAL PARTIES

Alleanza Nazionale (AN)   National Alliance

Centro Cristiano Democratico (CCD)   Christian Democratic Center

Cristiani Democratici Uniti (CDU)   Christian Democratic Union

Democratici di Sinistra (DS)   Left Democratic Party

Forza Italia (FI)   Italy Ahead

Lega Nord (LN)   Northern League

Partito Popolare Italiano (PPI)   Democratic Italian Party

Radicali   Liberal Party

Rifondazione Comunista (RC)   Communist Refoundation Party

Socialisti Democratici Italiani (SDI)   Socialist Democratic Party

L'Ulivo   (*lit.*, the olive tree) Alliance of Liberal Parties

Verdi   Green Party

EXERCISES
Adesso tocca a voi!

A   *Choose the Italian expression on the right that matches the English expression on the left:*

___ 1. separatists	a. la poltrona
___ 2. man of politics	b. la quercia
___ 3. bribe	c. essere moderato
___ 4. to be conservative	d. la Repubblica Italiana
___ 5. Democratic Party of the Left	e. le camicie verdi
___ 6. position of power	f. il senatore
___ 7. Italian Republic	g. la toga rossa
___ 8. magistrate	h. post fascista
___ 9. senator	i. l'uomo politico
___ 10. post-Fascist	j. la mazzetta

B   *Choose the correct abbreviations for the following Italian political parties:*

1. Democratic Italian Party (**AN/CCD/PPI**)

2. National Alliance (**FI/CDU/AN**)

3. Left Democratic Party (**AN/PPI/DS**)

4. Italy Ahead (**CCD/FI/DS**)

5. Christian Democratic Union (**CCD/PPI/CDU**)

C *Translate the following names of ministries into English:*

1. Ministero di Grazia e Giustizia: ———————————————

2. Ministero della Pubblica Istruzione: ————————————

3. Ministero degli Affari Esteri: —————————————————

4. Ministero della Sanità: —————————————————————

5. Ministero della Difesa: —————————————————————

Press, Magazines, and Books

abbonarsi   to subscribe ■ **Mi sono abbonato ad una rivista sugli animali.** I have subscribed to a magazine on animals.

l'album delle figurine   sticker album

gli annunci personali   personals ■ **Devo mettere un annuncio personale sul giornale.** I have to put a personal ad in the newspaper.

l'articolo (m)   article ■ **L'articolo sulla politica era molto interessante.** The article about politics was very interesting.

il biglietto della lotteria   lottery ticket

le colonne   columns

il *Corriere* (il *Corriere della Sera*)   the *Courier* (the *Courier of the Evening*) ■ **Mi prenderesti il *Corriere*?** Would you pick me up the *Courier*?

> NOTE: The ***Corriere della Sera*** is printed in Milan and is the most widely read newspaper in Italy.

la cronaca   local news ■ **Le notizie di cronaca sono sempre fasulle.** Local news events are always false.

la cronaca nera   crime news ■ **La cronaca nera mi fa venire i brividi.** Crime news gives me the shivers.

la cronaca rosa   tabloids

dare un'occhiata   to take a look, to glance (fam.) ■ **Più tardi darò un'occhiata al giornale.** Later I will take a look at the newspaper.

il direttore   editor-in-chief ■ **Il direttore non è d'accordo con quell'articolo.** The editor-in-chief doesn't agree with that article.

l'economia (f)   economics

l'edicola (f)   newsstand ■ **Dove è l'edicola?** Where is the newsstand?

edizione locale   local edition

edizione nazionale   national edition

edizione straordinaria   extra

gli esteri   foreign affairs

le figurine   stickers   ■ **Da piccolo scambiavo sempre le figurine con i miei amici a scuola.** When I was little I always traded stickers with my friends at school.

i fumetti   comics

la gazzetta (la *Gazzetta dello Sport*)   sports paper (fam.)

> NOTE: The *Gazzetta dello Sport* is a popular sports newspaper that is printed on pink paper.

il giallo   (*lit.*, yellow) detective story

un giornalaccio   rag (fam.)

il giornalaio   news vendor

il giornale   newspaper   ■ **Oggi non ho comprato il giornale.** Today I didn't buy the newspaper.

il giornaletto   newsletter

il/la giornalista   journalist

il gratta e vinci   scratch-and-win lotto   ■ **Gioco sempre al gratta e vinci ma non vinco mai. Che fregatura!** I always play scratch-and-win lotto, but I never win. What a rip-off!

la guida TV   TV guide

l'inserto (m)   supplement

l'intervista (f)   interview

leggere   to read   ■ **Leggo il giornale quasi tutti i giorni.** I read the newspaper almost every day.

leggiucchiare   to skim (fam.)

il lettore   reader

il *Manifesto*   the *Manifesto*

> NOTE: This is the newspaper of the Communist Party in Italy, which circulates nationally. It is generally read by those with the same political philosophy.

il *Messaggero*   the *Messenger*

> NOTE: This Roman newspaper also circulates in other parts of central and southern Italy.

il mensile   monthly publication

la *Nazione*   the *Nation*

NOTE: This Florentine newspaper is not widely read outside of the Tuscan capital.

la pagina culturale   cultural page ▪ **Ho letto una recensione di uno spetta-colo interessante sulla pagina culturale.** I read a review of an interesting play on the cultural page.

le parole crociate   crossword puzzle ▪ **Faccio sempre le parole crociate quando viaggio in treno.** I always do the crossword puzzle when I travel by train.

politica   politics ▪ **Gli articoli di politica sono spesso noiosi.** Articles on politics are often boring.

il porno/il pornazzo   porno mag (fam.) ▪ **Dove hai nascosto i pornazzi, Pierino?** Where did you hide the porno mags, Pierino?

la prima pagina   front page

la pubblicità   advertisement

la pulce   (*lit.*, the flea) magazine for buyers and sellers of secondhand merchandise (fam.)

il quotidiano   daily paper

la redazione   editorial staff ▪ **Domani il giornale non uscirà perché la redazione è in sciopero.** Tomorrow the newspaper will not come out because the editorial staff is on strike.

la *Repubblica*   the *Republic*

NOTE: The ***Repubblica*** is one of the most widely read newpaper in Italy.

una rivista di moda/attualità   fashion/current events magazine

una rivista da quattro soldi   (*lit.*, a four-coin magazine) a cheap maga-zine (fam.)

scienze   sciences

scrivere da Dio   to write like a god ▪ **Quel giornalista scrive da Dio.** That journalist writes like a god.

scrivere coi piedi   (*lit.*, to write with the feet) to write poorly

il settimanale   weekly publication

sfogliare il giornale   (*lit.*, to "de-leaf" the newspaper) to leaf through the newspaper

il *Sole 24Ore*   the *Sun 24Hours*

scrivere coi piedi

167

NOTE: This is a nationally circulating economic newspaper printed on light orange paper.

spettacoli   entertaiment

sport   sport ▪ **Sulla pagina dello sport c'erano le probabili formazioni della nazionale di calcio.** On the sports page there were the probable rosters of the national soccer team.

la *Stampa*   the *Press*

> NOTE: This newspaper is from the city of Turin and has a national circulation. It is one of the top three most widely read newspapers along with **il *Corriere della Sera*** and **la *Repubblica*.**

il tabloid   tabloid ▪ **Non compro mai tabloid.** I never buy tabloids.

il titolo di testa   headline

Topolino (*lit.*, little mouse) Mickey Mouse

> NOTE: *Topolino* is the name of an extremely popular monthly publication of Disney comics in Italy.

l'*Unità*   the *Unity*

> NOTE: This is a widely read left-wing national newspaper.

uscire   to come out ▪ **Questo mese esce il primo numero di *Altolà*.** This month the first issue of *Altolà* is coming out.

BOOKS

l'appendice   appendix

il bestseller   bestseller ▪ **I libri di Calvino sono tutti bestseller.** Calvino's books are all bestsellers.

la bibliografia   bibliography

le bozze   drafts ▪ **Dovrei mandare le bozze dell'articolo alla casa editrice.** I should send the drafts of the article to the publishing house.

i classici   classics

i capitoli   chapters ▪ **La mia tesi di dottorato ha quattro capitoli.** My Ph.D. thesis has four chapters.

la collana   series

la copertina   cover ▪ **La copertina di questo libro è molto bella.** The cover of this book is very nice.

il critico   critic

il dizionario   dictionary   ▪ **Mi passeresti il dizionario?** Could you give me the dictionary?

l'editor (m)   editor

fare la recensione   to review   ▪ **Luca ha fatto numerose recensioni di romanzi italiani.** Luca reviewed numerous Italian novels.

le illustrazioni   pictures

l'impaginazione (f)   layout

l'introduzione (f)   introduction   ▪ **Questa introduzione è molto interessante.** This introduction is very interesting.

il libercolo   book of little or no value (fam.)

un libraccio   foul book (fam.)   ▪ **Ignazio, come fai a leggere questo libraccio?** Ignazio, how can you read this foul book?

la libreria   bookstore

il libro   book

un libro di cucina   (*lit.*, a book of the kitchen) cookbook   ▪ **Voglio regalare alla mamma un bel libro di cucina per il suo compleanno.** I want to give mom a nice cookbook for her birthday.

un libro di fantascienza   sci-fi novel

un libro di poesie   book of poetry   ▪ **Ho perso il mio libro di poesie di Gozzano.** I lost my book of Gozzano's poetry.

il libro di testo   textbook

il manuale   manual

il manoscritto   manuscript   ▪ **Il manoscritto Landiano della** *Divina Commedia* **è datato 1336.** The Landiano manuscript of the *Divine Comedy* is dated 1336.

il mattone   (*lit.*, brick) a long and/or difficult book   ▪ **Questo libro è un mattone.** This book is long and difficult.

le note   notes

le pagine   pages   ▪ **Questo libro ha 787 pagine.** This book has 787 pages.

la prefazione   preface   ▪ **Il professor Cima ha scritto la prefazione di questo libro.** Professor Cima wrote the preface of this book.

la pubblicazione   publication   ▪ **A febbraio uscirà la mia prima pubblicazione.** My first publication will come out in February.

la raccolta/l'antologia (f)   anthology

la ristampa   reprint

il romanzo   novel ▪ **Mi piacciono molto i romanzi di Eco.** I like Eco's novels a lot.

la selezione   selection

lo scrittore/la scrittrice   writer ▪ **Umberto Eco è uno scrittore famoso.** Umberto Eco is a famous writer.

il sommario/l'indice (m)   summary

la trama   plot ▪ **La trama del libro è piuttosto complicata.** The plot of the book is rather complicated.

in vetrina   shop window ▪ **Il libro di Stefano è già in vetrina!** Stefano's book is already in the shop window!

EXERCISES
Adesso tocca a voi!

A *Translate the following expressions into English:*

1. fare la recensione _____

2. il giornale _____

3. leggiucchiare _____

4. sfogliare il giornale _____

5. dare un'occhiata _____

6. l'articolo _____

7. l'edicola _____

8. le parole crociate _____

9. l'inserto _____

10. il giallo _____

B *Choose the word in parentheses that best completes each sentence:*

1. Pablo Neruda era uno (scrittore/editore) famoso.

2. Gianluca ha scritto la (prefazione/copertina) di questo libro.

3. Quel negozio vende solo (libracci/capitoli) da quattro soldi!

4. Mi è piaciuta molto la (trama/note) dell'ultimo romanzo di Camilleri.

5. Non riesco più a trovare (ristampe/bibliografia) del *Pro Archia* di Cicerone.

C *Match each word in the following list with its equivalent below:*

l'antologia   il quotidiano   l'indice

1. la raccolta _____

2. il sommario _____

3. il giornale _____

Religion

CHURCHES

la basilica   basilica

la cappella   chapel

la cattedrale   cathedral

il convento   convent

il duomo   dome, cathedral ■ **Il Duomo di Milano è una delle più belle chiese che siano mai state costruite.** The cathedral in Milan is one of the most beautiful churches that has ever been built.

il monastero   monastery

la parrocchia   parish

la sacrestia   vestry

CLERGY AND RELIGIOUS PEOPLE

l'ACR (azione cattolica ragazzi) (f)   Catholic children's organization

andare a Roma e non vedere il papa (*lit.*, to go to Rome and not see the Pope) failing to see the forest for the trees

il cardinale   cardinal

il chierichetto   altar boy ■ **Quasi tutti i bambini in Italia fanno il chierichetto.** Nearly all young boys in Italy are altar boys.

chiudersi/ritirarsi in convento   to withdraw to a convent ■ **Lo sapevi che Beatrice ha avuto una crisi mistica e ha deciso di ritirarsi in convento?** Did you know that Beatrice had a religious crisis and decided to enter a convent?

i ciellini   Catholic activists

andare a Roma e non vedere il papa

NOTE: The **Comunione e Liberazione** is one of the most important and influential Catholic organizations in Italy, and its followers are called **i ciellini** because of the organization's initials.

il conclave   conclave ▪ **Durante il conclave è difficile per i cardinali essere subito d'accordo su un nome per l'elezione del Papa.** During the conclave it is difficult for the cardinals to come to an agreement on the election of a new pope.

il corvo   (*lit.*, crow) priest (*fam.*)

NOTE: In Italy the priests wear black, and the anticlerical population will sometimes refer to them as crows.

un cristiano   (*lit.*, a Christian) a person who believes in Christ (*fam.*)

l'esorcista (m)   exorcist

essere anticlericale   to be anticlerical

essere ateo   to be an atheist

essere un bacchettone   to be a moralist ▪ **Mio padre è un gran bacchettone! Non vuole che mi metta la minigonna!** My dad is such a moralist! He doesn't want me to wear a miniskirt!

essere un bigotto/bizzocco   to be sanctimonious, a religious hypocrite ▪ **Credo che Luciano sia proprio un bigotto. Non si perde una messa ma non ha un vero senitimento religioso.** I think that Luciano is really a religious hypocrite. He never misses a mass but he's not really a religious person.

essere un mangiapreti   (*lit.*, to be a priest eater) to be strongly anticlerical ▪ **Ogni volta che si parla della Chiesa cattolica tu dici solo cose cattive! Sei un mangiapreti!** Every time we talk about the Catholic church you only say negative things! You're so anticlerical!

essere papabile   to be likely to be elected pope, worthy candidate (in general) ▪ **È difficile dire chi sarà il nuovo presidente della banca. Ci sono molti candidati papabili.** It is difficult to say who will be the new president of the bank. There are many worthy candidates.

essere tutto casa e chiesa   (*lit.*, to be home and church) someone that only stays home and goes to church ▪ **Non vedo mai in giro la sorella di Maria. Penso che sia un tipo tutto casa e chiesa.** I never see Maria's sister around. I think she's the type that only stays at home and goes to church.

fare una cosa/andare in un posto a ogni morte di papa   (*lit.*, to do something/go somewhere whenever a pope dies) to do something once in a blue moon/to do something very rarely ▪ **Da quando mi sono trasferito a Firenze, vado a trovare i miei genitori a ogni morte di papa e loro sono molto arrabbiati con me.** Since I moved to Florence, I rarely go to visit my parents and they are really mad at me.

il frate   friar

la fumata bianca   white smoke signal   ■ **Fumata bianca! Abbiamo il nuovo Papa!** A white smoke signal! We have a new pope!

la fumata nera   black smoke signal

> NOTE: When the conclave is not able to reach an agreement on the next pope, a black smoke signal comes from a chimney in the Vatican. When they have chosen a pope, the white signal is sent up.

la guardia svizzera   Swiss Guard

il missionario   missionary

la monaca di clausura   cloistered nun

il monaco   monk

Morto un papa se ne fa un altro.   (*lit.*, When the Pope dies they make another one.) There are other fish in the sea.   ■ **Ma cosa fai, piangi perchè il tuo fidanzato ti ha mollato? Non preoccuparti! Morto un papa se ne fa un altro!** What are you doing, crying because your boyfriend dumped you? Don't worry! There are other fish in the sea!

il padre   father

il Papa/il Pontefice/il Santo Padre   the Pope

il parroco   parish priest

la perpetua   priest's housekeeper   ■ **La perpetua del nuovo parroco sembra proprio antipatica!** The housekeeper of the new parish seems really mean!

> NOTE: The word **perpetua** comes from the well-known Italian novel *I Promessi Sposi*, written by Alessandro Manzoni. It was the proper name of Don Abbondio's housekeeper.

un povero Cristo   (*lit.*, a poor Christ) a very unfortunate person (fam.)   ■ **C'è un povero Cristo che fa la carità in piazza.** There is a very unfortunate person who begs in the square.

predicare bene e razzolare male   to preach one thing and practice another   ■ **È facile per te dire agli altri che devono lavorare quando tutta la settimana non fai niente e ti diverti! Predichi bene e razzoli male!** It's easy for you to say that other people should work when you don't do anything all week but enjoy yourself! You preach one thing and practice another!

il reverendo   reverend

il sacerdote/il prete   priest

il sagrestano   sacristan

il seminario   seminary ▪ **Marco è andato in seminario per otto anni, ma poi ha deciso di non diventare prete.** Marco went into the seminary for eight years but then he decided not to become a priest.

il seminarista   seminary student

stare come un papa   (*lit.*, to feel like a pope) to live like a king ▪ **Questo appartamento mi piace proprio. Ci sto proprio come un papa!** I like this apartment so much. I live like a king here!

la suora   nun

il vescovo   bishop

SAINTS, CEREMONIES, AND FEASTS

l'apparizione (f)   apparition ▪ **La Chiesa cattolica è molto prudente con le apparizioni.** The Catholic Church is really careful concerning apparitions.

avere santi in paradiso   (*lit.*, to have saints in Heaven) to know influential people ▪ **Marco è riuscito a fare una carriera brillante in così poco tempo. Mi sa che ha parecchi santi in paradiso!** Marco was able to make a brilliant career in little time. I guess he knows a lot of influential people!

avere un santo dalla propria parte   (*lit.*, to have a saint by one's side) to have a guardian angel ▪ **Michela ha avuto tre gravi incidenti stradali e non si è mai fatta niente. Deve avere proprio un santo dalla propria parte!** Michela had three bad car accidents and she didn't have a scratch on her. She certainly must have a guardian angel.

il battesimo   baptism

la benedizione   blessing ▪ **Sono stato in Vaticano ed è stato molto emozionante assistere alla benedizione Urbi et Orbi del Papa.** I was in the Vatican City and it was really exciting to take part in the *Urbi et Orbi* blessing by the Pope.

bestemmiare   to curse, to blaspheme

bestemmiare come un turco   to swear like a Turk ▪ **Il mio amico Giovanni è proprio una gran brava persona. Peccato che dica sempre parolacce e che bestemmi come un turco!** My friend Giovanni is a great person. It's a shame that he always cusses and swears like a Turk!

la comunione   Communion

la cresima   confirmation

l'estrema unzione (f)   last rites

fare la santarellina   to act like a saint

il funerale   funeral

il matrimonio   wedding

la messa   mass

non c'è santo che tenga   at all costs, no matter what ■ **Il prossimo anno vado in vacanza alle Hawaii. Non c'è santo che tenga!** Next year I am going to Hawaii on vacation, no matter what!

non essere uno stinco di santo   (*lit.*, not to be a saint's shin) to be far from being a saint ■ **Conosco il fidanzato di tua figlia. Dille di stare attenta perché non è uno stinco di santo.** I know your daughter's boyfriend. Tell her to be careful because he is far from being a saint.

non sapere più a che santo votarsi   (*lit.*, to no longer know which saint to pray to)   to not know which way to turn ■ **Mio marito sta cercando lavoro ma non riesce a trovarlo. Le ha provate tutte, ma ora non sa più a che santo votarsi.** My husband is looking for a job but he can't find one. He tried everything but now he doesn't know which way to turn.

il pellegrinaggio   pilgrimage

la processione   procession

> NOTE: Throughout the year there are many religious processions all over the country, but the most important one is the procession for Good Friday.

la reliquia   relic

tirare giù un moccolo   to curse (fam.) ■ **Ero così arrabbiato e nervoso che ho tirato giù un moccolo di fronte a tutti!** I was so angry and nervous that I cursed in front of everybody!

tirare giù uno zirlo   to curse (fam.)

SUPERSTITION

il corno/cornetto   horn

> NOTE: In Italy, especially in the south, people will carry around small horns to keep bad luck away.

essere uno iettatore   to be a jinx ■ **Lucio è proprio uno iettatore. Ogni volta che lo incontro mi succede qualcosa di strano.** Lucio is a serious jinx. Every time I meet him something strange happens to me.

essere superstizioso/a   to be superstitious ■ **Mio padre è così superstizioso che non inizia mai le cose di martedì o di venerdì solo perché c'è quel vecchio proverbio che dice di non farlo.** My father is so superstitious that he won't start anything on a Tuesday or Friday only because of that old wives' tale that says not to do it.

fare le corna   to make the sign of the horns   ■ **Hai visto? È passato un carro funebre. Facciamo le corna.** Did you see? A hearse just passed. Let's make the sign of the horns for luck.

> NOTE: Italians make this gesture every time they think that something will bring them bad luck.

fare gli scongiuri   to touch wood for luck

fare il malocchio/una fattura   to give someone the evil eye   ■ **Giuseppe negli ultimi tempi sembra un altro. Non mangia, sta male, piange sempre. Sembra che qualcuno gli abbia fatto il malocchio.** Lately Giuseppe seems like someone else. He doesn't eat, he's sick, he cries all the time. It seems as if someone has given him the evil eye.

farsi benedire   to be blessed by someone   ■ **Questo ragazzo è proprio sfortunato! Perché non lo portiamo a farlo benedire?** This boy is really unlucky! Why don't we take him to get blessed by someone?

incrociare le dita   to cross one's fingers   ■ **Domani devo dare un esame importante. Incrociamo le dita!** Tomorrow I have to take an important exam. Let's cross our fingers!

portare sfiga   to bring bad luck (vulg.)   ■ **Non farmi gli auguri prima di un esame! Porta sfiga!** Don't wish me luck before the exam! It brings bad luck!

toccarsi le palle   to touch one's balls for luck (vulg.)   ■ **Hai visto? Un gatto nero ha attraversato la strada. Tocchiamoci le palle.** Did you see? A black cat just crossed our path. Let's touch our balls for luck.

toccare ferro   to touch metal for luck

togliere il malocchio/una fattura   to lift the curse of the evil eye

EXERCISES

Adesso tocca a voi!

A *Match each word or expression with its opposite:*

_____ 1. bizzocco

_____ 2. la fumata bianca

_____ 3. il funerale

_____ 4. portare sfiga

a. la fumata nera

b. benedire

c. toccarsi le palle

d. togliere una fattura

_____ 5. fare il malocchio   e. il battesimo

_____ 6. bestemmiare   f. mangiapreti

B   *Translate the following expressions into English:*

1. Morto un papa se ne fa un altro.

   _____

2. fare una cosa a ogni morte di papa

   _____

3. predicare bene e razzolare male

   _____

4. avere santi in paradiso

   _____

5. non c'è santo che tenga

   _____

6. non sapere più a che santo votarsi

   _____

7. stare come un papa

   _____

8. andare a Roma e non vedere il papa

   _____

C   *Match each word in the following list with its related term below:*

il battesimo	la reliquia	il papa
la suora	la basilica	

1. il conclave _____

2. l'apparizione _____

3. la cattedrale _____

4. ll frate _____

5. la cresima _____

Romance

LOVE'S GOOD SIDE: WINNING LOVE

andare all'imbrocco/in battuta   (*lit.*, to go to the pick up) to go out looking to pick up (fam.)

andare a donne   (*lit.*, to go to women) to go out looking to pick up women (fam.) ▪ **Stasera Gianni e Luigi vanno a donne.** Tonight Gianni and Luigi are going out to pick up women.

andare dietro a uno/una   (*lit.*, to go behind a guy/girl) to go after a guy/girl (fam.) ▪ **Ho il sospetto che quel ragazzo vada dietro a tua cugina.** I suspect that guy is going after your cousin.

l'appuntamento (m) date ▪ **Non posso venire perché ho un appuntamento con Vittorio.** I can't come because I have a date with Vittorio.

avere il ragazzo fisso/la ragazza fissa   (*lit.*, to have the fixed boy/girl) to have a steady boyfriend/girlfriend

avere una cotta per qualcuno   (*lit.*, to have a crush for someone) to have a crush on someone ▪ **Detesto quando le ragazze brutte hanno una cotta per me.** I hate it when ugly girls have a crush on me.

colpo di fulmine   (*lit.*, strike of lightning) love at first sight

il dongiovanni   Don Juan

il donnaiolo   lady-killer ▪ **Smettila di fingerti un donnaiolo.** Stop pretending to be a lady-killer.

essere innamorato/a pazzo/a   to be madly in love

essere l'amore della mia/tua/sua vita   to be the love of my/your/his or her life ▪ **Sei l'amore della mia vita, te lo giuro!** You are the love of my life, I swear!

essere l'uomo/la donna della mia/tua/sua vita   to be the man/woman of my/your/his or her life

essere pazzo/a di qualcuno   to be crazy about someone ▪ **Sono proprio pazzo di te.** I am really crazy about you.

essere un rubacuori (*lit.*, to be a heart thief) to be a heartbreaker ▪ **Si crede di essere un rubacuori, ma tutte le donne lo ignorano.** He thinks he's a heartbreaker, but all the women ignore him.

essere un sogno to be a dream

fare colpo su qualcuno (*lit.*, to make a blow on someone) to be a hit with someone (fam.)

fare gli occhi dolci a qualcuno (*lit.*, to make the sweet eyes at someone) to make eyes at someone (fam.)

fare il filo a qualcuno (*lit.*, to do the string to someone) to have one's eye on someone (fam.)

fare il piedino a qualcuno (*lit.*, to do the little foot to someone) to play footsie with someone

fare la civetta (*lit.*, to act like an owl) to flirt

fare la corte/corteggiare qualcuno to court someone ▪ **Non mi piace quando i miei amici corteggiano mia sorella.** I don't like it when my friends court my sister.

fare l'occhiolino (*lit.*, to do the little eye) to wink

fidanzarsi in casa (*lit.*, to get engaged in the house) to announce one's engagement to the family

il fidanzato/la fidanzata fiancé ▪ **Il mio fidanzato di si chiama Guerino.** My fiancé's name is Guerino.

> NOTE: The term **fidanzato/a**, which literally means "fiancé," is used rather loosely in Italian. As soon as someone introduces their current boyfriend or girlfriend to their family, the term **fidanzato/a** may be used to describe them, even if there has been no marriage proposal or intent to marry.

fissare un appuntamento to set up a date

flirtare to flirt ▪ **Non sono buono a flirtare con le estranee.** I'm not good at flirting with strangers.

frequentarsi (*lit.*, to frequent each other) to date

garbare a qualcuno to be liked by someone (fam.)

imbattersi in qualcuno to run into someone

imbroccare to pick up (fam.) ▪ **Ho imbroccato una ragazza svedese.** I picked up a Swedish girl.

mangiare qualcuno con gli occhi (*lit.*, to eat someone with the eyes) to devour someone with one's eyes (fam.) ▪ **Le sue studentesse lo mangiano con gli occhi.** His female students devour him with their eyes.

mettersi insieme (*lit.*, to put oneself together) to go steady

non avere occhi che per lui/lei (*lit.*, to not have eyes but for him/her) to only have eyes for him/her

perdere la testa per qualcuno (*lit.*, to lose the head for someone) to lose your head over someone ▪ **Ho perso la testa per una ragazza di diciassette anni.** I lost my head over a seventeen-year-old girl.

i piccioncini (*lit.*, little pigeons) lovebirds

prendere una bella cotta per qualcuno (*lit.*, to get a beautiful crush for someone) to get a big crush on someone

prendere una sbandata per qualcuno (*lit.*, to skid out of control for someone) to get a crush on someone ▪ **Mia zia ha preso una sbandata per il nuovo bagnino che lavora alla piscina comunale.** My aunt got a crush on the new lifeguard who works at the public swimming pool.

sbavare dietro a uno/una (*lit.*, to drool behind a guy/girl) to drool over a guy/girl (fam.)

prendere una sbandata per qualcuno

stare con qualcuno (*lit.*, to stay with someone) to go steady with someone ▪ **Lo sapevi che Marcella sta con Ugo?** Did you know that Marcella is going steady with Ugo?

uscire con un tipo/una tipa to go out with a guy/gal ▪ **Domani esco con quel tipo che ho conosciuto domenica in discoteca.** Tomorrow I'm going out with that guy I met Sunday at the disco.

vedersi con qualcuno (*lit.*, to see oneself with someone) to see someone

LOVE'S BAD SIDE: LOSING LOVE

avere il muso to be sulky (fam.)

bidonare to stand someone up (fam.) ▪ **Pensavo che fosse venerdì, quindi ho bidonato il professore senza volerlo.** I thought it was Friday, so I stood up the professor without meaning to.

dare il pacco a qualcuno (*lit.*, to give someone the package) to stand someone up (fam.) ▪ **Detesto quando le donne mi danno il pacco.** I hate when women stand me up.

essere fregato/a to be screwed

essere giù to be down

essere il terzo incomodo (*lit.*, to be the third inconvenience) to be a third wheel

fare le corna a qualcuno (*lit.*, to do the horns to someone) to be unfaithful to someone ▪ **Pensavo che mi avesse fatto le corna, ma mi sono sbagliato.** I thought he/she had been unfaithful to me, but I was mistaken.

fare una scenata to make a scene ▪ **Lei ha detto che se non stavo zitto avrèbbe fatto una scenata.** She said that if I did not shut up she would make a scene.

fregare il ragazzo/la ragazza a qualcuno (*lit.*, to rub someone's boyfriend/girlfriend) to steal someone's boyfriend/girlfriend (fam.) ▪ **Peppino mi ha fregato la ragazza due volte.** Peppino stole my girlfriend twice.

mollare qualcuno (*lit.*, to let go of someone) to break up with someone (fam.)

mollarsi (*lit.*, to let go of each other) to break up (fam.) ▪ **Se quei due si mollano, io vado dietro a lui, e tu a lei.** If those two break up, I'll go after him, and you go after her.

pedinare to stalk ▪ **Il mio ex-ragazzo mi sta pedinando. Devo chiamare la polizia.** My ex-boyfriend is stalking me. I must call the police.

il pedinatore   stalker

prendere il pacco (micidiale)   (*lit.*, to get the deadly package) to be stood up (big-time) (fam.)

rimanere incinta   (*lit.*, to remain pregnant) to get pregnant ■ **Temevo di essere rimasta incinta.** I feared that I had gotten pregnant.

tirare il bidone a qualcuno   (*lit.*, to throw the drum at someone) to stand someone up (fam.)

tirarsela   (*lit.*, to pull it oneself) to think you're hot stuff (fam.)

GENERAL VOCABULARY

un abbraccio   hug

accarezzare   to caress

un bacio in bocca/sulla guancia   kiss one on the mouth/cheek ■ **Ieri Monica mi ha dato un bacio in bocca per la prima volta.** Yesterday Monica kissed me on the mouth for the first time.

il bacino   little kiss

la carezza   caress ■ **Volevo solo una carezza e un bacino, ma lui non ha voluto darmeli.** I just wanted a caress and a little kiss, but he did not want to give them to me.

coccolare   to cuddle

fare le coccole   (*lit.*, to do the cuddles) to cuddle

fare un succhiotto a qualcuno   (*lit.*, to do a hickey to someone) to give someone a hickey (fam.) ■ **Non bisogna mai fare i succhiotti agli uomini sposati.** You should never give hickeys to married men.

farsi toccare   (*lit.*, to make oneself touched) to let oneself be touched (fam.)

mordicchiare l'orecchio   to nibble on the ear ■ **Non mi piace farmi mordicchiare l'orecchio.** I don't like having my ear nibbled on.

il petting   heavy petting ■ **Ho visto una coppia che faceva petting alla festa di Guglielmo.** I saw a couple who were all over each other at Guglielmo's party.

sbaciucchiarsi   to make out

tastare/palpare qualcuno   to feel someone up

tenersi per mano   (*lit.*, to keep each other by hand) to hold hands ■ **Quei due piccioncini si tengono sempre per mano.** Those two lovebirds are always holding hands.

tesoro mio/amore mio/caro mio/cara mia my treasure, my love, my dear ▪ **Non ti preoccupare, amore mio, sono qui con te.** Don't worry, my love, I'm here with you.

EXERCISES
Adesso tocca a voi!

A *Choose the Italian expression on the right that matches the English expression on the left:*

_____ 1. I went after her.

_____ 2. I've got a date.

_____ 3. He winked at me.

_____ 4. I've got a crush on two people.

_____ 5. She's the woman of my life.

_____ 6. Her fiancé is boring.

_____ 7. She really thinks she's hot stuff.

_____ 8. I don't want to be a third wheel.

_____ 9. I saw them making out.

_____ 10. We broke up.

a. **Il suo fidanzato è noioso.**

b. **Mi ha fatto l'occhiolino.**

c. **Lei è la donna della mia vita.**

d. **Li ho visti sbaciucchiarsi.**

e. **Se la tira davvero.**

f. **Non voglio essere il terzo incomodo.**

g. **Ho una cotta per due persone.**

h. **Ci siamo mollati.**

i. **Ho un appuntamento.**

j. **Le sono andato dietro.**

B *Select the best translation for each of the following sentences:*

1. **Quello lì mi ha fregato la ragazza.**
   a. That guy kissed my girlfriend.
   b. That guy stole my girlfriend.
   c. That guy stole my fiancée.

2. **Hai mai fatto le corna a qualcuno?**
   a. Have you ever been a third wheel?
   b. Have you ever broken up with someone?
   c. Have you ever cheated on someone?

3. Il mio ragazzo mi ha dato il pacco.
   a. My boyfriend gave me the package.
   b. My boyfriend stood me up.
   c. My fiancé stood me up.

4. Smettila di sbavare dietro a mia cugina!
   a. Quit drooling over my cousin!
   b. Quit stalking my cousin!
   c. Quit courting my cousin!

5. L'amica di mia madre faceva il piedino a mio padre.
   a. My father's friend was playing footsie with my mother.
   b. My mother's friend was playing footsie with my father.
   c. My mother's friend was playing poker with my father.

6. Lo sai che garbi al mio amico?
   a. Do you know that my friend likes you?
   b. Do you know that I like your friend?
   c. Does my friend know that you like me?

7. Non fare una scenata a casa dei miei genitori.
   a. Don't cheat on me at my parents' house.
   b. Don't rehearse your scene at my parents' house.
   c. Don't make a scene at my parents' house.

8. Le ho dato un bacino sulla guancia.
   a. I gave her a hickey on the neck.
   b. I French-kissed her.
   c. I gave her a little kiss on the cheek.

C *Indicate whether the following phrases are properly translated:*

1. Someone felt me up.

   Qualcuno mi ha palpato.   YES/NO

2. Today I am really sulky.

   Oggi sono proprio giù.   YES/NO

3. I don't have a steady boyfriend.

   Non ho la ragazza fissa.   YES/NO

4. Maurizia and Vincenzo are seeing each other.

   Maurizia e Vincenzo si vedono.   YES/NO

5. I picked up a philosophy student.

   Mi sono imbattuta in una studentessa di filosofia.   YES/NO

Sex

GAY SEX

There are many slang words in Italian for homosexual: **bucaiolo, buco, checca, cula, culattone, dama, diverso, effeminato, femminella, femminuccia, finocchio, frocio, invertito, mezzafemmena, orecchione, pederasta, pervertito, pigliain-culo, recchione, ricchione, rottinculo, sodomita, succhiacazzi, viados.** Most of these words for "homosexual" are very likely to cause offense, but members of the gay community in Italy refer to themselves as **gay.**

l'Arcigay (m) Italian Gay Association

il bar dei froci queer bar (vulg.)

il bar/locale gay gay bar/nightclub ▪ **Ci siamo incontrati in un bar gay.** We met in a gay bar.

dichiararsi gay (*lit.*, to declare oneself gay) to come out of the closet

diventare frocio to become queer (vulg.) ▪ **Luigi è diventato frocio.** Luigi has become a queer.

essere dell'altra sponda (*lit.*, to be from the other bank/shore) to be gay (fam.) ▪ **Non sapevo che fosse dell'altra sponda.** I did not know he was gay.

essere gay/frocio to be gay/a fag (fam.) ▪ **Pippo mi sembra un po' frocio. Secondo te?** Pippo kind of seems like a fag to me. What do you think?

essere inculato/inchiappettato to be sodomized (vulg.)

farselo sbattere/schiantare in/nel culo (*lit.*, to make it slammed in one's ass) to let oneself be slammed in the ass (vulg.)

farsi inculare/inchiappettare (*lit.*, to make oneself sodomized) to let oneself be sodomized (vulg.) ▪ **A Fabiano piace farsi inculare.** Fabiano likes to be sodomized.

farsi sfondare il culo (*lit.*, to make oneself break down the ass) to let one's ass be broken down (vulg.)

il giochetto dei frati (*lit.*, the little game of the friars) sodomy (fam.) ▪ **Il giochetto dei frati è un problema serio per il Vaticano.** Sodomy is a serious problem for the Vatican.

inculare, inchiappettare, metterlo in/nel culo (*lit.*, to put it in the ass), **schiantarlo tra le chiappe** (*lit.*, to crash it between the butt cheeks), **sbatterlo in/nel culo** (*lit.*, to slam it in the ass), **metterlo di dietro** (*lit.*, to put it behind), **infilarlo in/nel culo** (*lit.*, to slip it in the ass), **sfondare il culo** (*lit.*, to break down the ass), **sodomizzare** to sodomize (*vulg.*)

inculare con la Vaselina to buttfuck with Vaseline (*vulg.*)

il locale per froci queer nightclub (*vulg.*)

mettersi a novanta (*lit.*, to put oneself at ninety) to bend over (*vulg.*) ▪ **Non mi sono mai dovuto mettere a novanta.** I have never had to bend over.

l'omosessuale homosexual

omosessuale dichiarato (*lit.*, declared homosexual) openly gay ▪ **L'arcivescovo della chiesa episcopale è un omosessuale dichiarato.** The archbishop of the Episcopal church is openly gay.

pigliarlo/prenderlo in/nel culo to take it in the ass (*vulg.*) ▪ **Franco mi ha detto che l'ha preso nel culo per la prima volta.** Franco told me he took it up the ass for the first time.

scoprirsi gay (*lit.*, to discover oneself gay) to realize that one is gay ▪ **Claudio recentemente si è scoperto gay.** Claudio recently discovered he is gay.

succhiare il cazzo to suck the dick (*vulg.*)

LESBIAN SEX

camionara (*lit.*, female truck driver) lesbian (*vulg.*) ▪ **Non sapevo che Maria Pia fosse una camionara.** I did not know that Maria Pia was a lesbian.

essere lesbica to be a lesbian

fare un ditalino (*lit.*, to do a little thimble) to fingerfuck (*vulg.*) ▪ **La mia ragazza mi ha fatto un ditalino per la prima volta.** My girlfriend fingerfucked me for the first time.

farsi fare un ditalino (*lit.*, to have oneself make the little thimble) to have oneself fingerfucked (*vulg.*)

leccare la fica/figa to lick the pussy (*vulg.*) ▪ **Se mi lecchi la fica mi fai un piacere enorme, ne ho davvero bisogno.** If you lick my pussy you'll be doing me a huge favor; I really need it.

la lesbica lesbian

lesbicare (*lit.*, to "lesbianate") to have lesbian sex

lesbicona (*lit.*, big lesbian) lesbian (*fam.*) ▪ **Chiara è una lesbicona.** Chiara is a lesbian.

mangiare la fica/figa   to eat the pussy (vulg.)

rapporto saffico   sapphic relationship ▪ **Non sono mai stata coinvolta in un rapporto saffico.** I have never been involved in a sapphic relationship.

saffista   sapphist

> NOTE: The words for "lesbian" listed above should be used with great discretion as they will cause offense in most contexts.

MAKING LOVE

l'AIDS (m/f)   AIDS

attizzare   (*lit.*, to light) to turn (someone) on (fam.) ▪ **Quella bionda mi attizza un monte.** That blond really turns me on.

avercelo duro   (*lit.*, to have it hard) to be hard (vulg.) ▪ **Ce l'hai duro?** Are you hard?

avercelo moscio   (*lit.*, to have it flaccid) to not be erect (vulg.)

avercelo ritto   (*lit.*, to have it erect) to be erect (vulg.)

aver voglia di farsi qualcuno   (*lit.*, to feel like doing oneself someone) to feel like doing someone (vulg.)

aver voglia di figa   to want some pussy (vulg.)

aver voglia di scopare   to feel like fucking (vulg.) ▪ **Ho così tanta voglia di scopare che mi sembra di impazzire.** I want to fuck so badly that I feel like I'm going crazy.

baciare   to kiss

baciarsi   to kiss each other ▪ **Gli italiani si baciano spesso in pubblico e nessuno dice niente a riguardo.** Italians often kiss each other in public and nobody says anything about it.

bisessuale   bisexual ▪ **Conosco poche persone bisessuali.** I know few bisexual people.

bisex   bi

cornuto/becco   cuckold (fam.) ▪ **Quel becco di Gino non lo sa che sua moglie va a letto con tutti.** That cuckold Gino does not know that this wife goes to bed with everybody.

essere cornuto   (*lit.*, to have horns) to be a cuckold (fam.)

> NOTE: The act of "throwing the horns" is a common gesture in the United States, often associated with an expression of approval or amusement. In Italy this ges-

ture is very offensive, as it suggests that someone's spouse or significant other is unfaithful to them.

il dildo dildo

eccitarsi (*lit.*, to excite oneself) to become aroused

eiaculare to ejaculate

eiaculatio precox/eiaculazione precoce premature ejaculation ▪ **La eiaculatio precox è un problema che può essere imbarazzante.** Premature ejaculation is a problem that can be embarrassing.

l'esibizionista (m/f) exhibitionist

essere allupato (*lit.*, to be wolfed) to be horny (fam.)

essere arrapato to be horny (fam.) ▪ **Non me ne frega se sei arrapato. Vattene a casa e fatti una doccia fredda.** I don't care if you're horny. Go home and take a cold shower.

essere facile to be easy (fam.) ▪ **Mi avevi detto che era una ragazza facile, ma quella non la dà neanche se preghi.** You had told me that she was an easy girl, but she does not even put out if you pray.

fare l'amore to make love ▪ **Quando ero più giovane non avevo idea di cosa volesse dire fare l'amore.** When I was younger I had no idea what it meant to make love.

fare il sessantanove to do a sixty-nine ▪ **Mi eccita un monte fare il sessantanove.** It really excites me to do a sixty-nine.

fare sesso to have sex

fare lo scambio di coppia (*lit.*, to do the couple exchange) to swap mates ▪ **Mia moglie voleva fare lo scambio di coppia, ma la coppia in questione non mi piaceva.** My wife wanted to swap mates, but I did not like the couple in question.

fare un bocchino (*lit.*, to do a little mouth) to give a blow job (vulg.)

fare un pompino (*lit.*, to do a little pump) to blow (vulg.) ▪ **Non ho mai fatto un pompino a qualcuno. L'idea mi innervosisce molto.** I have never blown someone. The idea makes me very nervous.

farlo alla pecorina (*lit.*, to do it little sheep-style) to do it doggie-style (vulg.)

farlo in posizione canonica (*lit.*, to do it in the canonic position) to do it in the missionary position (fam.) ▪ **Mio marito non ha nessuna fantasia. Vuole sempre farlo in posizione canonica: lui sopra e io sotto.** My husband has no imagination. He always wants to do it in the missionary position: him above and me below.

farsi le pugnette   (*lit.*, to make oneself the little fists) to jerk off (vulg.)   ∎ **Riccardo, smettila di farti le pugnette!** Riccardo, stop jerking off!

farsi una sega   (*lit.*, to make oneself a saw) to jerk off (vulg.)

farsi una sveltina   (*lit.*, to have oneself a quickie) to have a quickie (fam.)   ∎ **Mia moglie è passata in ufficio e ci siamo fatti una sveltina sulla scrivania.** My wife came by the office and we had ourselves a quickie on the desk.

godere   to experience sexual pleasure

il goldone   condom (fam.)

il guardone   (*lit.*, the big watcher) Peeping Tom   ∎ **Per fortuna non conosco guardoni.** Luckily I don't know any Peeping Toms.

il guanto   (*lit.*, glove) condom (fam.)

herpes genitale   genital herpes

macchina da sesso   sex machine   ∎ **Luana è una macchina da sesso.** Luana is a sex machine.

maiala   (*lit.*, sow)/**vacca**   (*lit.*, cow) slut (fam.)

maiale   pig (fam.)

maniaco sessuale   (*lit.*, sexual maniac) sex maniac   ∎ **Quello sporcaccione di Vito è un maniaco sessuale.** That pervert Vito is a sex maniac.

masturbarsi   to masturbate   ∎ **Masturbarsi è una cosa più che normale.** Masturbating is more than normal.

il morto di figa   (*lit.*, dead of pussy) heterosexual male who never has sex (vulg.)

morto di seghe   (*lit.*, dead of saws) male who masturbates excessively (vulg.)   ∎ **Avevi ragione, Terenzio è un morto di seghe che non avrà mai la ragazza fissa.** You were right, Terenzio is a man who masturbates constantly and will never have a steady girlfriend.

perdere la verginità   (*lit.*, to lose the virginity) to lose one's virginity   ∎ **Ho perso la verginità quando avevo diciassette anni.** I lost my virginity when I was seventeen.

pomiciare/slinguarsi   to French-kiss (fam.)

i preliminari   (*lit.*, preliminaries) foreplay   ∎ **I preliminari sono un elemento essenziale di un rapporto fisico.** Foreplay is a fundamental element of a physical relationship.

il preservativo/profilattico   condom

la prima volta   the first time   ■ **Ero molto nervoso, perché per me era la prima volta e non sapevo cosa fare.** I was really nervous, because it was the first time for me and I did not know what to do.

il sadomaso, il sadomasochismo   sadomasochism

il/la sadomasochista   sadomasochist

la sborra   jizz (*vulg.*)

sborrare   to jizz (*vulg.*)

lo scambista   (*lit.*, "switcher") swinger

lo scolo   clap

scopare   (*lit.*, to sweep), **trombare, fottere, caricare**   (*lit.*, to load), **sbatterlo tra le cosce/gambe** (*lit.*, to slam it between the thighs/legs), **sbatterlo in figa** (*lit.*, to slam it in the pussy) to fuck (*vulg.*)

scopare alla pecorina   (*lit.*, to fuck little sheep-style) to fuck doggie-style (*vulg.*)   ■ **Non capisco perché lei vuole sempre farlo alla pecorina. Ci sono tante posizioni interessanti.** I don't know why she always wants to do it doggie-style. There are many interesting positions.

scopare come ricci   (*lit.*, to fuck like hedgehogs) to fuck like rabbits

scopare da dietro   to fuck from behind (*vulg.*)

il segaiolo   (*lit.*, saw vendor) chronic masturbator (*vulg.*)

sfondare la fregna   (*lit.*, to break down the pussy) to fuck (*vulg.*)

la sgualdrina/troia   slut (*vulg.*)   ■ **Ferdinando mi tratta come una sgualdrina e io non lo sopporto più.** Ferdinando treats me like a slut and I can't stand him anymore.

sieropositivo   HIV positive   ■ **Ho fatto l'esame del sangue e mi hanno detto che non sono sieropositivo.** I got a blood test and they told me I'm not HIV positive.

la sifilide   syphilis

simulare   (*lit.*, to simulate) to fake it

simulare/fingere l'orgasmo   to simulate/fake orgasm   ■ **Non ho mai simulato l'orgasmo e non vedo perché dovrei.** I have never faked an orgasm and I don't see why I should.

la Spagnola   (*lit.*, the Spanish woman) the act of rubbing one's breasts on a penis (*vulg.*)

sporcaccione (*lit.*, big nasty dirty) pervert (fam.) ■ **Perché finisco sempre con questi sporcaccioni maledetti? Dove sono gli uomini normali?** Why do I always end up with these perverts? Where are the normal men?

succhiare i capezzoli to suck the nipples (fam.)

sverginare (*lit.*, to "de-virginize") to take someone's virginity (vulg.)

toccare to touch (fam.)

toccarsi (*lit.*, to touch oneself) to masturbate (fam.) ■ **Non ti toccare che diventi cieco.** Don't touch yourself or you'll go blind.

trombaiolo (*lit.*, trumpet vendor) stud (vulg.)

venire to come ■ **Se sono preoccupato non riesco mai a venire.** If I'm preoccupied I can never manage to come.

il vibratore vibrator ■ **Regaliamo un vibratore a Vittoria.** Let's give Vittoria a vibrator as a gift.

PROSTITUTION

la bocchinara (*lit.*, little mouth vendor) cocksucker (vulg.)

fare marchette to turn tricks (vulg.)

la marchetta (*lit.*, little token) sexual act performed by a prostitute (fam.)

cento a marchetta (*lit.*, one hundred per little token) one hundred for sex (fam.)

> NOTE: The word **marchetta** refers to a little token given to women who worked in houses of prostitution for each sexual service performed.

Quanto vuoi? How much do you want? (fam.)

pompinara (*lit.*, little pump vendor) blow-job artist (vulg.)

prostituta prostitute

puttana, baldracca, bagascia, battona, lucciola (*lit.*, firefly), **marchettara, mignotta, zoccola** whore (vulg.) ■ **Lanfranco dice sempre che va a puttane, ma io non gli credo.** Lanfranco always says that he goes to whores, but I don't believe him.

squillo (*lit.*, telephone ring) call girl (fam.) ■ **La polizia ha arrestato venti ragazze squillo.** The police arrested twenty call girls.

EXERCISES
Adesso tocca a voi!

A *Write the English equivalent for each of the following Italian expressions:*

1. diventare frocio _____

2. segaiolo _____

3. succhiare il cazzo _____

4. camionara _____

5. aver voglia di scopare _____

6. essere arrapato _____

7. morto di figa _____

8. sborrare _____

9. pomiciare _____

10. farsi una sega _____

B *Match each word in the following list with its equivalent below:*

slinguare	pompinara	sbatterlo in figa	sporcaccione
mignotta	venire	essere arrapato	cornuto
essere dell'altra sponda		prenderlo in culo	

1. bocchinara _____

2. baciarsi _____

3. fottere _____

4. zoccola _____

5. essere allupato _____

6. sborrare _____

7. becco _____

8. essere uno di quelli _____

9. essere inchiappettato ⎯⎯⎯⎯⎯⎯⎯⎯⎯

10. maiale ⎯⎯⎯⎯⎯⎯⎯⎯⎯

C *Choose the word in parentheses that best fits each sentence:*

1. Gustavo è (camionara/ uno di quelli).

2. Marco mi ha detto che (ha voglia di scopare/morto di seghe) con Claudia.

3. Fabio sta sempre addosso alle ragazze: è proprio un (morto di figa/sifilide)!

4. Roberto è andato in ospedale perché pare abbia un (herpes genitale/sgualdrina).

5. Luisa è una grandissima (maniaco sessuale/pompinara)!

6. Ieri la polizia ha arrestato un (esibizionista/vibratore) al Parco Sempione.

7. Povero Giuliano, tutti sanno che è (scambista/cornuto)!

Sports

PRACTICING A SPORT

appendere le scarpe/la bicicletta/i guantoni/il casco al chiodo   to hang up one's shoes/bike/gloves/helmet ▪ **Per molti campioni del calcio che devono ritirarsi è veramente duro appendere le scarpe al chiodo.** For many soccer champions who must retire it is really hard to hang up their cleats.

l'arrivo al fotofinish (m)   photo finish

avere classe   to have class, style ▪ **Quel calciatore non ha un gran fisico ma, mio Dio, ha molta classe!** That soccer player doesn't have a great physique, but my God, what style!

l'avversario (m)   the competition/competitor, adversary

il campione del mondo   the world champion

il campione italiano/europeo/olimpico   the Italian/European/Olympic champion

il controllo antidoping   drug testing

il detentore del record   record holder

il dilettante/l'amatore   amateur ▪ **Mi piace molto giocare a calcio e mi alleno tutti i giorni, ma sono solo un dilettante.** I like to play soccer a lot and I practice every day, but I'm only an amateur.

il fondista   long-distance runner

essere al massimo della condizione   to be in top condition ▪ **Quando sei al massimo della condizione, tutto è più facile.** When you are in top condition, everything is easier.

essere drogato   to be drugged up ▪ **Secondo me, quel ciclista è drogato. Va troppo forte negli ultimi tempi.** I think that cyclist is using performance-enhancing drugs. He's been much too strong lately.

il fuoriclasse   star player, one who is a head above the competition ▪ **Del Piero e Totti sono due fuoriclasse.** Del Piero and Totti are two star players.

il/la maratoneta   marathon runner

la nazionale national team ▪ **La nazionale italiana di calcio ha vinto tre campionati del mondo.** The Italian national team has won three world championships.

non essere in forma to be out of shape ▪ **Quel ciclista non riesce più a tenere il passo degli altri. Mi sa che non è in forma in questo momento.** That cyclist is no longer able to keep pace. I believe he is out of shape right now.

l'outsider (m/f) underdog ▪ **Lance Armstrong può vincere il Tour de France ma ci sono molti outsider.** Lance Armstrong can win the Tour de France but there are a lot of underdogs.

il palmarès record of achievement ▪ **Pochi atleti possono vantare la vittoria di due medaglie d'oro alle Olimpiadi nel loro palmarès.** Very few atheletes can boast two gold medals at the Olympic games on their records of achievement.

passare il testimone to pass the baton ▪ **Quando mio padre andrà in pensione e non potrà più dirigere l'azienda, passerà il testimone a me.** When my father retires and can no longer run the company, he will pass the baton to me.

> NOTE: This expression is frequently used in everyday conversation to express the passing on of a responsibility.

perdere smalto to run out of steam ▪ **Il campione italiano era in testa fino a dieci minuti fa ma ora sta perdendo smalto ed è in fondo al gruppo.** The Italian champion was leading until ten minutes ago but now he's running out of steam and is falling behind the group.

il/la professionista professional

il record mondiale/nazionale/europeo world/national/European record ▪ **Sai per caso chi detiene il record mondiale di salto in alto?** Do you know who holds the world record in high jump?

il record personale personal record

le sostanze dopanti illegal substances, performance drugs

lo/la sprinter, il/la velocista sprinter

l'under 21 (f) national team on which no one can be older than twenty-one

SOCCER/FOOTBALL

l'arbitro (m) referee

calciare al volo to hit the ball while still in the air

il calciomercato (*lit.*, player market) when teams buy and sell players during the off-season

il capocannoniere   top scorer

colpire di testa   to head the ball ▪ **Solo i grandi attaccanti sanno colpire bene di testa e fare molti gol.** Only great forwards can head the ball well and score lots of goals.

il contropiede   counteroffensive

crossare   to cross

il dribbling   dribbling

l'espulsione (f)   ejection from the game

essere in fuorigioco   to be offside

giocare a pallone   to play soccer (football)

il guardalinee   linesman

mangiarsi un gol   (*lit.*, to eat a goal) to miss on an open net ▪ **Il centravanti si è mangiato un gol che anche io sarei riuscito a segnare.** The center forward missed a goal that even I could have scored.

il marcamento a uomo   man-to-man defense

il marcamento a zona   zone defense ▪ **Negli ultimi anni nel campionato italiano, molte squadre preferiscono il marcamento a zona al marcamento a uomo.** In the last few years of the Italian soccer league, many teams have preferred zone defense to man defense.

mangiarsi un gol

la moviola   slow-motion replay ▪ **Molte decisioni dell'arbitro dovranno essere riviste questa sera alla moviola.** Many of the referee's decisions will have to be reviewed this evening in slow-motion replay.

il mister/l'allenatore   coach

l'occasione da gol (f)   chance for a goal ▪ **Nonostante abbia avuto molte occasioni da gol, l'Inter non è riuscita a segnare e ha perso la partita.** In spite of the many occasions for a goal, Inter was not able to score and lost the game.

il pallonetto   lob

il panchinaro   benchwarmer ▪ **Quel giocatore non è mai entrato in campo durante il campionato. È un panchinaro.** That player never even played during the season. He's a benchwarmer.

prendere un cartellino giallo/rosso   to get a yellow/red card (to get booked)

la rete, il gol   goal

salvarsi in corner   to give up a corner kick ▪ **La difesa della Roma stava avendo molti problemi e si è salvata in corner.** Rome's defense was having many problems and gave up a corner kick.

scartare   to fake the defender out, to juke the defender

segnare un gol in zona Cesarini   to score a goal in the last five minutes of a game ▪ **Il Milan stava vincendo uno a zero, ma la Juventus ha segnato un bellissimo gol in zona Cesarini e ha pareggiato.** Milan was winning one to zero, but Juventus scored an amazing goal in the last five minutes and tied the game.

> NOTE: Cesarini was a soccer player famous for scoring a goal in the last few minutes of a game.

i tempi supplementari   overtime

il tiro dalla bandierina   corner kick

il totocalcio   betting pool

FORMULA-ONE AUTO RACING

l'autodromo (m), il circuito (m)   the motor speedway/circuit

la bandiera a schacchi   checkered flag

la bandiera gialla   caution flag

il box   pit

il collaudatore   test driver

il giro   lap

la partenza   start

il pilota   racecar driver

il pitstop   pit stop

le prove   qualifications, speed trials ▪ **Durante le prove i piloti non sono andati molto forte a causa della pioggia.** During the speed trials the drivers were not able to go very fast due to the rain.

la scuderia   the racing team ▪ **I piloti della Ferrari sono bravi, ma tutta la scuderia è di altissima qualità.** The Ferrari drivers are excellent, but the racing team as a whole is of the highest quality.

il warm-up   the warm-up

CYCLING

andare in fuga   to break away ▪ **Un ciclista è andato in fuga e ormai nessuno può raggiungerlo.** A cyclist broke away from the group and no one is able to catch up with him.

il capitano   captain

il ciclista dopato   cyclist who uses performance-enhancing drugs

la cronometro   time trial ▪ **Di solito gli scalatori non vanno molto bene nelle cronometro.** Usually climbers don't do very well in the time trials.

il doping   drug use ▪ **Nonostante tutti gli sforzi compiuti per combatterlo, il doping è ancora un problema nel ciclismo.** Despite all the efforts made to fight it, drug use is still a problem in cycling.

fare l'andatura/tirare il gruppo   to lead the pack

fare il ventaglio   (*lit.*, to do the fan) to bunch up and spread out alternatively

il giro d'Italia   Italian Tour

il gregario   teammate ▪ **I ciclisti più forti possono vincere le gare solo se hanno dei buoni gregari.** The best cyclists can win the races only if they have good teammates.

la maglia rosa   (*lit.*, the pink jersey) leader of the race during the Giro d'Italia ▪ **Con la tappa di oggi, l'attuale capo della classifica potrèbbe perdere la maglia rosa.** In today's leg, the current leader of the race could lose his pink jersey.

mettersi a ruota   to draft ▪ **Se vuoi fare meno fatica e vincere la gara, devi metterti a ruota.** If you want to do less work and win the race, you need to draft.

lo scalatore   climber

succhiare la ruota (*lit.*, to suck the wheel) to draft (fam.) ▪ **Quel ciclista vince sempre perché è molto furbo. Durante la gara succhia la ruota degli avversari e poi li sconfigge negli ultimi chilometri.** That cyclist always wins because he is very clever. During the race he drafts and then beats them in the last few miles.

la tappa leg of a race ▪ **Il giro d'Italia di quest'anno avrà venti tappe.** The Giro d'Italia this year will have twenty legs during the race.

il velocista sprinter

BASKETBALL

il basket/la pallacanestro basketball

il palleggio dribbling

il rimbalzo rebound

la schiacciata slam dunk ▪ **L'azione della pallacanestro più spettacolare è la schiacciata.** The most spectacular move in basketball is the slam dunk.

la stoppata block

TENNIS

la battuta serve

il campo da tennis tennis court

il doppio doubles match ▪ **Ci sono molti giocatori che non sono molto bravi nel singolo ma che sono assolutamente eccezionali nel doppio.** There are many players that aren't very good at singles but are absolutely brilliant during doubles matches.

il doppio misto mixed doubles

giocare a fondocampo to play at the baseline

giocare sull'erba to play on grass

giocare sul sintetico to play on Astroturf/fake grass

giocare su terra battuta to play on clay ▪ **Quella tennista gioca benissimo su terra battuta ma quando gioca sull'erba o sul sintetico è un vero disastro.** That tennis player plays really well on the clay, but when she plays on grass or Astroturf it's a real disaster.

il match point match point ▪ **Il match point è senza dubbio il momento più emozionante della partita!** The match point is without a doubt the most exciting part of the game!

la palla da tennis   tennis ball

la parità   deuce

il set point   set point

scendere a rete   to come up to the net ▪ **Gioco piuttosto bene a tennis, anche se gioco molto meglio a fondo campo che quando scendo a rete.** I play tennis quite well, although I play better at the baseline than when I come up to the net.

il singolo   singles match

il/la tennista   tennis player

il tie-break   tiebreaker

vincere in due set/tre set   to win two/three straight sets

SPORTS FANS

seguire la squadra in trasferta   to follow the team to an away game ▪ **Sono proprio un gran tifoso del Milan. Se avessi abbastanza soldi seguirei sempre la squadra in trasferta.** I am a huge fan of Milan. If I had enough money I would always follow the team to away games.

i tifosi   supporters, fans ▪ **La Juventus è la squadra italiana che ha il maggior numero di tifosi in Italia.** Juventus is the Italian team that has the largest number of fans in Italy.

gli ultrà   fanatic supporters ▪ **Gli ultrà sono molto importanti per lo spettacolo durante le partite. Peccato che qualche volta siano violenti.** The fanatic supporters are very important because they make a scene during the game. It's a shame that they are sometimes so violent.

TRAINING

fare la preparazione   to train ▪ **Di solito le squadre durante l'estate fanno la preparazione in montagna.** Usually teams train in the mountains during the summer.

il massaggiatore   masseur

il medico sociale   team doctor

la preparazione fisica   physical training

EXERCISES

Adesso tocca a voi!

A *Write the idiomatic Italian translation for each of the following expressions:*

1. to hang up one's shoes _____

2. to pass the baton _____

3. to draft _____

4. to lead the pack _____

5. to miss an open net _____

6. to follow the team to an away game _____

7. to score a goal in the last five minutes of a game _____

8. to run out of steam _____

9. to hit the ball while still in the air _____

10. to be out of shape _____

B *Match the Italian with the English expressions:*

_____ 1. i tifosi
     a. supporters

_____ 2. la scuderia
     b. fanatic supporters

_____ 3. il fuoriclasse
     c. the racing team

_____ 4. l'outsider
     d. benchwarmer

_____ 5. il collaudatore
     e. underdog

_____ 6. il gregario
     f. test driver

_____ 7. la tappa
     g. teammate

_____ 8. il panchinaro
     h. leg of a race

_____ 9. gli ultrà
     i. one who is a head above the competition

_____ 10. il dilettante
     j. amateur

C *Create an expression by joining words from the two columns:*

_____ 1. avere   a. supplementari

_____ 2. fare il   b. bandierina

_____ 3. la maglia   c. dopanti

_____ 4. le sostanze   d. ventaglio

_____ 5. il tiro dalla   e. rosa

_____ 6. i tempi   f. classe

_____ 7. essere in   g. rosso

_____ 8. prendere un cartellino   h. fuori gioco

_____ 9. il marcamento a   i. erba

_____ 10. giocare sull'   j. uomo

Travel and Transportation

TRAINS AND TRAIN STATIONS

il binario tracks ■ **È vietato attraversare i binari!** It is forbidden to cross the tracks!

il controllore ticket police

la cuccetta sleeper cabin

l'eurostar high-speed express train

fare il pendolare (*lit.*, to do the pendulum) to commute back and forth to work ■ **Sono stufo di fare il pendolare!** I'm sick and tired of commuting back and forth to work!

l'intercity (m) fast train that stops only in the larger cities

l'interregionale (m) interregional train that stops in the smaller towns

l'orario ferroviario (m) train schedule

fare il pendolare

il pendolino   (*lit.*, pendulum) high-speed train that runs back and forth between two cities

il posto prenotato   reserved seat

il regionale   regional train that stops at every station

il sottopassaggio   underground walkway

lo sportello   ticket booth

la stazione   the station

il treno   the train

il vagone ristorante   restaurant car

OTHER MEANS OF TRANSPORTATION

l'ape (f)   (*lit.*, the bee) three-wheel pickup truck

> NOTE: The quite popular **Ape** is the model name of this small and convenient vehicle.

la bicicletta da corsa   racing bike

la bicicletta da passeggio   city bicycle, a three-speed bicycle

il motorino, lo scooter, la Vespa   (*lit.*, wasp) motor scooter

la mountain bike   mountain bike

essere nella stessa barca   to be in the same boat ▪ **Bisogna aiutarci perché siamo tutti nella stessa barca!** We need to help each other because we're all in the same boat!

una barca di . . . a lot of, a ton of ▪ **Ho una barca di libri da leggere.** I have a ton of books to read.

TIMING YOUR TRAVEL

alta stagione   high season, tourist season

bassa stagione   low season, off-season

incrociare le braccia   (*lit.*, to cross one's arms) to go on strike ▪ **Gli operai della ferrovia statale incrociano le braccia domani dal mezzogiorno fino alle otto di sera.** The state railroad workers are going on strike tomorrow from noon until eight o'clock.

il ponte   long weekend

il rientro (*lit.*, re-entry) the return (from vacation) ▪ **Lunedì non lavoro per fare il ponte. Così farò il rientro per martedì.** Monday I'm not going to work so I can have a long weekend. This way, I'll make my return on Tuesday.

lo sciopero the strike

EXERCISES
Adesso tocca a voi!

A *Match each of the words or expressions on the left with the correct definition on the right:*

_____	1. il sottopassaggio	a. ticket police
_____	2. il ponte	b. train schedule
_____	3. la Vespa	c. to commute back and forth to work
_____	4. lo sportello	d. underground walkway
_____	5. fare il pendolare	e. sleeper cabin
_____	6. l'orario ferroviario	f. long weekend
_____	7. la cuccetta	g. to be in the same boat
_____	8. l'ape	h. motor scooter
_____	9. il controllore	i. three-wheel pickup truck
_____	10. essere nella stessa barca	j. ticket booth

Vacations

l'abbronzatura suntan

la barca a vela sailboat

il deltaplano hang glider

la lampada (*lit.*, lamp) tanning bed/lamp

il parapendio paragliding

il pattinaggio a rotelle Rollerblading or roller-skating

i pattini a rotelle roller skates

praticare il surf to surf

praticare il windsurf to windsurf

prendere il sole, stare sdraiato al sole to sunbathe, to lay in the sun ▪
Ho preso molto sole durante le vacanze! I got a lot of sun during the vacation!

i roller blades Rollerblade

lo sci alpino alpine skiing

lo sci di fondo cross-country skiing

la tavola da surf surfboard

la tavola da windsurf sailboard

EXERCISES
Adesso tocca a voi!

A *Complete the following sentences with an appropriate Italian word or phrase. In some cases, more than one answer may be possible.*

1. Vorrei andare al mare per _____ ma la mia
_____ è rotta.

2. Al mare io _____ molto sole, e quindi devo
   farmi la lampada quando rientro perché non voglio perdere
   _____ .

3. Preferisco andare in montagna d'inverno quando posso fare
   _____ o magari
   _____ .

4. Oggi è una bellissima giornata, e voglio andare a fare
   _____ ma non riesco a trovare i miei
   _____ .

Weather

WEATHER GREETINGS

Che bel tempo!   What nice weather we're having!

Che tempaccio!   What nasty weather!

Che tempo da cani!   (*lit.*, What dog's weather!) What terrible weather!

Che tempo di merda!   What shitty weather! (vulg.)

Si sta schiarendo!   It's clearing up!

RAINY WEATHER

l'acquazzone, lo scroscio di pioggia   downpour

diluviare   to deluge, to rain down ■ **Non possiamo uscire ora perché fuori diluvia!** We can't go out right now because it is pouring outside!

il diluvio   deluge, downpour

essere inzuppato, essere zuppo fino al midollo   (*lit.*, to be soaked to the bone marrow), **essere bagnato fradicio** to be soaked, to be drenched ■ **C'è stata un'acquazzone! Sono bagnato fradicio!** There was a downpour! I'm drenched!

grandinare   to hail

la grandine   hail

lampeggiare   to lightning

nuvoloso, coperto   (*lit.*, covered)   cloudy, overcast ■ **Portati l'ombrello perché fuori il cielo è tutto coperto.** Take the umbrella with you because it's overcast outside.

NOTE: The word **scoperto**, or "uncovered," means it is clear outside.

piove sul bagnato   (*lit.*, to rain on something already wet) when it rains, it pours

piove sul bagnato

piovere a catinelle, piovere a secchie   to rain buckets

piovere a dirotto   to pour

piovigginare   to drizzle

prendere/trovare acqua   to get rained on   ■ **Secondo le previsioni, doveva piovere ieri, ma non abbiamo trovato acqua, per fortuna!** According to the weather forecast, it was supposed to rain yesterday, but we didn't get rained on, thank goodness!

lo scoppio di tuono   a peal or clap of thunder   ■ **Quell'ultimo scoppio di tuono mi ha fatto prendere un colpo!** That last clap of thunder made me jump!

scrosciare   to pelt (with rain)

Su questo, non ci piove!   (*lit.*, On this, it doesn't rain!) There's no doubt about it!

il temporale, la tempesta, la bufera, la burrasca   storm

tuonare, rimbombare   to thunder   ■ **I ragazzi hanno paura perché fuori lampeggia e rimbomba.** The kids are afraid because it's thundering and lightning out.

Viene giù come Dio la manda!   (*lit.*, It's coming down as God sends it!) It's really coming down!

HOT WEATHER

afoso   sultry, hazy   ■ **Il concerto in piazza è stato bello, ma era troppo afoso per goderselo!** The concert in the square was beautiful, but it was too sultry to enjoy it!

Che giornata torrida!   What a scorcher!

essere appiccicoso   to be sticky   ■ **Oggi è troppo umido. È tutto appiccicoso fuori!** Today it's too humid. It's all sticky outside!

essere umido   to be humid

fare un caldo della Madonna   to be hot as hell (fam.)

fare un caldo micidiale   to be dangerously hot   ■ **Porca miseria! Non si può stare fuori perché fa un caldo micidiale!** My oh my! You can't even stay outside because it is dangerously hot!

la foschia   haze   ■ **Se non fosse per la foschia, si potrebbe vedere l'altra sponda del lago da qui.** If it weren't for the haze, you could see the other shore of the lake from here.

l'ondata di caldo (f)   heat wave ▪ **C'è stata un'ondata di caldo fino a qualche giorno fa, ma ora si è rinfrescato un po'.** There was a heat wave up until a few days ago, but now things have cooled off a bit.

lo scirocco   a strong, hot wind that blows from the southeast (the Sahara desert) and brings with it heat and humidity

> NOTE: The word **scirocco** is of Arab origin, and has spawned other terms like **sciroccata** (noun, a storm that comes from the southeast) and **sciroccoso** (adjective, hot and humid weather).

il solleone   high-noon summer heat

Il sole picchia!   The sun burns! ▪ **Se esci, mettiti un cappello perché il sole picchia oggi!** If you go out, put a hat on because the sun will burn you!

FROM COOL TO COLD WEATHER

al fresco   cool spot ▪ **Mettiamoci al fresco sotto quell'albero!** Let's find a cool spot under that tree!

fare freschetto/freschino   to be nippy or chilly ▪ **Non uscire senza una maglietta perché stasera fa freschetto.** Don't go out without a sweater because tonight it's nippy.

fare un freddo boia   (*lit.*, to be cold like an executioner) to be cold as hell

fare un freddo cane   (*lit.*, to be dog cold) to be cold as hell ▪ **Andiamo dentro perché qui fuori fa un freddo cane!** Let's go inside because out here it's as cold as hell!

freddoloso   sensitive to the cold, always cold ▪ **Ci sono tre coperte sul letto perché mia moglie è freddolosa.** There are three blankets on the bed because my wife is always cold.

gelare   to freeze

rinfrescarsi   to cool down ▪ **Dopo il temporale, si è rinfrescato molto!** After the storm, it cooled down a lot!

WINDY WEATHER

alzarsi il vento   to become windy ▪ **Si è alzato il vento mezz'ora fa, e ora continua a tirare!** It became windy a half an hour ago, and now it is still blowing!

la raffica di vento   gust of wind ▪ **Una raffica di vento mi ha portato via il compito!** A gust of wind blew away my homework!

soffiare/tirare il vento   to be windy

la tramontana   a cold, dry wind that blows from the north

NOTE: The word **tramontana** has come to indicate not only the northern wind but also north as a general direction (**a tramontana**) and is used in the expression **perdere la tramontana**, which means "to lose one's bearings" or "to lose control of oneself in anger."

ululare   to howl ■ **Non ho dormito bene perché il vento ha ululato tutta la notte!** I didn't sleep well because the wind howled all night long!

ventoso   windy

EXERCISES
Adesso tocca a voi!

A *Indicate to which category of weather the following comments refer:*

_____ 1. Si è rinfrescato!

_____ 2. Sta diluviando!

_____ 3. Che raffica di vento!

_____ 4. Fa un caldo micidiale!

_____ 5. Siamo bagnati fino
       al midollo!

_____ 6. Che giornata afosa!

_____ 7. Senti come ulula fuori!

_____ 8. Ma come si gela!

a. rain

b. sun or heat

c. cool/cold

d. wind

B *Translate the following expressions into English:*

1. Fa un freddo boia!

_____

2. Che caldo della Madonna!

_____

3. Sono bagnato fradicio!

_____

4. Piove a secchie!

_____

5. Che giornata torrida!

_____

6. Tira forte il vento!

_____

7. Fa un po' freschetto fuori!

_____

8. Che diluvio!

_____

The World of Work

WORK AND THE WORKPLACE

attaccare   to start work (fam.)

andare a guadagnarsi la pagnotta   (*lit.*, to go to earn bread) to earn wages ▪ **Che sacrificio andare tutti i giorni a guadagnarsi la pagnotta!** What a sacrifice to go every day to earn my bread!

l'aumento in busta paga (m)   pay raise ▪ **Ho avuto un aumento di cento euro in busta paga!** I got a pay raise of one hundred euro!

la busta paga   paycheck

la catena di montaggio   assembly line

la fabbrica   factory

lavorare in proprio   to work for oneself (to be the owner)

lavorare sotto padrone   to work under a boss ▪ **Mi sono stancato di lavorare sotto padrone! Voglio aprire un negozio tutto mio!** I'm sick of working for a boss! I want to open my own store!

il lavoro nero/il lavoro in nero   illegal work ▪ **Per molti immigrati l'unico modo di guadagnare dei soldi è il lavoro in nero.** For many immigrants the only way to earn money is illegal work.

montare   to start work, to start a shift (fam.)

il negozio   store

smontare/staccare   to get off work (fam.) ▪ **Stasera stacco alle sette.** Tonight I get off work at seven.

gli straordinari   overtime ▪ **Durante l'ultimo mese ho fatto sempre gli straordinari. Avrò una busta paga altissima.** During this last month I've always worked overtime. I'll have a huge paycheck.

il supermercato   supermarket

l'ufficio (m)   office

la tredicesima   bonus

NOTE: In Italian, the expression **la tredicesima** means "the thirteenth" and is used to refer to annual or Christmas bonus pay. It can be the equivalent of one month's pay, and for this reason, one might feel that he/she has received a "thirteenth" monthly paycheck.

WORK AND THE WORKERS

ammazzarsi di lavoro   to kill oneself (with work) ■ **Devo prendere qualche giorno di vacanza. È un mese che mi sto ammazzando di lavoro in fabbrica!** I have to take a few vacation days. I've been killing myself in this factory for a month!

battere la fiacca   to slack, to shirk

il capo/il boss   boss, chief ■ **Ho un nuovo capo che viene da Milano. È molto gentile e disponibile.** I have a new boss from Milan. He's really nice and approachable.

essere buono/a a nulla   to be good-for-nothing

essere un pigrone   to be extremely lazy

essere uno scansafatiche   to be a slacker ■ **Non vai mai a lavorare! Sei proprio uno scansafatiche!** You never go to work! You're such a slacker!

essere stanco morto   to be dead tired ■ **Sono stanco morto! Voglio dormire per dieci ore di seguito!** I am dead tired! I want to sleep for ten hours in a row!

essere uno sgobbone   to be a hard worker ■ **Non ho mai visto uno sgobbone come Tommaso! Lavora dalla mattina alla sera senza fermarsi un minuto.** I've never met a hard worker like Tommaso! He works day and night without stopping for a minute.

essere uno stacanovista   to be a workaholic

farsi il culo   to bust one's ass (vulg.) ■ **Basta, mi licenzio! Non vale la pena farsi il culo per guadagnare così poco!** Enough! I'm going to quit! It's not worth it to bust my ass for such little money!

lavorare come uno schiavo   to work like a slave

lavorare sodo   to work hard

mangiapane a tradimento   (lit., person who eats someone else's bread) one who earns money but does no work ■ **Ti pago tremila euro al mese e tu non fai nulla per me! Sei un mangiapane a tradimento!** I pay you three thousand euro a month and you don't do anything for me! You earn without working!

mettersi all'opera   to put oneself into one's work   ■ **Basta scherzare! È ora di mettersi all'opera perché dobbiamo finire presto questo lavoro!** Stop joking around! It's time for us to put ourselves into our work because we have to finish this job now!

non fare un fico secco   (*lit.*, not to do a dry fig) to be idle (fam.)

ridursi uno straccio dalla fatica   to feel like a wet rag, to be worn out

rimboccarsi le maniche   to roll up one's sleeves   ■ **Rimbocchiamoci le maniche e iniziamo a lavorare!** Let's roll up our sleeves and start working!

riuscire a sbarcare il lunario   to make ends meet   ■ **Mi sono rimasti solo trecento euro. Spero di riuscire a sbarcare il lunario.** I only have three hundred euro left. I hope I can make ends meet.

rompersi la schiena   to break one's back

rompersi le ossa dalla fatica   (*lit.*, to break one's bones with fatigue) to have physical pain due to work

rubare lo stipendio   to steal one's paycheck   ■ **In questo momento c'è così poco lavoro in fabbrica che mi sembra di rubare lo stipendio.** Right now there's so little work in the factory that it feels like I'm stealing my paycheck.

scaldare il posto   (*lit.*, to warm one's seat) to do nothing at work   ■ **Nel mio ufficio non devo fare quasi nulla. Devo solo scaldare il posto!** In my office I never have to do anything. I only warm my seat!

sgobbare   to work hard

sputare sangue   to spit blood (fam.)   ■ **È durissimo fare il minatore. Devi sputare sangue per otto ore al giorno!** Working in a mine is really hard. You have to spit blood for eight hours a day!

stare con le mani in mano   (*lit.*, to be with your hands in your hand) to do absolutely nothing   ■ **Ho lavorato con Paolo ma ho fatto tutto io. Lui è stato tutto il giorno con le mani in mano.** I worked with Paolo but I did everything. The whole day he did absolutely nothing.

sudare sangue   to sweat blood

sudare sette camicie   (*lit.*, to sweat seven shirts) to work really hard   ■ **Ho sudato sette camicie per scaricare i mattoni dal camion.** I worked really hard to unload the bricks from the truck.

tirare la carretta   (*lit.*, to pull the cart) to slave away   ■ **In famiglia chi tira la carretta sono io!** I slave away for this family!

sudare sette camicie

HIRING/GETTING AHEAD

essere un crumiro   to be a scab, a person who refuses to go on strike

essere un leccaculo   (*lit.*, to be an ass licker) to be an ass kisser, brown-noser, suck up (vulg.) ▪ **Giancarlo è proprio un leccaculo! Sta tutto il giorno a fare i complimenti al capo!** Giancarlo is a serious suck-up! He spends the whole day complimenting the boss!

essere un leccapiedi   (*lit.*, to be a feet licker) to be a brownnoser

essere licenziato in tronco   to be fired abruptly

essere licenziato su due piedi   (*lit.*, to be fired on two feet) to be fired without any notice ▪ **Sono stato licenziato su due piedi, senza neanche una telefonata di preavviso!** I was fired without any notice, not even a phone call!

essere un raccomandato   to be a person with connections ▪ **Se non sei raccomandato da persone influenti è molto difficile avere un buon posto di lavoro.** If you don't have connections to influential people it's really hard to find a job.

essere un ruffiano   to be a flatterer

mettere alla porta   (*lit.*, to put someone at the door) to fire someone ▪ **Il proprietario della fabbrica di frigoriferi ha messo alla porta venticinque operai.** The owner of the refrigerator factory fired twenty-five workers.

217

mandare a spasso (*lit.*, to send someone for a walk) to fire ■ **Spesso le aziende non si preoccupano di mandare a spasso i loro impiegati e i loro operai solo per tagliare qualche spesa!** Often companies don't care if they fire their white-collar and blue-collar workers if it saves them money!

perdere il posto to lose one's job

EXERCISES
Adesso tocca a voi!

A *Match each expression in the following list with its equivalent below:*

il lavoro illegale	essere un ruffiano	licenziare	farsi il culo
andare a lavorare	essere un pigrone	non lavorare per niente	
mangiapane a tradimento			

1. essere un leccapiedi _____

2. mettere alla porta _____

3. andare a guadagnarsi la pagnotta _____

4. lavorare moltissimo _____

5. stare con le mani in mano _____

6. una persona che guadagna soldi ma non fa niente _____

7. il lavoro nero _____

8. essere uno scansafatiche _____

B *Create an expression by joining words from the two columns:*

_____ 1. mettersi		a. a spasso
_____ 2. rubare		b. di lavoro
_____ 3. mandare		c. il posto
_____ 4. rompersi		d. all'opera
_____ 5. sputare		e. lo stipendio

_____ 6. scaldare   f. sangue

_____ 7. ammazzarsi   g. le ossa

C   _Choose the word or phrase in parentheses that best fits each sentence:_

1. Ho lavorato tutto il giorno: stamattina mi sono (scaldato il posto/fatto il culo) in fabbrica e durante il pomeriggio ho lavato tre automobili.

2. Quel nuovo impiegato è proprio antipatico. Fa sempre gli straordinari ed è un gran (leccaculo/pigrone).

3. La fabbrica sta licenziando molti lavoratori e io ho paura di (perdere il posto/essere uno sgobbone).

4. È ora di metterci all'opera! Rimbocchiamoci (il lunario/le maniche) e iniziamo!

5. Tuo padre lavora sempre, giorno e notte. È proprio uno (sgobbone/scansafatiche).

Answer Key

Acronyms and Initials

A. 1. e 2. d 3. c 4. f 5. g 6. h 7. i 8. a 9. b 10. j

B. 1. TG 2. APT 3. PPI 4. KO 5. RAI

Animals

A. 1. i 2. a 3. h 4. b 5. d 6. j 7. c 8. f 9. e 10. g

B. 1. c 2. c 3. c 4. b 5. a

C. 1. b 2. c 3. a

Art

A. 1. g 2. a 3. e 4. i 5. b 6. h 7. c 8. j 9. d 10. f

B. 1. cinefilo 2. giallo 3. vip 4. fuori moda 5. scene, lira

C. 1. (Secondo me) il film è una cazzata. 2. Che palle quello spettacolo!
3. (Mia madre) pensa troppo all'antica per capire. (Mia madre) è troppo di
vecchio stampo per capire. 4. (Nella mia opinione) Benigni è stato mitico!
5. Il ristorante è molto chic. 6. È una produzione da non perdere!

Beauty

A. 1. avere le tette rifatte 2. avere le labbra siliconate 3. avere le tette piccole
4. rifarsi il culo 5. rifarsi il naso 6. rifarsi le tette 7. rifarsi le labbra 8. avere le
tette cadenti 9. avere le borse sotto gli occhi 10. avere il doppio mento

B. 1. peso/balena 2. gonfiato/armadio 3. mettere su/metta 4. tenerti in
forma/fitness 5. parrucchiera/colpi

C. 1. di muscoli 2. un chiodo, un grissino 3. di lardo 4. che lungo 5. ossa

Business

A. 1. il palazzinaro 2. il tirapiedi 3. la grana, i quattrini, il denaro 4. sgobbare
5. la carta 6. mettere alla porta, mandare a spasso, dare gli otto giorni 7. essere
al verde 8. essere a spasso 9. fare quattrini

B. 1. (a) pushes drugs (b) earn/make a living 2. (a) cost an arm and a leg
(b) a rip-off 3. (a) The blue-collar workers (b) top brass 4. (a) A good con
artist (b) swindling/conning (c) child's play

Cars and Driving

A. 1. l'incidente stradale, lo schianto, il tamponamento (a catena)   2. andare a sbattere contro   3. sfasciare la macchina, distruggere la macchina   4. andare a tutto gas, andare a tutta birra, andare a tavoletta

B. 1. e   2. g   3. i   4. f   5. h   6. b   7. j   8. c   9. a   10. d

City

A. 1. un affare   2. l'autista   3. lo scontrino   4. una fregatura   5. il marciapiede   6. la bancarella

B. 1. i saldi   2. a due passi   3. fare lo shopping, fare acquisti   4. tirare sul prezzo   5. il pirata della strada

C. 1. andare a spasso   2. battere le strade   3. concedersi   4. costare un occhio della testa   5. convalidare il biglietto

Clothing

A. 1. b   2. c   3. b   4. a   5. c

B. 1. Non ho uno straccio da mettermi.   2. mettersi in ghingheri   3. sudare sette camice   4. togliersi tanto di cappello   5. vestirsi sbracato

Coffee Shops

A. 1. caffè ristretto   2. caffè corretto   3. caffè freddo   4. caffè shakerato   5. latte macchiato

B. 1. e   2. c   3. h   4. a   5. b   6. d   7. f   8. g

C. 1. schiuma   2. cornetto   3. al bar   4. banco   5. pasticceria

Conversations and Invitations

A. 1. b   2. a   3. b   4. a   5. a

B. 1. dare buca, tirare il bidone   2. il leccaculo   3. beccare un raffreddore   4. essere stanco morto   5. il tempo di merda   6. fare storie   7. fare girare le palle a qualcuno

C. 1. to go dutch   2. to not look well   3. to be healthy as a horse   4. to be cold as hell   5. to fuck around   6. to get in touch   7. to break someone's balls   8. to fucking bug someone

Disputes

A. 1. b   2. c   3. b   4. a   5. c   6. a   7. b   8. c   9. b   10. a

B. 1. incazzarsi   2. metterci una pietra sopra   3. dare dello stronzo a qualcuno   4. vai a farti fottere   5. menare   6. spaccare la testa a qualcuno   7. essere beccato   8. piedipiatti   9. spaccone   10. disgraziato

Drinking and Smoking

A. 1. to have oneself a joint   2. to bum a smoke   3. to smoke constantly
4. to stick two fingers down one's throat   5. to hit the bottle   6. to puke
7. Do you want a smoke?   8. to have a drag   9. Do you have a light?   10. match

B. 1. fumare troppo   2. fumatore abituale   3. un pacchetto al giorno
4. un pacchetto da dieci   5. mi fai accendere?

C. 1. b   2. c   3. a   4. c   5. b

Education

A. 1. compito in classe/andare a ripetizione   2. voto/fare sega   3. copiare/nota sul
registro   4. si ammazza di studio/secchione   5. bucato/scena muta

B. 1. spremersi le meningi   2. ammazzarsi di studio   3. scaldare il banco
4. essere una cima   5. essere un somaro, un asino

C. 1. la supplente   2. borsa di studio   3. quarto d'ora accademico   4. mensa
5. trenta e lode

Emotions

A. 1. culo   2. girati   3. le staffe   4. tasca   5. le mani   6. la bocca amara

B. 1. d   2. e   3. f   4. c   5. a   6. b

C. 1. to have a long face   2. to beat someone's face   3. to make a fool of oneself, to
commit a faux-pas, to lose face   4. to be born under a good sign   5. to keep at it
6. to shit oneself, to shit one's pants

Entertainment

A. 1. il film hard   2. tirar fuori, sganciare   3. il buttafuori   4. strappare gli
applause   5. godersi la vita, darsi alla pazza gioia   6. la bettola, il buco   7. buttare
giù, tracannare   8. il must, da non perdere   9. l'after   10. fare due salti, pogare

B. 1. How boring!   2. We were bored to death!   3. Oh! I can't take this!   4. It was
as dull as dishwater!   5. One is having a great time!   6. It's the best/most!

Food and Eating

A. 1. X   2. 2   3. X   4. X   5. 2   6. 2   7. +   8. 2

B. 1. Mario e Giulia hanno buttato giù tutto come un lavandino!   2. Riccardo,
invece, è molto difficile nel mangiare.   3. Carlo ha mangiato come un bufalo,
mentre Geppina ha mangiucchiato un po'.   4. Gianni è una buona forchetta.
5. Massimo deve avere un verme!   6. Pietro e Stefano hanno si sono abbuffati
tutta la sera.   7. Monica ha solamente stuzzicato qua e là.   8. Io mi sono
abbuffato! Mi sono riempito le budella!

C. 1. d   2. g   3. h   4. c   5. f   6. a   7. b   8. e

Geography

A. 1. fiorentina 2. genovesi 3. potentino 4. bolognesi 5. napoletani
6. trevigiana 7. parmigiane 8. barese 9. campobassano 10. triestini

B. 1. piemontese 2. calabrese 3. sardi 4. lucano 5. marchigiano 6. pugliese
7. ligure 8. molisani 9. valdostana 10. laziali

C. 1. montagna 2. fiume 3. montagna 4. fiume 5. montagna 6. lago
7. fiume 8. mare 9. montagna 10. mare 11. lago 12. fiume 13. montagna

Health

A. 1. e 2. f 3. d 4. g 5. h 6. a 7. c 8. b

B. 1. c 2. b 3. a 4. c

C. 1. c 2. b 3. a

Hobbies and Pastimes

A. 1. un melomane 2. un topo di biblioteca 3. la filatelia 4. la numismatica
5. il fai da te 6. il modellismo 7. il cinefilo

B. 1. essere ossessionato/a con 2. essere negato/a per 3. sapersi arrangiare
4. avere talento per

C. 1. le mani d'oro 2. melomane 3. impazzisce 4. dilettante 5. fai da te

The Human Body

A. 1. penis: verga, salame, fava, bastone, cazzo, uccello, mazza, pisello 2. vagina:
fregna, topa, vulva, sorca, ciccia, sgnacchera, passera

B. 1. d 2. f 3. e 4. g 5. h 6. b 7. a 8. c

Immigrants and Immigration

A. 1. il vu cumprà 2. le carrette del mare 3. il fondamentalismo 4. il rimpatrio
forzato 5. il clandestino

B. 1. + 2. 2 3. 2 4. + 5. 2 6. 2 7. 2 8. 2 9. 2 10. X 11. 2 12. X

C. 1. c 2. d 3. b 4. a 5. e

D. 1. c 2. b 3. c 4. c 5. c

Information Technology

A. 1. Internet/sito 2. virus/dischetto 3. indirizzo/e-mail 4. stampante
5. collegamento/modem/scaricare

B. 1. b 2. c 3. b

Music

A. 1. il paroliere   2. cantare dal vivo   3. il podio   4. il vinile   5. il turnista
6. il saltarello

B. 1. It's always the same old song.   2. Change the subject!   3. to lead people by setting a standard   4. to be out of one's mind   5. to be out of tune

C. 1. gruppo spalla   2. strimpellatore   3. palasport   4. suono   5. rock duro
6. fiasco   7. disco d'oro   8. jazzofilo   9. ninnananna   10. loggionisti

Names

A. 1. c   2. a   3. b   4. c   5. c   6. a   7. b

People

A. 1. d   2. f   3. g   4. h   5. a   6. c   7. b   8. e

B. 1. tizia/tipa   2. schiappa   3. capellone   4. mani di burro   5. polentone
6. naso a maialino

Politics

A. 1. e   2. i   3. j   4. c   5. b   6. a   7. d   8. g   9. f   10. h

B. 1. PPI   2. AN   3. DS   4. FI   5. CDU

C. 1. Ministry of Justice   2. Ministry of Education   3. Ministry of Foreign Affairs
4. Ministry of Health   5. Ministry of Defense

Press, Magazines, and Books

A. 1. to review   2. newspaper   3. to skim read   4. to leaf through the newspaper
5. to glance   6. article   7. newsstand   8. crossword puzzles   9. insert, supplement
10. detective story

B. 1. scrittore   2. prefazione   3. libracci   4. trama   5. ristampe

C. 1. l'antologia   2. l'indice   3. il quotidiano

Religion

A. 1. f   2. a   3. e   4. c   5. d   6. b

B. 1. There are other fish in the sea.   2. to do something very rarely   3. to preach one thing and practice another   4. to know influential people   5. at all costs
6. to not know which way to turn   7. to live like a king   8. failing to see the forest for the trees

C. 1. il papa   2. la reliquia   3. la basilica   4. la suora   5. il battesimo

Romance

A. 1. j 2. i 3. b 4. g 5. c 6. a 7. e 8. f 9. d 10. h

B. 1. b 2. c 3. b 4. a 5. b 6. a 7. c 8. c

C. 1. yes 2. no 3. no 4. yes 5. no

Sex

A. 1. to become queer 2. chronic masturbator 3. to suck dick 4. lesbian
5. to feel like fucking 6. to be horny 7. heterosexual male who never has sex
8. to jizz 9. to French-kiss 10. to jerk off

B. 1. pompinara 2. slinguare 3. sbatterlo in figa 4. mignotta 5. essere arrapato
6. venire 7. cornuto 8. essere dell'altra sponda 9. prenderlo in culo
10. sporcaccione

C. 1. uno di quelli 2. ha voglia di scopare 3. morto di figa 4. herpes genitale
5. pompinara 6. esibizionista 7. cornuto

Sports

A. 1. appendere le scarpe al chiodo 2. passare il testimone 3. mettersi a ruota,
succhiare la ruota 4. tirare il gruppo, fare l'andatura 5. mangiarsi un gol
6. seguire la squadra in trasferta 7. segnare in zona Cesarini 8. perdere smalto
9. calciare al volo 10. non essere in forma

B. 1. a 2. c 3. i 4. e 5. f 6. g 7. h 8. d 9. b 10. j

C. 1. f 2. d 3. e 4. c 5. b 6. a 7. h 8. g 9. j 10. i

Travel and Transportation

A. 1. d 2. f 3. h 4. j 5. c 6. b 7. e 8. i 9. a 10. g

Vacations

A. 1. praticare il surf/praticare il windsurf, tavola da surf/tavola da windsurf
2. ho preso, l'abbronzatura 3. lo sci alpino, lo sci di fondo (or vice versa)
4. il pattinaggio a rotelle, pattini a rotelle

Weather

A. 1. c 2. a 3. d 4. b 5. a 6. b 7. d 8. c

B. 1. It's cold as hell! 2. It's hot as hell! 3. I'm drenched! 4. It's raining buckets!
5. What a scorcher! 6. The wind is blowing hard! 7. It's a bit nippy out!
8. What a downpour!

The World of Work

A. 1. essere un ruffiano   2. licenziare   3. andare a lavorare   4. farsi il culo
5. non lavorare per niente   6. mangiapane a tradimento   7. il lavoro illegale
8. essere un pigrone

B. 1. d   2. e   3. a   4. g   5. f   6. c   7. b

C. 1. fatto il culo   2. leccaculo   3. perdere il posto   4. le maniche   5. sgobbone

Italian-English Dictionary/Index

Numbers refer to the page numbers of entries in the main thesaurus, where further details on literal translations, register, and usage; example sentences; and related terms may be found.

Note: the following words are not initially alphabetized within an entry:
  definite and indefinite articles: **un, uno, una, il, la, lo, l', gli, i**
  the prepositions: **a, al, alla, all', in**
  avere, essere and their forms.

il 33 giri LP, long-playing record 147
il 4 per 4 off-road or 4 x 4 vehicle 38

l'abbigliamento clothes, garments 43
l'abbonamento bus pass 42
abbonarsi to subscribe 165
un abbraccio hug 183
l'abbronzatura suntan 207
abbuffarsi to stuff oneself, to gorge oneself, to pig out 115
l'abbuffata big meal, blow out, binge 115
l'abito (m) suit 53
l'abito non fa il monaco don't judge a book by its cover 49
abruzzese from Abruzzo 121
accarezzare to caress 183
l'accattone (m) beggar 156
accendersi una sigaretta to light oneself a cigarette 83
l'accendino (m) lighter 83
Accidenti! Holy Cow! Holy Smokes! 65; Wow! Holy cow! My goodness! 99
Accidenti a te! Damn you! 72
ACI [Automobile Club Italiano] Italian equivalent of AAA 5
È acqua passata! It's water under the bridge! 71
l'acquazzone downpour 209
l'acquolina in bocca to have one's mouth water 113
l'ACR (azione cattolica ragazzi) (f) Catholic children's organization 172

l'affare (m) thingamabob 35; deal 43
l'affarista (m) wheeler-dealer 33
gli affettati sliced salami and/or lunchmeat 111
affondare l'acceleratore to put the pedal to the metal 40
afoso sultry, hazy 210
l'afro-beat (f) afro-beat 151
l'after (m) after-hours club 106
l'agente (m/f) agent 150
agevolare le difficoltà to grease the wheels, to facilitate 30
l'aggeggio (m) contraption 35
l'agnellino (m) little lamb 8
l'AIDS (m/f) AIDS 188
l'album (m) album 150
l'album delle figurine stickers album 165
l'alcolizzato lush, drunkard, alcoholic 79, 106
allacciare la cintura to buckle/put on the seat belt 38
Alleanza Nazionale (AN) National Alliance 162
allegare un documento/video/ un'immagine ad un' e-mail to attach a document/video/image to an e-mail 144
l'allenatore coach 198
allocco: Non essere un allocco! Don't be stupid! 11
allocco: Perché fai sempre la figura dell'allocco? Why do you always come off as being stupid? 11
allocco: Sono rimasti come un allocco. They were left stunned. 11
allodole: È uno specchietto per allodole. It is a lure/a decoy. 11
Allora? What's up? 64
allungare il muso to have a long face 98
allungare un dritto to punch 102
allungarsi to buy 43
essere allupato to be horny 189
alta stagione tourist season 205
l'altalena (f) swing 91
gli alti ufficiali top brass, high officials 32
altoatesino from Alto Adige 123

bastonare to beat up 72
il bastone penis 135
battere la fiacca to slack, to shirk 215
battere le strade to work the streets in prostitution 46
il battesimo baptism 175
la battona whore, hooker 106, 192
la battuta serve 200
avere la bava alla bocca to be foaming at the mouth (with rage) 96
beato blessed, lucky 101
beccare un monte di botte/cazzotti/ schiaffi to catch a hell of a beating 74
beccare/beccarsi un raffreddore to catch a cold 63, 125
beccare una valanga di schiaffoni to catch a hell of a beating 74
essere beccato to be caught 76
becco cuckold 188
essere un beduino to look unsophisticated 138
la befana ugly woman, hag 157
bello/bella beautiful (person) 64
ben cotto well done (meat) 112
essere bene in carne to be plump 114
la benedizione blessing 175
bere to drink 80
bere alla salute di qualcuno to drink to someone's health 80
bere come una spugna to drink like a fish 80
bere un bicchiere di troppo to drink one glass too many 80
il Berlusca Silvio Berlusconi, Italian Prime Minister 154
i bermuda bermuda shorts 54
il berretto hat 51
bestemmiare to curse, to blaspheme 175
bestemmiare come un turco to swear like a turk 175
i bestemmie blasphemous cursing 99
bestia: Lui lavora come una bestia. He works like a beast. 13
il best-seller bestseller 168
la bettola dive, hole in the wall 108
la biancheria intima lingerie 53
il bibliofilo book lover, avid reader and collector 131
la bibliografia bibliography 168
il bicchierino shot glass 81
la bicicletta da corsa racing bike 205
la bicicletta da passeggio city bicycle, a 3-speed bicycle 205

il bidello/la bidella janitor 88
bidonare to stand someone up 182
bigiare la scuola to skip class 89
la biglietteria ticket office 45
il biglietto ticket 42
il biglietto della lotteria lottery ticket 165
il Bignami *Cliff's Notes* 154
il bignè cream puff 57
essere un bigotto to be sanctimonious, religious hypocrite 173
il bikini bikini 54
i binari tracks or rails (for both trains and subways) 45
il binario tracks 204
il biondo blond guy 157
birra alla spina beer on draft 80
la birretta beer 66
Bis! Encore! 107
il bis encore 151
bisessuale bisexual 188
bisex bi 188
bisticciare to squabble, to bicker 102
bisticciarsi to bicker 71
essere un bizzocco to be sanctimonious, religious hypocrite 173
bloccarsi to crash 143
il boccale di birra a mug of beer 80
le bocce breasts 135
la bocchinara cocksucker 192
il bocchino cigarette holder 83
essere bocciato/a to fail 89
il boccone bite (to eat) 66, 111
il body-building bodybuilding 128
il bollide hot-rod 38
bolognese from Bologna 120
una bomba a hit, a smash, a great show 18
il bomber flight jacket 51
il bombolone a fried pastry with cream inside 57
il bordello brothel, whorehouse 106
la borsa di studio scholarship 92
avere le borse agli/sotto gli occhi to have bags under the eyes 23, 49
il borseggiatore pickpocket 42
il boss boss, chief 32, 215
una botte very fat 157
la bottega workshop 43
una bottiglia o lattina di . . . a bottle or can of . . . 80
il box pit 198
i boxer boxers 53
le bozze drafts 168
i bracci arms 134, 135

il bracciante labourer, unskilled worker 32
le brache trousers 51
il brandy brandy 80
il brano song 150
essere brillo/un po' brillo to be tipsy/ a little tipsy 81
brindare to toast/make a toast 80
la brioche croissant 57
la brodaglia slop, nasty food 112
la bronza smelly fart, asphyxiating fart 136
il browser browser 145
il brufolo person with acne 157
la bruschetta bruschetta (toasted bread, garlic, fresh tomatoes, basil, and olive oil) 111
avere una brutta cera to not look well 63; to look ill 125
essere brutto come la fame to be as ugly as hunger 113
la bua the boo-boo 127
bucare lo scritto to fail, bomb a written test 93
bucarsi to shoot up 128
buciaiolo homosexual 186
il buco dive, hole in the wall 108; homosexual 186
la bufera storm 62, 210
il bullo bully 91
a buon mercato at a good price 43
essere una buona forchetta to be a hearty eater 114
Buona sera! Good evening! 64
Buonanotte ai suonatori! That's that! 148
Buonanotte! Good night! 64, 67
Buondì! Good day! Hello! 64
Buongiorno! Good day! Hello! 64
essere buono come il pane as good as gold 116
essere buono/a a nulla to be good-for-nothing 215
il burino redneck 156
la burrasca storm 210
il bus city bus 42
buscarne/buscarle to receive a beating 75
la busta paga paycheck 214
la bustarella bribe, kickback 160
il buttafuori bouncer 76, 106
buttare fuori il fumo dal naso to blow the smoke out of the nose 83
buttare giù to throw down (a drink), to have a drink 106
buttare giù tutto come un lavandino to eat everything in sight/within reach 114

buttarsi to dive or throw oneself into something 97
essere buttato fuori to be thrown out 76
il buzzurro hillbilly, ignorant person 156

C'hai il fuoco? Do you have a flame? 83
la cabriolet/la cabrio convertible 38
cacciare to cough up, or fork out (money) 109
il caffè coffee 56; café 58
il caffè americano american coffee 56
il caffè corretto espresso coffee with a little bit of liquor 56, 106
il caffè corretto con sambuca/grappa/crema al whisky coffee spiked with sambuca, grappa, cream of whisky 80
il caffè freddo iced coffee 56
il caffè lungo opposite of caffè ristretto; more water, less coffee 56
il caffè macchiato espresso coffee with a touch of milk 56
il caffè ristretto a small and dense espresso coffee, very creamy and strong 56
il caffè shakerato coffee shaken with ice 56
il caffè valdostano valdostano coffee 80
il caffelatte part coffee, part milk 56
la caffetteria coffee shop and breakfast bar 58
cagarsi adosso/sotto to shit oneself, to shit one's pants 100
il cagasotto a person who shits oneself, a person who shits one's pants (for every little thing) 101
cagliaritano from Cagliari 120
il cagnolino doggy 10
calabrese from Calabria 122
calare le brache to surrender 50
calcare le scene to be an actor, to tread the boards 17
calciare al volo to hit the ball while still in the air 196
il calciofilo soccer lover 132
il calciomercato When teams buy and sell players during the off-season 196
i calzettoni di lana wool socks 54
cambiare disco to change the subject 148
il cambio di etichetta label change 150
il cambio manuale stick shift, manual transmission 39
la Camera dei Deputati Congress 160
il camerino dressing room 107
la camicia hawaiana Hawaiian shirt 54

le **camicie verdi** separatists 160

camionara lesbian 187

cammello: Puzza come un cammello! He stinks like a camel! 13

la **campagna elettorale** electoral campaign 160

la **campanella** schoolbell 88

il **campanile** penis 135

campano from Campania 122

il **campione del mondo** the World Champion 195

il **campione italiano/europeo/olimpico** the Italian/European/Olympic champion 195

il **campo da tennis** tennis court 200

campobassano from Campobasso 120

Cane non mangia cane. There's honor among thieves. 10

cane: C'era un cane. There was no one there. 10

cane: Che vita da cani! What a terrible life! 10

cane: Dai, smetti di menare il cane per l'aia e arriva al punto. Come on, stop beating around the bush and get to the point. 10

cane: Era solo come un cane. He was all alone. 10

cane: Ha fatto un lavoro da cani. He/She did a very poor job. 10

cane: Lavora come un cane. He/She works a lot. 10

cane: Lo tratti sempre come un cane! You always treat him poorly! 11

cane: Marco e Lucia sono come cani e gatti. Marco and Lucia argue constantly. 10

cane: Mondo cane! Damn it all! 10

cane: Non temere, Mario, cane che abbaia non morde. Don't worry, Mario, a barking dog does not bite. 10

cane: Piove sempre, che tempo da cani! It always rains, what bad weather! 10

cane: Sei un cane! You're a despicable person! 10

cane: Te l'ho detto di non svegliare il cane che dorme. I told you to let sleeping dogs lie. 10

cane: Tu hai sette vite come i cani. You have seven lives like dogs. 10

cannare lo scritto to fail, bomb a written test 93

il **cannolo** single cannoli 57

il/la **cantante** singer 150

cantare dal vivo to sing or play live 148

cantare in play-back to lip-sync, mime 150

il **cantautore/la cantautrice** singer-songwriter 150

il **cantiere edile** building site 32

i **cantucci/cantuccini** small biscotti made with almonds 82

la **canzone** song 150

CAP [codice avviamento postale] zip code 5

la **capa** head 135

il **capellone** longhair 157

il **capitano** captain 199

il **capitano d'industria** tycoon, mogul 32

i **capitoli** chapters 168

il **capo** boss, head, chief 32, 135, 215

il **Capo del Governo** Head of Government 160

il **capocannoniere** top scorer 197

il **capoccia** boss, head 32, 135

il **capolinea** end of the line 42

il **capomastro** foreman 32

il **caporale** slave driver 33

il **caposquadra** foreman 32

la **cappella** chapel 172

il **cappello da baseball** baseball hat 54

il **cappuccino/cappuccio** cappuccino 56

il **capretto** little goat 8

i **carabinieri** military police force 76

i **caramba** military police force 76

avere un caratterino to have a temper 96

la **carcassa** wreck 38

il **cardinale** cardinal 172

la **carezza** caress 183

caricare to fuck 191

la **Caritas** Catholic humanitarian organization 138

la **carne tritata** ground or minced meat 111

caro mio/cara mia my treasure, my love, my dear 184

caro/cara, carissimo/carissima dear or very dear (person) 64

il **carpentiere** carpenter 32

la **carretta** jalopy, old clunker 38

le **carrette del mare** old rusty boats 138

la **carta** buck, bill 30

cartine lunghe/corte long/short papers 83

la **casa chiusa** brothel, whorehouse 106

la **casa dello studente** dorm 92

il **casino** brothel, whorehouse 106; mess, utter shambles 109

la **cassa** cash register 43

la **cassetta** cassette tape 147

convalidare to validate or stamp (your ticket) 42

il convento convent 172

la convivenza living together, cohabitation 139

la copertina cover 168

coperto cloudy, overcast 209

copiare to cheat 88

il copione copycat, not original 18

Coraggio! Have courage! 98

il cordiale cordial 81

il cornetto croissant 57

il corno/cornetto horn (for good luck) 176

cornuto cuckold 72, 188

essere cornuto to be cuckolded 188

correre to speed 39

la corriera city bus 42

il *Corriere* (il *Corriere della Sera*) the *Courier* (the *Courier of the Evening*) newspaper 165

il corrimano handrail 45

Corte Costituzionale Constitutional Court 160

Corte dei Conti Court of Accounts 160

corteggiare qualcuno to court someone 180

il cortile playground 91

essere a corto di tempo to be short of time 67

il corvo priest 173

corvo: È sempre il solito corvo del malaugurio. He's always the person who brings back luck. 11

cosa da nulla child's play, a piece of cake 35

così così so-so 125

il coso thingamabob 35

Costa un occhio! It's expensive! 2

costare un occhio della testa to cost an arm and a leg 30, 43

la Costituzione the Constitution 160

il costume da bagno bathing suit 54

avere una cotta per qualcuno to have a crush on someone 179

cotto medium well (meat) 112

il cranio head 134, 135

la crema del caffè crema, i.e. the white foam on top of an espresso shot 56

crepare to croak/kick the bucket 128

crepare dal ridere to die laughing 101

crepare dalla bile to be consumed with anger and envy 96

la cresima confirmation 175

cretino cretin 72

CRI [Croce Rossa Italiana] Italian Red Cross 5

Cristiani Democratici Uniti (CDU) Christian Democratic Union 162

un cristiano a person 173

il critico critic 168

la croce rossa red cross 128

la cronaca local news 165

la cronaca nera crime news 165

la cronaca rosa tabloids 165

la cronometro time trial 199

crossare to cross 197

i crostini toasted bread served with various spreads 111

un crucco kraut 140

essere un crumiro to be a scab, a person who refuses to go on strike 217

la cubista professional dancer who dances onstage or in cages at nightclubs 107

la cuccetta sleeper cabin 204

il cucciolo/cucciolino puppy 10

cula/culattone homosexual 186

avere culo to be a lucky son-of-a-bitch 101

il culo bottom 135, 136

avere culo all'esame/nel compito in classe to be lucky during a test 88

curarsi to take care of oneself 63

da qualche parte somewhere, some place 66

Dai! Come on! 97

dama homosexual 186

dare buca to stand someone up 66

dare dello stronzo a qualcuno to call someone a turd 72

dare di stomaco/gozzare to throw up/to puke 81, 127

dare fastidio (a qualcuno) to bother/irritate (someone) 60, 71

dare gli esami to take exams 92

dare gli otto giorni to fire, to can, to sack 34

dare il la to lead people by setting a standard/to be the first one to do something 148

dare il pacco (a qualcuno) to stand someone up 66, 182

dare lo smalto alle unghie to paint one's nails 27

dare un calcio to kick 75

dare un party to throw a party 108

dare un sacco di botte/cazzotti/schiaffi to get/give a hell of a beating 75

dare un'occhiata to glance 165

la **fregatura** a rip-off 33, 44
la **fregna** vagina 136
frequentare l'università/non frequentare l'università to attend/not attend college or university 92
frequentarsi to date 180
al **fresco** cool spot 211
frignare to whine 61
il **frignone** a whiner, a crybaby 61
fringuellino: Canta come un fringuellino. He/She sings happily. 11
friulano from Friuli 122
frocio homosexual 186
essere frocio to be gay/a fag 186
fumare to smoke 84
fumare come un turco/come una ciminiera to smoke constantly 84
fumare poco to smoke a little 84
fumare troppo to smoke too much 84
fumare un pacchetto al giorno to smoke a pack a day 84
fumare una volta ogni morte di papa to smoke very rarely 84
fumarsi uno spinello to have oneself/smoke oneself a joint 84
la **fumata bianca** white smoke signal 174
la **fumata nera** black smoke signal 174
fumatore abituale habitual smoker 84
fumatore incallito inveterate smoker 84
fumatore occasionale occasional smoker 84
i **fumetti** comics 166
fumo negli occhi smoke in the eyes 84
il **funerale** funeral 175
essere fuori corso to be a second/third/fourth, etc. year senior 92
fuori moda out of style or fashion 19
il **fuoriclasse** star player, one who is a head above the competition 195
essere in fuorigioco to be offside 197
il **fuoristrada** off-road or 4 x 4 vehicle 38
furoreggiare to be all the rage 19

galletto: Lui fa sempre il galletto. He always plays the gallant. 9
la **gallina vecchia fa un buon brodo** there's many a good tune played on an old fiddle 116
gallina: Abbiamo trovato una gallina dalle uova d'oro. We found a gold mine. 9
gallina: andare a letto con le galline e svegliarsi col gallo early to bed, early to rise 9

gallina: Sei un cervello di gallina! You're not smart! 9
il **galoppino** gofer, errand boy 32
in gamba with it, hip, alert 19
In gamba! On your toes! Stay sharp! 68
il **garantismo** guaranteeism 161
garbare a qualcuno to be liked by someone 180
gatta: C'è una brutta gatta da pelare. There's a big problem to be solved. 10
gatta: Qui gatta ci cova. I smell a rat here. 9
gatta: Tanto va la gatta al lardo che ci lascia lo zampino. Curiosity killed the cat. 10
il **gattino** kitty 9
gatto: Hanno nove vite come i gatti. They have nine lives like cats. 9
gatto: Luciano è un gatto. Luciano is smart. 9
gatto: Siamo quattro gatti. We're very few. 9
gay homosexual 186
essere gay to be gay/a fag 186
la **gazzetta (la *Gazzetta dello Sport*)** a sports paper 166
gelare to freeze 211
essere un genio dei computer/dell'informatica to be a computer whiz 143
Genova Genoa 120
genovese Genovese 120
ghiotto gluttonous, greedy 115
il **ghiottone/la ghiottona** glutton 115
la **giacchetta** jacket 51
il **giallo** detective story 19, 166
il **giardinaggio** gardening 130
il **gigolo** gigolo, womanizer 16
il **gilè** vest 51
il **gin** gin 81
i **ginocchi** knees 135, 136
il **giobba/giobbone** boaster 156
giocare a fondocampo to play at the baseline 200
giocare a pallone to play soccer 197
giocare su terra battuta to play on clay 200
giocare sul sintetico to play on astroturf/fake grass 200
giocare sull'erba to play on grass 200
il **giochetto dei frati** sodomy 186
il **gioco da ragazzi** child's play, a piece of cake 35
un **giornalaccio** rag 166
il **giornalaio** news vendor 166

il giornale newspaper 166
il giornaletto newsletter 166
il/la giornalista journalist 166
avere i giorni contati to have one's days numbered, to be not well 63
le giostre park rides 108
la gippone Sport Utility Vehicle 38
giraffa: Sei una giraffa! You're super tall! 13
giraffa: Vedi quella ragazza alta come una giraffa? Do you see that girl who's tall like a giraffe? 13
girare la testa to spin 63
girare un film to shoot or make a film 17
il giro lap 198
il giro d'Italia Italian Tour 199
i girotondini grass-roots reform movement 161
la gita field trip 89
essere giù to be down or depressed 63, 182
un Giuda a Judas, a traitor 154
giuliano from Venezia Giulia 122
avere/non avere la giustificazione to have/not to have an absent note 88
Giusto un goccio. Just a drop. 3
la gnocca vagina 136
lo gnomo shorty, very short person 158
la gobba hump 157
il gobbo hunchback 157
godere to experience sexual pleasure 190
godersi la vita to live it up 108
il gol goal 198
il goldone condom 190
il gommone rubber dinghy 139
essere gonfiato to be overly muscular 25
graffiare to scratch 75
la grana dough, money 30
granchio: Temo di prendere un granchio. I'm afraid to make a mistake/to mess up. 12
il grande capo boss 33
il grande schermo the silver screen, the big screen 16
i grandi magazzini department store 44
i grandi stilisti famous fashion designers 51
grandinare to hail 209
la grandine hail 209
essere grasso/a to be fat 24
essere grassoccio/a, grassotello/a to be plump 114
il gratta e vinci scratch and win lotto 166
il gregario teammate 199
il grissino very thin person 157

il grosso nome a big name 20
i gruppi parlamentari parliamentary groups 161
il gruppo band 147
il gruppo spalla opening act 147
guadagnarsi il pane to earn one's living, to earn one's keep 30
i guadagni earnings 30
il guanto condom 190
il guapone boaster 156
il guardalinee linesman 197
guardare dall'alto in basso to look down upon 17
guardare la morte in faccia to look death in the face 126
guardare le vetrine to window shop 44
il guardaroba coat check 107
la guardia svizzera Swiss Guard 174
il guardone peeping tom 190
gufare: Non mi gufare! Don't bring me bad luck!/Don't jinx me! 11
gufo: Sei un gufo. You're a person who brings bad luck. 11
la guida TV TV guide 166

Hai da accendere? Do you have a light? 84
Hai l'accendino? Do you have a lighter? 84
handicappato handicapped 157
l'happy hour happy hour 80
l'hard disk (m) hard drive 143
herpes genitale genital herpes 190

idiota idiot 73
l'idraulico plumber 32
iena: S'incazza come una iena. He/She gets pissed like a hyena. 13
essere uno iettatore to be a jinx 176
illudersi to deceive oneself 104
le illustrazioni pictures 169
imbattersi in qualcuno to run into someone 180
Imbecille! imbecile 73
imbestialirsi to fly into a rage 71
l'imbianchino painter 32
imbroccare to pick up 180
imbrogliare to swindle, to con 33
l'imbroglio (m) scam 34
l'imbroglione (m) swindler, con artist 34
l'immagine (f) style, image, look 27
immatricolarsi to register for classes 92
l'immigrato/a immigrant 139
l'immigrato/a irregolare illegal immigrant 139

Minerva, il coglione di riserva Minerva, the spare nut 154

una minestra riscaldata old hat 117

Ministero degli Affari Esteri Ministry of Foreign Affairs 162

Ministero dei Lavori Pubblici Ministry of Public Works 162

Ministero del Commercio con l'Estero Ministry of Foreign Trade 162

Ministero dell'Ambiente Ministry of Environment 162

Ministero dell'Industria, del Commercio e dell'Artigianato Ministry of Industry, Commerce, and Handicraft 162

Ministero dell'Interno Ministry of the Interior 162

Ministero della Difesa Ministry of Defense 162

Ministero della Pubblica Istruzione Ministry of Education 162

Ministero della Sanità Ministry of Health 162

Ministero delle Comunicazioni Ministry of Communications 162

Ministero delle Finanze Ministry of Finance 162

Ministero di Grazia e Giustizia Ministry of Justice 162

Ministero per i Beni e le Attività Culturali Ministry for Cultural Assets and Activities 162

il ministro minister 161

il missionario missionary 174

il mister coach 198

mitico mythical, legendary, of godlike proportions 20

il mito legend 20

la moca mokka 58

i mocassini moccasins 52

alla moda in fashion, all the rage 18

il modellismo modeling 130

il modello/la modella fashion model 52

il modem modem 145

essere un moderato to be liberal 160

molisano from Molise 122

mollare to let go or get rid of someone or something, to dump 67

mollare qualcuno to break up with someone 182

mollarsi to break up 182

Molto lieto! It's a pleasure (to meet you)! 65

la monaca di clausura cloistered nun 174

il monaco monk 174

il monastero monastery 172

essere una mongolfiera to be a balloon 24

il monitor monitor 143

essere una montagna di muscoli to be a mountain of muscles 25

le montagne russe roller coaster 108

montare to start work, to start a shift 214

montare in cattedra to start pontificating, to get on one's high horse 91

montarsi la testa to get a big head 18

morbide softpack (of cigarettes) 85

mordere to bite 75

mordicchiare l'orecchio to nibble on the ear 183

morire dal desiderio/dalla voglia di fare qualcosa to be dying to do something 104

morire di fame to die of hunger 113

Mortacci tua! Fuck your dead ancestors! 73

essere un morto di fame to be a nobody or a nothing 113

Morto di fame! You're a nobody! 73

il morto di figa heterosexual male who never has sex 190

morto di seghe male who masturbates excessively 190

Morto un papa se ne fa un altro. There are other fish in the sea. 174

mosca: Bobby è una mosca bianca. Bobby is a very rare person. 13

mosca: Ermanno non farebbe male a una mosca. Ermanno would not hurt a fly. 13

mosca: Non si sente volare una mosca. There's absolute silence. 13

la moschea mosque 141

avercelo moscio to not be erect 188

il motivo song 150

il motore di ricerca search engine 145

il motorino motor scooter 205

essere motorizzato to have wheels 39

la mountain bike mountain bike 205

il mouse mouse 143

la moviola slow-motion replay 198

il mozzicone cigarette butt 85

mulo: È carico come un mulo. He's loaded like a mule. 9

il muratore bricklayer 32

la musica classica classical music 151

la musica leggera pop/top 40/easy listening music 107, 150

la musica rap rap music 151

avere il muso to be sulky 182

un muso giallo Asian 140

il sadomaso, il sadomasochismo sadomasochism 191

il sadomasochista sadomasochist 191

saffista sapphist 188

il sagrestano sacristan 174

il salame penis 135

salato salty food 113

i saldi sales 44

il salone salon 26

il salone di belleza beauty parlor, salon 27

la salsiccia penis 135

saltare to skip 148

saltare alla corda to skip rope 91

il saltarello popular dance of central Italy 152

Alla salute! To our health! 80

salvare un documento/file/programma to save a document/file/program 146

salvarsi in corner to give up a corner kick 198

Salve! Greetings! 65

al sangue rare (meat) 112

avere il sangue freddo to have ice water in your veins 97

essere sano come un pesce to be healthy as a horse, to be in perfect health 63, 125

avere santi in paradiso to know influential people 175

Santo cielo! Good heavens! 100

avere un santo dalla propria parte to have a guardian angel 175

il Santo Padre the Pope 174

saperci fare con to really know how to do something, to be really good at something 131

saperci fare con i computer to be skilled with computers 144

sapere di niente to be bland 113

sapersi arrangiare to get by 131

la Sardegna Sardinia 122

sardo Sardinian 122

essere sazio to be full or satisfied 115

sbaciucchiarsi to neck 183

sbafare to gobble up, to polish off 116

la sbafata big meal, blow out, binge 115

lo sbafatore/la sbafatrice glutton 115

sbandare to skid, to slide 40

sbarcare to disembark, to land 140

sbattere le cicche to pack the smokes 85

sbatterlo in figa to fuck 191

sbatterlo in/nel culo to sodomize 187

sbatterlo tra le cosce/gambe to fuck 191

sbavare dietro a uno/una to drool after a guy/girl 181

gli sbirri the cops/the fuzz 77

lo sbirro cop 76

la sboba/sbobba bad food, slop 113

sboccare to puke 82

sbolognare to palm off, to unload 34

avere la sbornia to be sloshed/plastered 80

la sborra jizz 191

sborrare to jizz 191

sbronzarsi to get sloshed/plastered 82

essere sbronzo to be sloshed/plastered 81

lo scacciapensieri pastime 109

lo scafista navigator of ships carrying illegal immigrants 140

la Scala di Milano the major opera house in Italy 149

lo scalatore climber 199

scaldare il banco to sit around 90

scaldare il posto to do nothing at work 216

scaldarsi to get hot under the collar 72

lo scambista swinger 191

lo scanner scanner 144

scannerizzare to scan 144

essere uno scansafatiche to be a slacker 215

scaricare to drop off 40; to download 145

avere una scarpa e uno zoccolo to dress poorly, to wear clothes that clash 49

le scarpe coi tacchetti/da calcio shoes with cleats/soccer shoes 53

le scarpe da corsa running shoes 53

le scarpe da ginnastica gym shoes 53

le scarpe da tennis tennis shoes 53

uno scarpone incompetent person 50

scartare to fake the defender out, to juke the defender 198

scassaminchia/scassacazzo annoying, pain in the neck 70

scassare il cazzo/la minchia a qualcuno to break someone's balls 70

scassare la testa a qualcuno to break someone's head 76

scassare le palle/i coglioni a qualcuno to break (or bust) someone's balls/nuts 70

scassato beat up, junky 38

essere scazzato to be down in the dumps, to be without energy or emotion, to be depressed 63

scendere a rete to come up to the net 201

scendere in campo to enter the world of politics 161

lo schermo screen 144

succhiare la ruota to draft 200
sudare sangue to sweat blood 216
sudare sette camice to sweat profusely, to work very hard 50, 216
la sufficienza passing grade 90
essere sul letto di morte to be about to die 125
suonare dal vivo to sing or play live 148
suonarle a qualcuno to beat somebody up 149
essere suonato to be out of one's mind 149
il suono sound system 148
la suora nun 175
super super 110
il superalcolico hard liquor 82
il supermercato supermarket 45, 215
essere superstizioso/a to be superstitious 176
il supplente/la supplente substitute teacher 88
svendere to sell off (stolen goods) 33
svenire per la fame to faint from hunger 113
sverginare to take someone's virginity 192

il tabacco da pipa pipe tabacco 85
il tabacco da sigarette cigarette tobacco 85
il tabloid tabloid 168
TAC [tomografia assiale computerizzata] CAT scan 6
tagliare la strada to cut off 40
tagliarsi le unghie to cut one's nails 27
tagliarsi le unghie dei piedi to cut one's toenails 28
avere talento per to have a talent for something 131
tallonare to tailgate, to be hot on someone's tail 40
talpa: Sei cieco come una talpa. You're as blind as a bat. 14
il tamponamento (a catena) pile-up 37
tamponare to crash 37
il tanga thong 53
la tangente bribe, kickback 160
la tangentopoli kickback system 160
tanto fumo e poco arrosto a lot of show and little substance 117
la tappa leg of a race 200
il tappetino mouse pad 144
il tappo shorty, very short person 158
la tarantella popular dance of Naples 152
il tarchiato stocky guy 158
taroccato knock-off 45

avere le tasche bucate to have holes in one's pockets 49
tastare qualcuno to feel someone up 183
la tastiera keyboard 144
la tavola da surf surfboard 207
la tavola da windsurf sailboard 207
A tavola! Time to eat!, Dinner/Lunch is served! 115
il teatro theater 151
il teatro Ariston di Sanremo pop festival at Sanremo 150
la techno techno music 107, 148
la tele TV, tube 108
un temperamento d'artista an artistic temperament 18
la tempesta storm 62, 210
i tempi supplementari overtime 198
il tempo da cani terrible weather 62
il tempo di merda shitty weather 62
il temporale storm 62, 210
tenere duro to hang in there, to be strong or tough 98
tenero tender 113
tenersi duro to keep an erection 98
tenersi in forma to stay in shape 127
tenersi per mano to hold hands 183
tenersi su to keep one's spirits up 61
Teniamo le dita incrociate. Let's keep our fingers crossed. 3
il/la tennista tennis player 201
il terremoto something revolutionary or groundbreaking 20
il terrone peasant, southern Italian 156
la terza gamba penis 135
essere il terzo incomodo to be a third wheel 182
la tesi di dottorato doctoral disseration 93
la tesi di laurea graduation thesis 93
tesoro dear (person) 65
tesoro mio my treasure, my love, my dear 184
la tessera membership card 107
testa a pinolo pinhead 158
essere una testa calda to be a hothead 96
testa di cazzo dickhead 74
avere la testa per aria to have one's head in the clouds 17
testa: Avete grilli per la testa. You guys are full of fancy. 13
il testone head 135
le tette breasts 135
avere le tette cadenti to have sagging boobs 23

verme: Dovresti sentirti un verme! You should be ashamed! 13

verme: Sei un verme! You are despicable! 13

verme: Sono nudo come un verme. I'm stark naked. 13

Versami da bere! Pour me a drink! 3

versare to deposit 31

il verseggiatore/la verseggiatrice versifier, rhymester, versemonger 17

il vescovo bishop 175

la vespa motor scooter 205

vestirsi alla moda to dress in style 51

vestirsi firmato to wear brand name clothing 51

vestirsi sbracato to dress badly 52

i vestiti clothes, garments 43

il vestito suit 53

un vestito da quattro soldi a cheap outfit 49

vestito di stracci poorly dressed 49

il vestito firmato/di marca brand name clothing 52

in vetrina shop window 170

viados homosexual 186

viaggiare to speed 39

il vibratore vibrator 192

un vichingo Scandinavian 140

il video music video 151

Viene giù come Dio la manda! It's really coming down! 210

i vigili del fuoco firemen 76

il vigliacco/la vigliacca coward 101

vincere in due set/tre set to win two/three straight sets 201

il vinile vinyl record 148

il vino rosso e bianco red and white wine 82

il vinoteca wine bar 106

il vinsanto sweet, dessert wine 82

il/la vip very important person, VIP 20, 33

vipera: Mia sorella è una vipera! My sister is a snake! 14

il virus virus 145

avere visto giorni migliori to have seen better days 63

È una vita che non ci vediamo! Long time no see! 65

avere il vizio to have a habit 83

VM 18 [vietato ai minori di 18 anni] NC-17 6

la vodka vodka 83

aver voglia di farsi qualcuno to feel like doing someone 188

aver voglia di figa to feel like pussy 188

aver voglia di scopare to feel like fucking 188

aver voglia di una sigaretta to feel like a cigarette 83

volere to want 66

volpe: Tommaso è furbo come una volpe. Tommaso is clever like a fox. 14

voltare gli occhi to pass out 127

vomitare to vomit 83

vorrei un pacchetto di . . . I would like a pack of . . . 85

il voto grade 90; vote 162

il voto in condotta conduct grade 90

il vù cumprà foreign street vendor 140

la vulva vagina 136

Vuoi una cicca/una sigaretta? Do you want a smoke/a cigarette? 85

il warm-up warm-up 199

il whisky whisky 83

uno yankee yank 140

le zampe mitts, hands 134, 135

avere le zampe di gallina to have crow's feet (eye wrinkles) 23

zampe: Giù le zampe! Hands off! 16

uno zingaro gypsy 141

le zinne breasts 135

lo Zippo Zippo 85

la zoccola whore, hooker 106, 192

gli zoccoli clogs 52

la zona di traffico limitato limited traffic zone

la zuffa scrap, scuffle 91, 102

essere zuppo fino al midollo to be soaked, to be drenched 209